WOMEN LIVING SINGLE

Women Living Single

*Thirty Women Share Their Stories of
Navigating Through a Married World*

LEE REILLY

ff

Faber and Faber
BOSTON • LONDON

Library of Congress Cataloging-in-Publication Data

Reilly, Lee.
    Women living single : thirty women share their stories of navigating
through a married world / by Lee Reilly.
        p.   cm.
    ISBN 0-571-19888-0 (hardcover)
    1. Single women—Case studies.   I. Title.
HQ800.2.R45   1996
305.48'9652—dc20   95-42132
                                                                CIP

Jacket design by Trina Lion

Printed in the United States of America

To Fran—
To JoAnn—
To all the singular women.

Contents

Acknowledgments

Many people have had a hand in making this book. I am particularly grateful to the thirty ever-single women and their families who contributed their time, their histories, and their perceptions. Although I cannot name them, I do thank them, each and every one.

Other people offered direction and encouragement and helped me find resources. These include Nina Barrett, Ellen Blum Barish, Anne Cusick, Joe and Kathy Cusick, Laurel Doud, Allen Douglas, Cheryl Devall, Terry Guymon, Jacquie Harper, Eddy Harris, Lorraine Hart, Kip Hillman, Bob Kucera, Judy Kowal, Greg Martin, Jeannie Martinelli, John McDonnell, Leann Murphy, Doris Osbrook, Joe Scholten, Mary Ann Schwartz, Mary Ellen Sullivan, Peter and Pooja Vukosavich, Mary Ellen Waghorn, and members of my family.

Three women stand out. They listened, they read, they reread, they analyzed. Betsy Baer generously supported the idea and read early drafts. Esther Spodek read drafts and contributed a thoughtful analysis. Literary agent Frances Kuffel contributed her humor, enthusiasm, and considerable professional skills. In short, they made *Women Living Single* possible.

WOMEN LIVING SINGLE

Introduction

❧

We're on the way to Nana's house. Stuck in the middle seat in the back of the 1962 Buick, I'm leaning forward, my chin propped on the edge of the front seat. We're talking about marriage.

"Marriage is completion," my mother is saying. "Someday you'll understand that."

"But what about Miss Martin? She does okay."

"Miss Martin can't—doesn't have a full life," my mother says.

This is news. This is horrifying news. After all, Miss Martin is the nicest person I know. "Why not?" I ask. "Because she's not married?"

"And she doesn't have children," my mother says. "It's not a whole life without children."

I am dismayed. Miss Martin is the world's best second-grade teacher and I still visit her once a month even though I'm almost ten. She is tall and elegant and silver haired; her voice is low and musical; it's common knowledge she gets all the "difficult cases" at Ho-Ho-Kus Public School.

"You don't know that!" I argue. "You don't know!"

My father laughs.

"I do know," my mother says.

❧

But is it true?

Common wisdom—the same stuff that tells us to always look both ways before crossing the street and avoid frogs or we'll contract warts—says so. My

3

heart said so when I realized sometime in my thirties that in fact I had not married . . . and it repeated it as I watched a man I had thought I could marry (possibly, sometime, maybe) walk out. The world around me said so: it implied it in articles; it pronounced it in commercials; it proved it in movies.

It must be true.

Well, then, why not get married? I certainly had nothing against it. In fact, I'd served as a substitute wedding hostess, teaching social protocol to anxious brides and grooms, at the campus church my last year in college. Other women, women I knew and liked, had managed to marry. But there were studies telling me that I probably wouldn't, couldn't: there were just too many women like me and not enough men. And besides, there were all the specifics to work out, parallel careers and compatible values, complementing schedules for raising children and the existence of a certain Irish setter I was not willing to give up. And then, of course I'd have to meet him first . . . and then I'd have to fall in love. . . .

I went to a therapist. I sat in her beige-walled office in a pretty two-flat and went through the paces, the protracted education, the bewildering sense that somehow I'd reached a stage of adulthood—and passed it—without really noticing. She listened carefully, left the room to consult her notes, and returned with her recommendations. "You should learn to live your life as if you will always be alone," she said.

"*Always be alone,*" I heard her say, and then I heard my mother say, "*It's not a whole life.*" And then I heard the therapist say, "*Always be alone,*" and then I heard my mother say, "*It's not a whole life.*"

The echo whirled and whipped me into an emotional paralysis that lasted for almost a year. To *be alone,* I thought, to *be incomplete*—I couldn't move off the words. They expanded: alone, isolated, without connection; incomplete, unfulfilled, without purpose.

But then suddenly I asked, "Is it true? Is that what it is to be an unmarried woman?"

Answering that question has proved to be more complicated than asking it. Answering it means dealing with issues of expectation and failure: what do I really want in my life? Have I failed to get what I want? More critically, it means dealing with the definition of a feminine identity. Instinctively, I knew that the woman alone was somehow believed not to be a woman at all.

Instinct is putting it mildly; you'd have to be insensible not to notice it.

4

The bulk of western thought in novels and poetry and law draws on the definition of woman as man's love object and companion, the mother of sons, and the emotional center of the family. Virtually everywhere you turn, she exists largely in relation to others—she is rarely alone, rarely identified by something other than family. Property laws, marriage laws, employment laws; Shakespearean plays and Andy Hardy movies; Freudian thought and credit card rules: all have contributed at one time or another to the picture of woman entwined with, indeed *defined by* (and seeking definition from) the people around her.

Even recent feminists have contributed to the picture. In this psychological line of thinking, woman is defined by her nurturing role—by the way she connects with people and builds mock families as a little girl, by the fact that she brings children into the world and usually raises them, and by the apparent moral stature that her motherhood endows her with.

But there must be something more, something deeper, something more usable—something must be known about the woman alone! After all, Queen Elizabeth I was a woman alone. So was Jane Austen. Mary Cassatt. The first woman premier of Poland. Louisa May Alcott.

❦

This is not a book about consciously choosing to be single; single women in their sixties and seventies often tell me that marriage is still an option: "If the right man came along? Maybe," says Kate O'Connor, a straight-talking, confident woman in her sixties who has a ready laugh and a perceptive eye. But this is not a book about being single and doing everything you can to change that fact, either: "You mean settle? On a man? Just to get married?" asks Linda Schindler, a psychotherapist in her forties. "Never!"

This book is about a journey, the journey from girlhood, when expectations are usually clear and unquestionable, through a difficult time when the marriage choice looms large—and remains, for one reason or another—inactivated. The journey proceeds through a period of redefinition, a time of profound questioning and adjustment, when a woman consciously or unconsciously revises the place of marriage in her life and in her sense of self: she may confront, as the impressionist painter Mary Cassatt once did, the possibility that she cannot be herself and be in a *conventional* marriage; often she resolves feelings about the nature of identity, femininity, home, family, and intimacy.

Her journey ends in a time, a place, that could be called "singularity." In singularity, a woman finds a way to thrive comfortably in an unconventional situation; she finds an identity that can sustain partnership or forgo it. The singular woman likes herself, she values her place in the world, and she makes her way through the world without apology. Unlike her single sisters who have for one reason or another refused to journey, she has found herself to be worthy of her own story; she's no longer a supporting actress in someone else's movie, the single lady in perpetual waiting, the never-married woman whose marital status dominates her very sense of who she is.

But when I first started, I didn't know about singularity. I didn't know there was a journey. I didn't know to look for an alternative to the beat-beat-beat of the culture around us, the drumming, droning message that made single life appear unpalatable and nearly impossible for women. In fact, when I started, all I really wanted to know was that I wasn't alone in my fears and values—afraid of marrying the wrong guy, afraid of not marrying at all, hounded by images of spinsters shriveling into cardboard cutouts, confused by mixed messages I received in professional circles. I wanted to know who had gone before me and who was out there now.

At first I looked in all the conventional places.

The dictionary, for instance. Here, a "spinster" is "a woman past the common age of marriage." This definition floats in the wake of other events: wars, plagues, and economics all influence "the common age of marriage." In the seventeenth century, the legal age of marriage for girls was a mere twelve; you could be a spinster at nineteen. More recently, the common age of first marriage in the U.S. has drifted forward and back and forward again: from 22 in 1900, to 20.1 in 1956, to 24 in 1990. Hence, the dictionary spinster drifts in shifting cultural waters.

So I turned to the census. Today in the U.S., some nineteen million women over the age of eighteen are "drifting"—just over 19 percent of adult females. The percentage drops as age climbs: 12.6 percent of women in their late thirties have never been married, but only 8.4 percent of women in their early forties have never been married. The majority are white; a third are African American.

Our numbers swell and shrink depending on the time and place we live in. Among American women born in the ten years after the Civil War, 11 percent didn't marry; among those born during World War I, just under 5 percent didn't. In Asia the never-married woman is a rarity. In contrast, Western Europe seems to breed them: in 1860, in the Swiss canton of Obwalden, the rate was *48 percent.*

Finally I turned to the social scientists. The sociologists see us as a marginal group, a demographic anomaly in the population curve that is alternately vilified and celebrated. Traditionally the psychologists have been less kind: focusing on the definition of woman as nurturer and companion, they defined the never-married woman—the unnurturing, uncompanionable woman—as pathological until the 1960s.

The demographers are less quick to judge. They describe women who delay or forgo marriage through a statistical profile called the marriage gradient. It looks like this: in the so-called marriage market, especially at times when women outnumber men, women at the top end of the population in education and age are less likely than their younger and less accomplished sisters to find a mate. As a result, women who don't marry tend to be some of the most accomplished in the population.

Of all the demographic descriptions of women who don't marry, this is the most discussed. The marriage gradient is seen as a window into the psychological and cultural underpinnings of spinsterhood; everyone has an interpretation.

The classic interpretation is that older and accomplished women are less likely to marry because men traditionally marry "down": they marry women who are younger and less educated than they are—a phenomenon Samuel Johnson noted way back in the eighteenth century. This interpretation makes the never-married woman a kind of tragic heroine: she has developed herself, but she never wins the opportunity to share those developments.

Of course, some people, like author George Gilder, argue that women insist on marrying "up." Always looking upward toward older and more accomplished men, they squeeze the market, especially at the top, which leaves the older, accomplished woman with slim pickings—the choice to marry down or not at all. This interpretation makes the never-married woman a sort of socioeconomic prima donna. But it also goes against the grain of history, in which men have exerted most of the control in the marriage choice.

The popular media have an interpretation too. It goes like this: apparently because of their tunnel vision, college-educated and professional women have stupidly missed the marriage boat, and if they don't scramble soon, they'll be left alone on an emotional island. This is the message that appeared in a cover story in *Newsweek* in 1986, easily one of the most famous lifestyle stories the magazine has ever produced.

Newsweek's article portrayed a slow, creeping panic seizing the country as worried women discussed a new demographic disaster over the phone and at dinner: there were not enough men for all those college-educated women the baby boom had produced. "The dire statistics confirmed what everybody suspected all along," intoned *Newsweek*, "that many women who seem to have it all ... will never have mates." The doomsday tone alternately frightened and angered women across the country. "I was there when that article came out," one woman told me recently over the phone, "and I was furious." But in fact you didn't have to be there, spontaneously caught in the blaring media headlights—the study was still being quoted on the sitcom *Frasier* ten years later. *Newsweek*'s interpretation has far outlived the event—which was a poorly designed study that made marriage seem a near impossibility for college women born before 1950.

Interestingly, critics were often not as furious with the interpretation as they were with the actual statistics. The census weighed in first; then author and feminist Susan Faludi; then author Barbara Lovenheim, who still contests Faludi's statistics. Are there more women than men in this age group or that? Does a forty-year-old never-married woman have more chance of being hit by a terrorist than being married? Wading through the statistical methodologies was like balancing old checkbooks: when you were done, something had been accomplished, but what? All you realized is that you'd spent too much money twelve years ago.

In this case, a woman was likely to discover that she was born too early, she went to school too long, she had worked on her career too assiduously. Tragically, she was apt to apply the data derived from her entire generation to her specific life, an approach that was neither good for her soul nor helpful in making her marriage choice. Still, popular magazines picked up the resonant themes. In 1986 *Mademoiselle* boldly claimed that there was no man shortage; the next year *Mademoiselle* worried that the man shortage was making men arrogant.

Like the woman on the phone, I was there too, and I focused on the statistics too, until my friend Anne (now married) pointed out that the statistical hysteria was just plain stupid. She had done what she had wanted to do at eighteen and then twenty-two and then twenty-five. What was the alternative? Anne asked. Beat the marriage gradient by not going to college? By not attending graduate school in Italy? By not joining the Foreign Service?

She was right, but she was bucking a powerful, popular prejudice, the notion that women are completely passive in the marriage choice (after all, the *Newsweek* article was called "Too Late for Prince Charming?" and you can't get much more passive than Cinderella—unless, of course, you are Sleeping Beauty). She was also bucking the assumption that marriage, even a bad marriage, is something all women have traditionally craved above all things: "Many women have frankly come to terms with staying single," observed *Newsweek*, "perhaps *even* preferring it to settling for Mr. Wrong" (emphasis mine).

Anne was bucking popular thought, and she got me to thinking. She was talking about something essential, the question of what a woman is and how she makes choices. She was talking about identity, human identity; she was talking about how a woman declares herself outside the marriage contract— and, one hopes, holds on to herself once she is inside the marriage contract. Clearly I had looked in all the wrong places for an answer, for a real and living picture of what being a single woman meant. In fact, all I'd really done was get myself worked up.

The fact was, someone had gone before me. Women like Susan B. Anthony, Emily Dickinson, and Miss Martin had found wonderful, productive lives—had found themselves—outside marriage. They hadn't planned it, yet they'd done it. But how? I wondered. How? Did they avoid weddings? Did they go home for the holidays? What did they feel when they woke up in the morning? When they walked alone in the park? How did they choose their work? Their homes? Their friends? How did they find a female identity, a feminine life, when most people had to be telling them that marriage was the only route to womanhood?

That's when I decided to ask some real, living women.

𝕶

Today, as I write, my world is filled with voices, the voices of thirty women who shared their lives and their joy with me. They come from ten states across the country. They are interesting, lively women, travelers who have crossed through difficult territory; most, not all, have reached a destination called singularity. Others have it in their sights.

They are all heterosexual women who have not married. I focused on heterosexual women because marriage is a recognized rite of passage for heterosexuals; for a lesbian, a heterosexual marriage would most likely be uncomfortable, and at present she can't turn to a homosexual marriage. So her passage is different from that of a heterosexual woman, and the pressures, prejudices, and choices she encounters are different. This is a serious oversight in much of the research on never-married women: researchers have frequently failed to distinguish between lesbian women who may very well be in committed, primary, sexual relationships and heterosexual women who are not.

The voices I hear come from a wide age range—from thirty to seventy-six. I reached across this age range because I wanted to look forward, to see the life experiences of women who are forging ahead of me. This is an unusual approach: sociological and psychological studies typically work with something called "age cohorts"; by working with women in a particular age group, researchers can minimize influences caused by shifting social and political conditions. Being a writer and not a social scientist, I wasn't worried about shifting social and political conditions; they were part of the story, I felt. Similarly, I noted that most studies on never-married women focused on women in their sixties and older; the studies deal in memories thirty and fifty years past.

The voices I hear ring with a profound sense of continuity. This continuity is so deep and essential that I came to feel that the term "never-married," which is the phrase the government and social scientists use, was misleading. It suggests that these women failed in some way to do something; it suggests that they live in a state of not having done something, when in fact, many of them see themselves as living in the same state they were born in—single. That's why a better term for all women who have not married is "ever-single."

These ever-single voices—especially those who have reached the comfort and confidence of singularity—are filled with spirit and grit, with laughter and introspection. They are not shallow. They are not unaware of the choices made, the losses taken, or the joy created. They reflect a little-known phenomenon that sociologists and psychologists note every once in a while:

ever-single women show higher life-satisfaction rates than their male counterparts. In fact, they show higher life-satisfaction rates than divorced women, and they're often more satisfied than married women. "I think it all comes out even in the end," observes Maureen Cabot, sixty-eight. "There are good things about both; you're not going to find it perfect." She doesn't say this lightly. A retired public relations writer, she was certain when she took her first job as a stenographer that she would quit when she married. She knows the peculiarity of the path toward singularity.

She knows that to be singular, to be happy in her ever-single life, a woman must find a way to live outside the expected definitions and structures; she must create an identity and a life wholly of her own making, despite social and economic pressures, despite her own fears, despite the invisible losses she has suffered. That's why, in a world of increasing isolation, the singular woman becomes a model, a person who accepts the landscape of her life and builds on it, a woman who finds her way and makes it work, who creates a life of purpose and connection. "I think there's a great dignity to being single," one woman says.

So who are these women? They are teachers and daughters, sisters and friends. They are nursing in D.C. and researching in the Midwest. They are starting businesses, volunteering, working for the environment, raising children. They are making art on the eastern shore of Lake Michigan and making history in the Los Angeles Fire Department. Most live alone; some have extraordinary friendships; the happiest are close to their root families. Many have intimacy in their lives; all of them value their freedom.

And all are aware that everyone else thinks they're unhappy old maids—ugly, lonely, embittered women doing nothing worth writing about. So I asked them: if you were going to write a children's book about a single woman, what would she be like?

"She'd be strong and fun, and she'd be a teacher and a traveler," said Mary Stendahl, forty-four.

"She'd be her own person, making decisions based on what she wants to do and not . . . on what other people do," said Pat McDonald, fifty.

"She'd be witty. She'd have gone through some hard times, and she'd admit it," said Victoria Mason, thirty-nine, who has raised two children alone, "but she'd be funny."

"She'd be me," said Susan Ryerson, a forty-two-year-old fire fighter.

And I agreed.

And then I thought, how can the world that thinks they're unhappy old maids be so far off the mark?

And then I thought, what was I so scared about anyway?

CHAPTER ONE

The Cultural Mirror

"You will be married," he says with psychic certainty.

He pulls the wine cork out decisively and pours. This is our fourth date, and I've just begun to get comfortable with his kitchen, where kids' shoes and toys crowd the corners and counter tops, never quite under foot, but always in view.

He is sure. Of course, there's no reason for him to be sure of such a thing—he doesn't know me; he hasn't watched me struggle with income-tax forms or negotiate PMS; he hasn't seen the way I can sustain a depression or carry a grudge.

"Why do you say so?" I ask.

He hesitates. He shrugs. "Because," he says.

If my last name were Kennedy or Rockefeller, perhaps . . . If I had the temperament of Mother Teresa and the grace of Margot Fonteyn . . . If I were more talented than Meryl Streep and more gracious than the Queen Mother . . . perhaps. But no. To my mind, nothing about me guarantees that I'll marry.

I shrug.

He continues. "Because you're not—" He's gesturing at me.

"I'm not the spinster kind," I say.

He smiles. "Well, yeah."

This is condescension and compliment both, and I feel a vague gratitude (thank you, thank you for saying I'm not a spinster type!) mixed with a mounting anxiety (what do you mean by spinster type, anyway?).

I want to say something pointed and political. I want to make an astute
observation. I want my self-esteem to shine like a newly polished Porsche.
Instead, I take a drink of dry red wine and swallow.

꽃

Of course I know what he means. I know what one looks like, and I know I
don't want to be thought of as one. Given the research, my response is appropriate: stigma may well be one of the most virulent factors shaping and troub-
ling the lives of single people. For a woman, stigma may actually undermine
her very sense of being a feminine creature.

Yes, I well know what he means when he says "spinster type."

Despite the contemporary American prejudice against fat people, the
stigmatized spinster is not fat, but thin, paper thin, the kind of thin that suggests rigidity and frigidity; she has the bearing of a flagpole and the fashion
sense of a nun. She is usually standing in a classroom, holding a pointer (to
which she bears a remarkable resemblance), and she wears her hair in a bun
that hangs low at the nape of her neck. No one has to say it: she is clearly a
spinster.

No one has to say it because we know her so well. She is the apparition
poor, distraught George Bailey sees in the classic 1946 film *It's a Wonderful
Life* as he runs through the streets of nightmarish Pottersville, a town that has
lived without him, a town where greed and poverty have won and good people have turned to bad. Nick the bartender has become a cynic; Mr. Gower
the druggist has become a beggar—but oh! the worst, the most wrenching
fate is left for poor Mary Hatch. Because George Bailey never lived, she has
become a bespectacled, suspicious librarian who hurries in huddled, irrational
fear down the wintry streets of Pottersville, a frightened, fluttery thing who
runs away even from him, good George Bailey. "You won't like it," warns the
angel Clarence, and we don't: Mary is such a sad and pinched spinster.

Some women tell me it's the word that has the power; it's the word *spinster* that discriminates and objectifies.

"I hate that word," says Ellen Adams, a thirty-eight-year-old, fiercely independent environmentalist who has spent some of her career working on
commercial fishing vessels, living for four and six weeks at sea surrounded by,
say, five dozen Russian fishermen. She is by nature and by profession unflap-

pable. But say the word *spinster*—"That word," she chides me, "why do you keep using it?"

Several women have talked about buying their first houses and having to sign official papers that identified them as spinsters. "I talked to my female real-estate attorney about it," thirty-six-year-old Marguerite Ramanis recalls, "and she said, 'Don't worry about it.' But it annoyed me. I looked into it, and it can't be changed." She pauses, leaning against the wall of her commercial horse stable. Marguerite had postponed our meeting because she had to put up the hay, and already this morning she has cleaned the stables and worked the horses; now she stands at the doorway to her new office wearing clean shorts and a shirt and a mildly sarcastic expression. An M.B.A., Marguerite is quick witted and pragmatic. She grew up on a family farm, and just this summer she left a corporate job to pursue her lifelong love of horse training. Clearly she doesn't relate to the word *spinster* at all. But what can you do when your lawyer tells you that you're up against the forces of real estate and American law? "Just close your eyes and sign the paper," she tells me.

Women hate the word *spinster*. They never use it. Some of them shudder when they hear it. "I don't think I *am* a spinster!" one woman, forty-two, insists. But she is—she is past the common age of marrying. What she is not is the *picture* of a spinster. She is not shriveled or ramrod rigid; she is not excessively frightened. She is not even similar to more recent images: that is to say, she is not pathologically self-destructive, sexually dysfunctional, or in desperate need of a brain.

The words—*spinster, old maid, always a bridesmaid never a bride*—have power, but I think the pictures that they suggest have more power. In an increasingly visual society, it's the images that solidify the concepts and enshrine them; it's the images that influence our feelings about ourselves as young women forming our sexual and social lives; it's the images that nag us, that threaten to define us, that may even trap us into a decision we might not otherwise make.

The images threaten to trap us, and they trap other people too, people who come to expect some kind of visible evidence as to why the unmarried woman is unmarried. That's probably why, not long ago, a travel companion was confounded by Rosalie Morgan, seventy-five, and her ever-single sister. "You *never* married?" asked the traveler, apparently caught off guard by the living images of two attractive, vibrant women, one still employed in her seventies. She looked at each of them, Rosalie first, then her sister, then Rosalie, searching for visible evidence. "Is there something *wrong?*" she asked.

Such a question doesn't surprise Karen King. "The image of the single woman is a terrible image," she says, "and I think it comes from the culture." Jamaican-born, Karen came to the U.S. to go to college in the 1960s and was immediately struck by the way unmarried women are perceived here. Now she's in her fifties and looks like she's in her thirties; she's an ardent Dodgers fan who teaches high school English with a special mix of toughness and enthusiasm. Karen doesn't pull punches. In her description, America's spinster image is a refraction of the image of mainstream women. "The culture says what a woman is supposed to be," she points out. "Your life is supposed to be connected to a man's life. And if a person does not do that—either by choice or by intent or by whatever else causes it—people think of you as weak or wanting too much or having a flaw that is so insurmountable that no one wants you."

In a sense, society holds up a mirror to us, and what we see in that mirror is not who we are but how we're perceived. The mirror is influenced by economics, demographics, social norms, and, as Karen says, the status of mainstream women. Indeed, the image of the spinster is intimately tied to the social position of all women at any given time. The spinster is a weather vane, a kind of indicator.

I would like to redeem the word *spinster*. It's a nice, crisp noun like *husband* or *wife*, not an awkward adjective like *maiden* or *never-married* or even *ever-single*. But it has taken a terrible beating since the early twentieth century. It is, I think, irredeemable.

And the image? Perhaps I can reform the pictures that run through our heads and inform the people around us. First, I'll have to get a sense of how the cultural mirror works.

🦅

Without a doubt, one factor influencing the cultural mirror is demographics. The spinster is a minority in most societies; by nature, she's an exception to the way most women are and are supposed to be.

In England and the United States the norm has been, and still is, marriage. Most women marry: in the U.S. the percentage of women who remain single throughout their lives usually hovers between 3 and 10.

But, as Karen has observed, spinsters are not denigrated just because they're a minority. Marriage is much more than a norm. Up until the late twentieth century, it was an important girder in the social structure in England and the U.S. Believed to be seriously deficient in brain function and physical strength, women lived in a social and legal netherworld somewhere between male adults and children; they could not own property free and clear until the late 1800s, and although work was possible among the lower classes, it was scarce among the upper classes. That's why the marital use of the word *spinster* dates from a time when single women made money by spinning; the term for being unmarried is actually a term for work, for economic independence.

For most, spinsterhood loomed as a kind of economic and social black hole, and, as a result, early English novels are riddled with marriage stories: girls forced to marry men they dislike, daughters thrown into despair when their fathers lose their wealth, orphans left unclaimed and then rescued and placed into the warm confines of a financially stable marriage. These panic-ridden dramas were just this side of reality, and they were often written by women.

Among these writers was the obscure, acerbic, and conservative Jane Austen, a woman well acquainted with the fiscal urgency of marriage. She wrote *Pride and Prejudice* in the last years of the eighteenth century and re-vised it sixteen years later, when she was still single at thirty-seven. By that time, she'd had some field experience: having accepted a proposal from the well-born Harris Withers apparently for financial reasons, she'd unceremoni-ously dumped him less than twelve hours later, and retreated in a carriage in a whirling cloud of embarrassment. In her novel, she presents a middle-class man with five daughters to marry off, and she opens the story with the wry observation: "It is universally acknowledged that a single man in possession of a good fortune, must be in want of a wife."

In fact, a man wasn't in search of a wife so much as a father was in des-perate search of a son-in-law and a young woman was in desperate search of a place to call home. Austen knew this, and so did her readers.

Indeed, it was universally understood among Austen's readers that a fa-ther's best strategy was to marry his girls off early. In the writing of the eigh-teenth century, the marriageable woman is young and delicate; she is virginal both sexually and intellectually. She is a fresh, dainty flower waiting to be picked.

But when she is not picked, she is an unsightly problem: "the most Calamitous creature in nature," seventeenth-century advice writer Richard Allestee called her; "maidens withering on the stalk" was William Wordsworth's image; "uncultivated waste," was the term that came to mind when *Blackwell's* magazine tried to describe the unmarried women of Britain. But I think Alexander Pope said it best: "My soul abhors the tasteless dry embrace/Of a stale virgin with a winter face."

At first, you wonder how the sight of a twenty-five- or thirty-year-old woman could inspire such dismay, until you remember the economic imperative and the cultural mirror: if women are economically useful only when married and are most marriageable when they are young, then the aging single woman is an aberration, a social sin, a structural problem. As such, she inspires a social disgust tinged with sexuality and driven by the sense that the natural order has been violated.

Take John Milton's observation of Catholic countries where single women often became nuns. Convents, he said, were "convenient stowage for their wither'd daughters." As brutal as this seems, the comment here isn't personal—it's structural: the nun isn't a woman, but a withered daughter, a dependent; the convent isn't a vocation, but a form of storage, a place to put unused inventory.

For the ever-single woman looking into that antique cultural mirror, the primary message seems to be that she is ugly. But another message underlies it. The underlying message goes something like this: In a world where women are made useful by their roles in marriage, you have failed your purpose; you are useless. The connection between the image (the ugliness) and the indictment (the uselessness) is so seamless that it appears natural. The complete message is this: *usefulness is attached to beauty, and both are confirmed by marriage.*

That message—backlashing into the spinster image—persists even today. In fact, the image and the mechanism behind it have not changed much at all.

❧

Roxanne Walters arrives at the park wearing pink, green, and black spandex, a backpack, and cornrows; observant, exuberant, quick-thinking, she's a wind off the river, a political force, a personality to be reckoned with. A thirty-one-year-old filmmaker, she has worked with the director Robert Townsend, and she has founded a film organization for African Americans. She is frank, funny, self-aware. And whisking her athletic body through New York City streets, glistening a bit in the summer sun, she is beautiful. Especially when she smiles.

As a woman past the common age of marriage, Roxanne is not supposed to be this energetic or this body-confident. And, by the values of the cultural mirror, she will soon be judged faded, undesirable, a little suspect. "Yeah," she says with a roll of the eyes. "Yeah, I know."

We all know it: spinsters are ugly. Just take a look in the cultural mirror. You'll no doubt see a plain woman with close-cropped hair or a strict bun, empty eyes, and a dress destined for the dollar bin at the Salvation Army. She is Miss Quested, the flat-chested, sexually repressed heroine in E. M. Forster's 1924 novel A *Passage to India*. She is Miss Hathaway, the tall, awkward secretary in the 1960s sitcom *The Beverly Hillbillies*. She is Gunny, the monotoned military aide in the 1990s sitcom *Major Dad*.

The plainer and more out of date they are, the more immediately they're recognized as spinsters. They're clearly throwbacks: if a trend-conscious illustrator were to draw an ugly woman today, this pariah would undoubtedly be fat, not thin, and she'd be shorter rather than taller. It was way back in Charlotte Brontë's day that an ugly woman was thin: that's partly why the slim heroine of her 1847 novel *Jane Eyre* has such a rocky time of it. It's also why Jane Eyre's evil relatives go separate ways. Her attractive, *plump* cousin Georgiana is rewarded with a marriage, but her ugly, *angular* cousin Eliza is sent to a convent.

Now we are in another time, a time when American women drop millions of dollars a year in liposuction treatments just to have thighs the size of Jane Eyre's. Yet the Jane Eyre—ugly, paper-thin spinster image persists. Apparently, not only does marriage pass the spinster by, but time itself does; the spinster is irrevocably static. She's not a person at all, but a symbol, a symbol of ugliness frozen in time.

This timeless ugliness of the spinster reflects the persistent importance of beauty to all women. For the mainstream woman, beauty is a powerful force, a genetic accident that can determine the course of her life. It may affect whether she gets a good grade in reading, a prom date, a traffic ticket, a desirable job, and—as the poets, novelists, filmmakers, and historians tell us—an admirer. In fairy tales, beauty overcomes poverty and position. In television sitcoms, beautiful women turn heads and cause car accidents; in films, they make clever criminals make bad mistakes. Even in a cartoon movie, *Who Framed Roger Rabbit?* (1988), the beauty of Roger's well-endowed wife, Jessica, reduces powerful men into puddles of bubbling testosterone. By all indications, beauty is unstoppable, and it's one of the most important tools a woman has to achieve her presumed life goal: marriage.

This makes the ugliness of the spinster nearly axiomatic. She has failed to reach her life goal (marriage); therefore she must lack beauty. The axiom is so ingrained in us that it hounds even those who claim to feel good about themselves and their situation. One example occurred in a recent issue of *McCall's* magazine.

In an article called "Still Single at 38," Stephanie Brush, an accomplished writer, sets out to tell us what it's like to be an ever-single woman approaching middle age. But first, within the first twenty-five words, she hastens to assure us that she is good looking, or, as she puts it, "not unattractive enough to spoil any man's evening (or so I have been told)." Then she goes on to describe her life: leaving for China on twenty-four hours' notice, looking for condoms in all-night drug stores, and surviving dates during which each person tries to figure out what's wrong with the other. She calls this the "Secret Finger-Pointing Syndrome," and she seems to laugh at it—but only *after* she has established her credentials as a desirable woman, only after she makes it clear that nothing big (nothing physical) is wrong with *her*. The article ends with a tribute to the sanctity of marriage and the assurance that when she marries she will wear magenta. She doesn't explore why she would marry, what she's looking for in a marriage, or what she feels she would realistically gain or give up. She mentions only the dress.

But if that mishmash of self-doubt and self-proclamation were not confusing enough, Brush wrote a follow-up piece sometime later for the *Orlando Sentinel*. In it, she complains about the *McCall's* photo staff, who handled her makeup and gave her a $2,000 jacket to wear for the photograph that accompanied the article. Brush resents the magazine's emphasis on her appearance and sees the art direction as manipulation.

She's onto something here. But she fails to see her participation in it.

She—like the culture—apparently believes that something must be wrong with the unmarried woman, and it's probably the way she looks. Brush makes her first defense where she believes the first attack will be. Then she attacks others for doing the same. The result is a kind of furious cartoon scuffle in which the premise—*something must be wrong with the unmarried woman*—escapes attention.

Having spent untold hours in front of my own bathroom mirror measuring my impossible chin from every possible angle, I can't quite blame her. The attack on the single woman's appearance is real, and it's easily internalized, often in feelings about our bodies. "I tore myself inside out trying to—I thought, well if I lost two pounds . . ." Janice Patinkin, a thirty-eight-year-old dental hygienist, says of a particularly rough time in her twenties. "Where was my head at?" That's a good question. Athletic and graceful, Janice stands five feet tall at most, and I doubt she has ever achieved a three-digit weight. Her body is so lean and taut that she once mistook the slight bulge of a fibroid tumor for a stomach muscle. Above all, she is spontaneous, genuine, and laughs at herself with ease.

But to be beautiful is a pressure all women feel, and the charge of being ugly is an indictment most single women feel. Patricia McDonald, a fifty-year-old Michigan schoolteacher with a voice that could melt Antarctica, felt the indictment increase as she passed the common age of marriage. "My mother said, 'Such a pretty face,'" she recalls. "My father didn't say much about it." She pauses, and then she admits that her father did try to make deals with her: he'd pay off her car loan if she lost weight.

"So they connected your weight with your marital status," I say. I'm thinking of a number of overweight married women I know. "Do *you* feel that way?"

There are many things in Pat's life that I heard about later, individual events and choices that had influenced her life course: her connection to the church, her hesitance to join activities, her quiet life in a tiny town surrounded by wheat fields, her involvement with fully formed families. But at this moment, that old spot, the spot where she was hit most often, is exposed, and it is painful. At this moment, it's hard to separate reality from her reflection in the cultural mirror.

"I don't know" is all she says.

Of course there *are* beautiful ever-single women on television and in film. But the ever-single heroine who is endowed with beauty is inevitably endowed with other qualities that explain why she has "failed" to marry.

Most often, she is endowed with a brain the size of the average breath mint, which seems to account for her effervescent personality. On early television *My Friend Irma* established the type—a dumb, sexy blond, who, luckily for her continued survival on the planet, had a levelheaded roommate. Similarly, *The Gale Storm Show* had Susanna Pomeroy bubbling and bungling her way through life as the social director on a cruise ship. One wonders how these women manage to pay their parking tickets; not all of them are protected by concerned fathers as Rebecca Howe was on the eighties sitcom *Cheers*. Yet they are more common than compassionate doctors on prime-time TV—and that's saying a lot.

Flanking the breath mints are the bosses, the cranky, aggressive women who are just too difficult to attract and keep a man. These are worthy women, but defensive and slow to reveal their vulnerability. Margo Channing in the film *All About Eve* (1950) is such a type; so is Tess Harding in *Woman of the Year* (1942). Tess, a foreign correspondent who speaks a half dozen languages including Arabic and Serbian, is so assertive that her colleagues claim it's best to sign a nonaggression pact before dealing with her. Interestingly, she was raised by her ever-single aunt, "another difficult case."

In TV sitcoms, the most famous boss is *M*A*S*H**'s Margaret Houlihan—pretty, sexy, loudmouthed, and rigid, a woman so pungent that for years the only man who can connect with her is a self-indulgent, married wimp named Frank Burns. Less pungent but more lethal is Maggie O'Connell, the beautiful, self-reliant pilot in the 1990s series *Northern Exposure*. O'Connell is particularly bitchy toward the snobby, self-involved town doctor, who seems to deserve it. But that's not her crime. No, O'Connell has a worse fault: whenever she dates someone, he dies. She is a one-woman dating death squad. It is an imaginative twist on an old tradition.

In fact, Maggie O'Connell was lucky that *she* wasn't the one zapped by the writers. As researcher Diana Meehan has pointed out, TV is not kind to independent women. Reject a man, create an independent life, live alone, and it could be lethal. When an attractive woman tells Steven Kiley, the young, handsome doctor on *Marcus Welby, M.D.*, a 1960s evening drama, that she loves another man, she is quickly thrown from a horse and paralyzed from the waist down. The foolish woman who spurns Dr. Kildare, another sixties medical hunk, contracts leukemia and dies. On *Medical Center* a woman turns down her doctor and *boing!*—says Meehan—breast cancer.

In later years the penalties for singleness became rape, harassment, and violent death. This TV trend was so flagrantly misleading that it captured the attention of a U.S. senator, Paul Simon, who told a Chicago radio audience that television was just plain wrong on the subject of single women and violence: in the world of television, single women are the primary victims of violence, he said; in the real world, married women are.

Beautiful *but*—vulnerable. Stunning *but*—bossy. Attractive *but*—brainless. What are we to do with a woman like that? She may be pretty, *but* she's dangerously unattached. Which must mean she has no purpose.

A couple of years ago fire fighter Susan Ryerson investigated a juvenile incident. In a transient hotel where the hallways smelled of garbage, she found an eight-year-old girl and her mother, both of them polite and very frightened. The girl had accidentally burned them out of their home.

Kids set a lot of fires, dangerous ones, Susan tells me. Years before, she investigated fire scenes, and she remembers one in particular where a whole family died, trapped on the second floor. Now, sitting in this dingy hotel room, with a vase of fresh daisies on the table, she had a choice. She could pull out the in-your-face photos of children who died in fires—the lecture for school-aged kids—or she could go with her instincts. She pulled out a coloring book. The little girl relaxed. The mother smiled.

Right away I notice that there's a difference between Susan and just about every spinster image I've ever seen. It's not the badge or the attractive, breezy haircut or her basic respect for people. It's the fact that she's got a purpose. It would matter if Susan didn't show up.

Yet Susan *doesn't* show up in the cultural mirror. There, spinsters are frustrated, narrow-minded, and useless.

Just *how* useless?

As Anita Brookner's 1993 novel *Fraud* opens, British spinster Anna Durant has been missing for *four months* before anyone notices that she's gone. In a recent play by Alan Bennett, a middle-aged spinster sits in a chair and chats happily about her work as a clerk in a large corporation. As she ages, the highly replaceable clerk sinks into a terrifying, disabling disease, an emotional anonymity; of course, throughout it's clear to the audience that she will be easily forgotten by her colleagues. The play is called A *Woman of No Importance*.

And these are the kinder, gentler, more complex literary images. The characterization of spinsters as functional failures has dozens of simplistic paper-doll versions; it's everywhere in the society. Indeed, I think it comes from the society, not from the frontiers of artistic originality. It is what literary critics call a stock character; the purposeless spinster is shorthand for things extraneous, futureless, useless.

When *Forbes* magazine reports on a stalled and financially lonely corporate giant, the headline asks: "Ma Bell an Old Maid?" When *Business Week* reports on Stone Container's hesitation to choose a merger over going it alone, the magazine opines that Stone Container's hesitation has "*condemned it to life as an old maid*" (emphasis mine). The judgment here is that the company's failure to partner consigns it to a lack of productivity (as it does for a woman). In the children's card game, the old maid has no positive value; you get stuck with her, you lose. But I think current slang has summed it up the best in the Midwest, where an "old maid" is a kernel of non-popping popcorn—the very pinnacle of uselessness.

What's strange about all of this is that it flies in the face of history. The first women to work outside the home, to be *publicly* productive, were mostly formerly married and ever-single women. That's why so many of the pioneers that feminists have retrieved from the storm drains of history are single. Aphra Behn, a mediocre seventeenth-century playwright who is nonetheless celebrated as the first professional woman writer, was widowed. The Quaker abolitionist Sarah Moore Grimké, one of the first women in America to speak in front of a co-ed crowd, was ever-single. Elizabeth Blackwell, one of America's first woman doctors, was ever-single too.

Slowly, inexorably, as it became clear that warehousing wasn't going to work, so-called "excess" (unmarried) women opened major educational and occupational doors in the nineteenth and twentieth centuries. They took on new kinds of jobs; they developed new professions and institutions. This is productivity of the male kind. Yet in the cultural mirror, the old maid is still underfunctional, an expendable clerk performing a trivial task she doesn't know is trivial. The old maid's purposelessness is just as timeless as her ugliness.

Occasionally there *are* image blips, moments when purposeful spinsters achieve celebrity. They appear at times of political change for all women, and they inevitably end in a reaffirmation of marriage as the preferable state.

The most famous blip occurred around the turn of the twentieth century. If ever there was a time to be a spinster, this was it. "Oh, it was a wonderful time," says high school teacher Christi Wagner, who at age forty-five obviously didn't live it, but studied it as part of her master's program. She also once analyzed the images of women in five women's magazines. "It was a great era for the coming out of women, the vote and all that business," she says, "*and* the outspokenness." The problem, she adds in a tiny, lilting voice, "was those darned 1950s."

She's right. Between 1870 and 1920, single women left home in greater numbers than ever before; women's colleges were established; popular women's magazines proclaimed spinsterhood a viable lifestyle. It was a time when a woman could write seriously and without shame, "I want to be a spinster and a good one," and an article in a 1917 issue of the *Atlantic Monthly* magazine was unabashedly signed, "by an elderly spinster." Ellen Key, a Swedish writer, surveyed the scene and declared that spinsters had changed. No longer were they bitter old women, imbibing a "multitude of humiliations" as governesses, companions, and hangers-on. Here was a new type, she wrote in 1909: the joyous, active, independent unmarried woman, a "glorified spinster."

With this kind of endorsement behind them, glorified spinsters established settlement houses in London and Chicago; they explored Africa; they joined the faculties of universities. They were a leading edge in a vast social shift toward civil rights for women. They were indisputably productive.

And, as Christi notes, they were catching a ride on historical currents that were whisking mainstream married women into the modern age. The Victorian emphasis on duty was ebbing, and a greater emphasis on individual rights was burgeoning. Margaret Sanger initiated her campaign for contraception. And marriage was openly criticized in popular novels and women's magazines: "To be frank about it, the intelligent American girl is afraid of getting married," announced a 1909 editorial in *The Independent.* "She has reason to be. The veil has been taken from her eyes . . . and she is appalled by what she sees."

In both Britain and America the vote was achieved. The land-based, inheritance-oriented marriage contract that had burdened characters in Austen and Brontë novels was gone. Married women's lives were changing—and even though the spinster was still marginal, she lived in a margin that seemed to be heading in the same direction that the educated and married mainstream was going, or could at least tolerate.

But it was a blip. By the late 1920s currents had shifted, and ever-single women had shriveled into passive, unhappy types haunting the halls of elementary schools. Ironically, the sexual discussion that seemed to support the Age of the Spinster may have also contributed to its demise. While people like Margaret Sanger and her lover, sexologist Havelock Ellis, promised a future of sexual freedom, their more august contemporary Sigmund Freud raised the specter of sexual pathology—and it stuck.

The Depression, with its economic and social retrenchment, capped off the era. Add to this the social focus on our fighting men during World War II and the engineered familism of the 1950s—and it would be fifty years before another significant blip appeared and the ever-single woman would *look* purposeful again.

🌿

The next blip occurred in the 1970s, the era of *The Women's Room, An Unmarried Woman, The Turning Point,* and *Fear of Flying.* Amid these "women's" novels and movies, television gave us *The Mary Tyler Moore Show,* featuring Mary Richards, the first pretty, competent, ever-single woman who lived away from home and worked as anything other than a teacher or secretary. Turning the pretty-but-stupid formula on its ear, the show made Mary's colleague Ted Baxter, a square-jawed, silver-haired anchorman, indisputably incompetent. Mary, in turn, was allowed to do her job well. She was occasionally silly, but always responsible, and she was a good and steady friend.

She reflected her times. In America in 1970, mainstream women faced enormous social change. Between 1960 and 1970, the number of women working outside the home increased 35 percent. Marriages began to dissolve at an ever-increasing rate (the divorce rate actually doubled between 1966 and 1976), leaving many women single for the first time in their adult lives. Some were living alone, as Mary was. Many were dating, as Mary was. At the same time, the campaign for the Equal Rights Amendment was in full swing. Fueled by the pop do-what-you-want-as-long-as-it-doesn't-hurt-anybody ethos of the late sixties, the image of Mary Richards—a woman still single at thirty, engaged in a meaningful job, and relatively happy—was acceptable.

But in 1980 the nation elected the avuncular Ronald Reagan and began to court domestic images that had long since become economically impossible. During the second half of the decade, the status of mainstream women careened under contradictory messages that told them to be sexually alluring, but reach for success; work extraordinary hours, but focus on their husbands and children; become educated and competent, but accept the "mommy track." As the family stumbled under time pressures and the 1990 recession, news reports falsely suggested that large numbers of mainstream women were guiltily returning to the home to take up their neglected work as mothers and homemakers. The independent woman, the woman who was not caught up in this agonizing cycle, became increasingly suspect.

Film handed us a successful ever-single executive who miraculously "inherited" a baby and learned about real life. The Indiana Jones films gave us a profile of the decade, a downward progression in which the ever-single woman tumbled from likability into malevolence. The series started with the good-hearted and feisty ever-single Marion (*Raiders of the Lost Ark*, 1981); then moved to the beautiful, bland, and ever-helpless, ever-single Willie (*Indiana Jones and the Temple of Doom*, 1984); and finally concluded with the evil and manipulative ever-single Nazi, Elsa (*Indiana Jones and the Last Crusade*, 1989).

Under similar pressures, Christine Cagney, the competent, ever-single cop on the TV drama *Cagney and Lacey*, rode the whitewater shift in attitudes through the late eighties and finally sank. Although CBS allowed Cagney to turn down a marriage proposal, programming executives were uncomfortable with her. They struggled with her image, fidgeted over her robust character, canceled the show despite passable ratings, and then retracted. In the end, dedicated, fallible, pretty Christine Cagney proved unmanageable. You couldn't marry her off, and you certainly couldn't kill her. Her attractiveness was necessary for television stardom, and her toughness was appropriate for the job she was doing. And on top of all that, the woman wasn't unhappy.

How do you deal with a woman like that? The network finally canned the show.

And herein lies the last image in the cultural mirror. Even if we are beautiful, even if we are productive, even if we do have functioning brains and gentle spirits, the ever-single woman is perceived to be miserable, miserable, miserable.

❦

"I think it's insulting when people act as though if you're not married it had to be that nobody ever wanted you," says witty, opinionated Carrie Cunningham, a travel agent in her late fifties. She's one of the viewers who wrote CBS the first time *Cagney and Lacey* was canceled, and, despite the spinster stereotype, she is decidedly not miserable: "Maybe I have a gene missing?" she jokes.

The gene she's apparently missing is the Havisham gene, named for the grandmother of all modern-day rejected, dejected, and otherwise miserable spinsters. Born in Charles Dickens's imagination in 1860, Miss Havisham began to haunt my childhood a hundred years later, when I encountered her one Christmas Eve in the late 1960s. The opening of David Lean's 1946 film of *Great Expectations* is scary enough—we see nine-year-old Pip confronted by a runaway convict—but it was the eerie, unnatural wedding scene that did me in. As young Pip walks into a banquet hall, the camera reveals a long dining-room table inexplicably set for a formal dinner amid dust and cobwebs. As he scans the empty hall, he notices a mouse eating an ancient, moldy wedding cake. Abruptly, miserable old Miss Havisham, still wearing the white wedding dress she wore the day she was jilted, taps Pip on the shoulder—and I turned the TV off. That image stuck with me for thirty years, but since I was too chicken to see the rest of the film, I never knew which English classic it came from.

As a result, I only recently discovered the real horror of Miss Havisham. Her unmitigated bitterness is bad, but her greatest sin is the heartless girl she has raised to wreak revenge on men. For this, Dickens burns her in her dried wedding dress like an aging, flaking book and then lets her linger in pain for a few more chapters until she dies, a reformed but isolated old woman.

Luckily, most miserable spinsters have neither the resources nor the imagination of Miss Havisham. Usually they just chase and complain, and, by chasing and complaining, they confirm the primacy of marriage in the lives of women.

Miss Hathaway, otherwise a reasonable person, chases the stupid, Boy Scout–handsome Jethro Bodine. Sally Rogers, the clever comedy writer on the sixties sitcom *The Dick Van Dyke Show*, makes self-deprecating singles jokes to her senior colleague Rob Petrie—which in turn affirm the happy role of Rob's bubbly wife, Laura.

Ten years later the liberated Mary Richards is flanked by two single women whose unhappiness is firmly centered in their marital status: Sue Ann, the sugary and desperate star of a homemaking show, and Rhoda, a witty self-proclaimed fat girl. In the late seventies, miserable Margaret Houlihan indiscriminately throws herself at aging generals until she finally lands a career officer who later cheats on her. In the mid-nineties pretty, minty Kim of *Almost Perfect* asks a man she has dated twice whether he plans to marry her.

But at no time since Miss Havisham have ever-single women been more miserable than Alex Forrest, the beauty who dominates the hyper-violent 1988 film *Fatal Attraction*.

"Can I ask you something?" asks the attractive, married lawyer Dan Gallagher, whose wandering eye has fallen on blond, sexy Alex. "Why don't you have a date tonight? It's Saturday night." (Translation: what's wrong with you—you're beautiful, you're not a breath mint or a boss; why aren't you with a man?) Dan Gallagher is annoyed; some part of him resents having to "deal" with an attractive unmarried woman.

From then on, the ever-single thirty-six-year-old Alex plays the evil twin to Gallagher's wife, like a sexualized, updated Sally Rogers playing to a yuppie Laura Petrie. But Alex is much more shadowy than Sally. She is profoundly disconnected from the world: she never gets a phone call; although she is a successful book editor, she never actually works. There are pale shadows in her past—a father who died, a miscarriage some time ago—but for the most part Alex has no story and no real life. She is a neurotic paper doll, perpetually dressed in bridal white, sitting alone on her bed, calling, calling, calling Dan, while he—normal, married, connected—interacts with his dog and his secretary and his wife.

At one point Alex slits her wrists because Dan is going to leave her. Later, she threatens to kill his wife. At the end of the literal bloodbath that she wreaks, the camera lingers on an Ophelia image of her floating dead in the water, then pans over to a portrait of the Gallagher family, intact and healthy; here is the marginal woman and there the married woman, says the camera. *Choose one.*

"Haven't you seen *Fatal Attraction?*" Sam Baldwin demands when he finds out that his eight-year-old son has called a radio shrink in an effort to find him a new wife. It is five years later, and the Chicago audience watching *Sleepless in Seattle* breaks out in laughter. The joke is clear: we know what those single women are like. In this atavistic, romantic movie, the theme sounds once more: *those ever-single women are just kooky and miserable and desperate enough to be dangerous—or at least unpleasant.*

"If that's all people see, of course that's what they think of single women," observes thirty-year-old Felicia Collinet, who admits that she sometimes thinks those things too. She's a fund-raiser for a children's theater, the daughter of African-born parents who has laid the foundation for a promising career. But she is often sad and sometimes confused. It's difficult, she says, to filter these images.

Filtering is not easy. In fact, most women do their best to ignore the images altogether. Living on the West Coast, spending her evening hours trying to save the shoreline from development, Ellen Adams doesn't own a television and is only vaguely aware of magazines like *Cosmopolitan.* Teresa Sanchez, a professor of comparative literature, owns one, watches it, but refuses to watch sitcoms. Pat McDonald owns one, watches it, and finds herself arguing with the commercials. Others struggle more openly. When I first ran a newspaper ad to find ever-single women, one woman called specifically to complain about *Sleepless in Seattle;* she had counted the references to desperate women (four) and resented every one. Unsolicited, half a dozen women talked about the 1986 *Newsweek* article. One woman told me that when she first meets people she tells them that she's divorced.

Instinctively, this last woman seemed to know that ignoring the images just isn't enough. Even if we don't look into the mirror, other people do. They imbibe the images and the language, and many accept without questioning images that have no contradiction in their immediate lives—and then they interact with us. That's probably why they ask, "Why aren't you married?" as if this is an easy, impersonal question to answer; apparently, they believe that we'll draw our answer from any one of the four or five formulas TV has provided. Yet they'd be startled if we were to ask, "Why are you married?" and expect a similar kind of response.

More profoundly, the images inform women's fears of not marrying and of being around people who aren't married: I like to think that when my pregnant friend told me that she didn't want a baby girl because she didn't want to raise a spinster, she was thinking of Miss Havisham and not of me. "They think it's real. They see *Fatal Attraction* and that is what they think," says Teresa, forty-five. She is sitting in her university office with a copy of *Don Quixote*, the story of a man who fights windmills, in front of her; Teresa has some experience with crazy characters. "But no one," she says of Alex Forrest, "no one is *that* crazy."

Nor is anyone that desperate, and yet the image is part of our lives. When an auto mechanic referred to Katrina Baker, who is thirty-one, as an "old maid" recently, she challenged him. "Do I look like an old maid to you?" she asked him.

"No," he answered. "But years ago you would have been considered an old maid."

"Well I certainly don't consider myself that," she told him in her precise, well-spoken way. "I *like* the way I am."

The mechanic laughed loud and hard at this statement, apparently sure that she was mistaken. "Oh, man," he concluded. "We gotta find you a husband."

Indeed, as Teresa points out, a big body of evidence suggests that television viewers do in fact see TV as representing reality in areas as pervasive as relationships, behavior, and social status. This cultural onslaught requires of us a quiet strength, a kind of internal mirror that keeps us clear about and content with who we are.

Some women, the singular women, have this. Karen King, with her sharp, cross-cultural observations, seems to have been born with it; Marguerite Ramanis, the entrepreneur with the commercial horse barn, has developed it. But others, like many of the women in Barbara Levy Simon's 1987 study *Never Married Women*, cope by changing the reflection in their internal mirrors; they conform as closely as they can to the notion of the ideal woman, the nurturing, compliant, married woman, so that they can at least *appear* acceptable. It's a technique that works—but it's not necessarily comfortable. In fact, it can be quite uncomfortable, especially if a woman is driven by the haunting, internalized fear that there's something not quite right with her. "Like, why my sisters, why my friends, why not me? What have I done?" asks Janice, who has two sisters, one married and one divorced. "You know, you get crazy."

Even in the absence of these internal and external judgments, the media-drenched world does not make it easy for single women. Let's just say some vibrant ever-single woman—Roxanne Walters, for instance—manages to ignore the Alex Forrests and Miss Hathaways and deals only with people who filter their media in highly sophisticated ways—filmmakers and friends who understand imagery—and accept her individuality. Or maybe Roxanne changes just a little bit: maybe she softens her speech when a glitch occurs so that no one blames her anger on her marital status, or maybe she abdicates her leadership role when it might seem too "boss." Even then Roxanne lives in a world without popular models.

When I asked, "What do you do for role models?" there was a nearly universal shrug among the ever-single women.

That blankness is disturbing, I thought, sitting in the park listening to Roxanne. For the truth is, in the last year I have never met a woman who fulfilled the image of a spinster. I never met a breath mint or a boss, an unproductive woman, a withering schoolmarm. Mostly I met vibrant women, each with a strong sense of purpose and place in life. Similarly, I never met a woman who *chose* to take this unusual course through life. In large part, singleness happens to women—no one I met chose it wholesale, the way you choose a book to read or a college to attend. So how does such a woman proceed across the unexpected blankness without a positive image, without a road map?

Among the women I've talked to, most would like to fill in the blank—not with a prescription (most of these women are too independent for that, and many would like to be married), but with one or two or five enduring images. Just something to refer to on occasion, when the going gets rough, when the cultural mirror begins to nag. Just something to glance at and feel confirmation. Just something to counteract the impact of the cumulative social forces that affect single people.

An *accurate* mirror would do; a mirror that reflects the people we actually are—Marguerite Ramanis and Pat McDonald and Susan Ryerson—would do. A clear and uncompromised picture of what our expectations have been and what our lives are like now, one that includes the sadness and the happiness both, the loneliness and the freedom both. A mirror that shows our beauty and our purpose. That shows us what it is to be a singular woman.

It's time to start.

CHAPTER TWO

Expectations

🦅

She wants to be a bride. Of course she does. Every little girl does. Her best friend, Tonya, does.

Together Roxanne and Tonya play Barbie dolls. They play Barbie and Ken. They play Barbie and Ken Getting Married.

Later, in high school, Roxanne and Tonya vow to be each other's bridesmaids and they spend hours glued to the television watching Princess Di's wedding. "All that gaudy stuff," Roxanne recalls now. "We watched all of it, every second."

When it's time to look for dresses for the prom, they start small, but soon they're trying on bridal gowns, long ones, white ones, with satin trains and full-length veils. Roxanne's in love. Maybe she'll marry John Osterman.

"The images were very storybook," she says now, "because that's all I'd ever seen." But Roxanne's own story turned out differently. No longer a friend, Tonya got married a few years ago. Far away in Los Angeles, John died in a car accident. At thirty-one, Roxanne doesn't know whether she'll marry or not.

But she remembers the dreams, the bridal magazines she bought, the pictures she had in her mind. They're clearer than anything.

🦅

Whenever anyone asks, "Why didn't you get married?" I'm stumped. Ever since I was a little girl, I planned on marrying—no, not exactly planned. I *expected* it.

Indeed, most of the ever-single women I've met say that they expected to marry. "I never considered that I would be a single woman," says Mary Stendahl, forty-four, a New England schoolteacher who shares her home with a spunky Bernese mountain dog. "It's funny, because nobody ever asked me that. It never occurred to me that I would never get married. It's weird."

Her closest role model was her mother, who enjoyed a loving marriage; in the distance, there was a maiden aunt who visited once every ten years and wore outlandish clothes. She was Portland, Maine's, answer to Auntie Mame, and Mary was not impressed: "She was a little bizarre."

Single is foreign, complicated; married is familiar, simple. "See, I thought my life would be simple," says Christi Wagner, who lives in a trendy New York neighborhood and commutes to a wealthy New Jersey suburb to teach high school English. "Not easy, but simple. Long Island. I'd get married; I'd have kids; I'd teach people how to use the semicolon. That would be my life."

The expectation isn't surprising. In the late 1980s, when sociologist Ruth Sidel traveled the country asking young women between the ages of fifteen and twenty-five about their version of the American dream, nearly all expected to marry—despite the discouraging divorce statistics that had probably touched their lives already. In *Private Pages*, a compendium of women's diaries written between 1832 and 1979, the diaries of young girls who grew up to be ever-single are almost indistinguishable from those of the girls who grew up to marry. They talk about making friends, getting along with their parents, eating too much, wishing for adulthood and worrying about it. We are told that one young girl whose diary describes a series of profound crushes on her teachers discovered her homosexuality later in life, but for the most part the girls all seem headed in one direction—and they all seem to feel that it's the direction they're supposed to be headed in. None of the girls at age thirteen expects to be alone. All of them are concerned with fitting in, living peaceably and productively within their families, finding intimacy, and figuring out how to achieve marriage.

Our expectations have been—well, what you would expect.

Just take a look at the books on any little girl's bookshelf. I still have mine: *Rapunzel, Sleeping Beauty, Beauty and the Beast, The Frog Prince, The Lit-*

tle Mermaid, Cinderella, Snow White. As these traditional stories crisscrossed western culture, they carried their heroines to their final, lofty destiny: marriage. For psychoanalyst Bruno Bettelheim, this was necessary: these fairy tales, he believed, were stories of development, of maturation, and marriage was the normal—indeed necessary—culmination of late childhood. It is the thing the child reaches for, if only unconsciously.

Consciously, the message was much more dramatic, something filmmaker Walt Disney knew well. All alone in a forest, his young Snow White soulfully sings "Someday My Prince Will Come" to a crowd of birds who offer their pity; in a crowded ballroom, his Cinderella dances on fairy-dust air among well-dressed admirers. To be unmarried is to be mournful, incomplete; to be married is to be accepted, celebrated.

To modern adult eyes, the drama is almost comical, especially after, say, three or four consecutive readings of "Beauty and the Beast." With enough repetition, "Beauty" starts to look a lot like a lesson in feminine self-sacrifice, a kind of pre-Bradshaw codependency that transforms following orders and caring for a beast into a feminine art, the conversion of the world through love and patience. At the other end of the scale, "Cinderella" is something of a revenge fantasy: getting the prince would not be nearly as much fun if Cinderella didn't get the chance to leave those nasty, fat-footed, spinsterish stepsisters in the dust.

In fact, fairyland is paved with the defeats of evil spinsters—unmarried, infertile types who threaten the natural order. The witch in "Rapunzel" is not only single, she has a garden full of rampion, which her pregnant neighbor craves. To withhold the rampion is tantamount to sabotaging the pregnancy, we feel. And in fact she exacts an unethically high price for the stuff: she demands the child in return.

Sleeping Beauty is hounded by an apparent spinster too. The spinster's original spell would have killed Beauty (how's that for a metaphor?) if no one had intervened. Her motive: she has been slighted, excluded from the family circle.

And who can forget Dorothy's problems? In the 1939 film version of The Wizard of Oz, Miss Gulch is not only ugly, she's vindictive, and her fairyland counterpart, the Wicked Witch of the West, is downright evil. Unlike Glinda, who is characterized by her motherlike relationship to the Munchkins, the Wicked Witch of the West has only her sister, now dead. And that sisterly relationship is hardly tender: the first thing we see is anger. The next thing we see is greed.

Even if fairy tales don't create the expectation to marry, it would be safe to say they don't inspire many young girls to seek out the spinster's life either.

᛫

"When I was growing up, you just saw yourself as getting married, and then nothing else after that," remembers Carrie Cunningham, the woman who claims she's missing a "misery gene." "You know, you grew up and you went to school, and then you got married, and I do mean 'got married.' It was a state of being. It wasn't like you ever stopped and thought that you have to be married *to* somebody." In some cases, she says, it didn't seem to much matter *whom* a girl married just as long as she married at a respectable age. "I had one friend whose mother . . . thought you should get married at about eighteen. She was very sweet about it, but she was always reminding Sally to be marriageable." Whenever Sally had a fight with a boyfriend, her mother would counsel her to be careful, to be nice, to behave a certain way. "She'd say, 'You have to do that so he'll go on liking you,'" remembers Carrie, "'because having a man of your own is extremely important.'"

At seventeen, Carrie Cunningham watched with uncomprehending dismay. "I thought, oh God, this is awful."

Awful though it may have seemed to young Carrie, Sally's mother was actually invoking a long-standing tradition, the notions that a girl's worth and future depend on her marriageability, and that marriageability is a *learned* skill. Mothers and fathers and self-appointed advisors have been invoking these notions for hundreds of years, and many still do.

For the young girl growing up in the seventeenth, eighteenth, and nineteenth centuries, the message that a girl's worth was tied to marriage was primarily conveyed through her so-called education, which, for the most privileged classes, was a smorgasbord of etiquette, music lessons, embroidery, and general knowledge designed to increase her attractiveness—a sort of four-course meal without protein or carbohydrates. If she had liberal parents, she might learn to read; if she had unusual parents, she might learn to read Latin or Greek and do a little math. She might attend a girls' school, but often she studied at home, though rarely to the extent that her brothers did. This disparity fueled the eighteenth-century essays of feminist Mary Wollstonecraft, and it was justified in a series of essays by Edward Dickinson, father of the ever-single poet Emily. In the late 1870s, the disparity so frustrated the precocious Mary Kingsley that she finally stole her father's chemistry books and hid them until she'd finished reading them. Thus educated, she became a well-known explorer and biologist.

For girls like Mary Kingsley, training was supposed to focus on behaviors congruent with the social and economic necessity to marry. More bluntly, training taught girls how to please men without sacrificing their modesty. "An immodest woman is a kind of monster," notes Wendell Wilkes in his eighteenth-century bestseller A *Letter of Genteel and Moral Advice to a Young Lady*. By all accounts, modesty is characterized by silence and undermined by education. "Be ever cautious in displaying your good sense," advice writer John Gregory counsels young women in A *Father's Legacy to His Daughters*. "It will be thought you assume a superiority over the rest of the company. But if you happen to have any learning, keep it a profound secret, especially from the men." (Although ubiquitous, Gregory's book sometimes missed its mark. In the mid-1700s it was given to a young woman named Abigail Smith, who later married and rebelliously warned her revolutionary husband, John Adams, that if "ladies" were not given a voice in government, they would revolt.)

This constant advice was politely called "conduct literature" and it never let up; in one form or another, it advised and censured young women for centuries. Jane Austen read conduct literature; so did the fictional Jane Eyre. In post-revolutionary America, when adults began to worry that their daughters would not put up with this unpalatable writing, they turned it into bad fiction, novels such as *The Boarding School; or, Lessons of a Preceptress to her Pupils*. There readers met characters like Flirtilla, whose shameless coquetry dooms her to a gloomy and isolated life. They also met Lydia, who turns down a good marriage to take care of her mother. Predictably, good, self-sacrificing Lydia is rewarded with a guy whose marital résumé makes Bill Cosby look like Al Capone.

But the effort to mold women for marriage didn't stop there. In the twentieth century, the conduct tradition that Sally's mother vocalized was taken over by the women's magazines, which alternately counseled, cajoled, and criticized their readers about a whole string of feminine behaviors. In the

1950s, *Vogue* sounded much like Wendell Wilkes. "There are some rules: women are at least supposed to look down when sighting a strange man," notes one article, which goes on to list other specifications: "He wants her to be neat, smart, simply not fussily dressed, and displayed at her most attractive." The fifties woman must be elegant and more; like Wilkes's woman, she must be focused on her man: "Quite rightly he resents it when he senses (as he is quick to do) that she is dressing not to please him but for the approval of other women. Above all she must be feminine."

For women like me who were born in the mid-twentieth century, John Gregory and Wendell Wilkes sound so obvious, Edward Dickinson sounds so desperate, *Vogue* sounds so silly. It's easy to pinpoint the influences that shaped the expectations of *other* generations. Clearly contemporary experience is much more subtle: our economic freedom is so much greater, our choices more plentiful, our communications so multifaceted, so fast. But then I hear Carrie Cunningham's summation—"It was as if Sally was being told, you should just be whatever this other person wants you to be"—and I realize that the influences that shape our individual expectations don't stop with the copies of *Cinderella*, the broadcasts of Di's wedding, or even the latest issue of *Vogue*.

Now, just as way back when future First Lady Abigail Adams read books that told her to keep quiet, a girl's experience is cumulative, unpredictable, maybe even unfathomable. Whatever cultural influences swirl around us, whatever the media blare at us, the closer I move my camera in—toward nineteenth-century biologist Mary Kingsley, toward twentieth-century dreamer Roxanne Walters—the more incalculable these influences become. For we begin to slide down an emotional slope, past the courses in home economics, past the fairy tales—to that private place where cultural influences converge with individual temperaments, events, and families. There, what the world says about women and wives and femininity and achievement is amplified or dulled; there, in a kind of emotional blender, a girl's identity is formed and a personal sense of the future is created.

❧

"It was a good marriage," Roxanne observes. Her father worked for an auto manufacturer; her mother worked for an electronics company. Roxanne's parents encouraged her to find something to do, and she drifted into college.

Inevitably, what her parents had together influenced her: growing up in that household, coming home for Christmas, watching her parents work, go to church, and support their children, informed her sense of what her life was going to be like, and it wasn't until much later that things like racial fallout and gender politics began to intrude on this image. "I guess I want a man like my dad," she says, more cautiously than she might have five years ago. "My dad is a good man [and he] provided for his family."

Most of the women I met grew up in stable—although not always inti-mate—families. Most had stay-at-home moms. All had mothers who man-aged the household. A few had mothers who managed more than that: Karen King's mother raised seven young children after Karen's dad left early on; Ellen Adams's mother managed the upbringing of six children as well as two part-time jobs after her husband died when Ellen, the oldest, was just twelve.

Even in light of unusual family configurations, most women I met ex-pected a normal course of events. Katrina Baker, the woman who told her mechanic that she is happy just the way she is, thank you very much, remem-bers having ordinary expectations even though her Jamaican-born parents have been divorced most of her life. "I expected to be married and live in a big, huge house with a bunch of kids," she says. "I thought that was going to be me. And my family had expectations along those lines. That was going to be me."

But there are expectations—and there are expectations. Some of us *expect* marriage. Others—for reasons that are complex and not well under-stood—*count on* it. We stake our very selves on it. This difference, the differ-ence between expecting marriage and counting on marriage, seems to have a hand in the way an ever-single woman manages the pain and pleasures of her single status. And it may be a significant key in understanding how we feel as adolescents, young adults, and women facing choices concerning marriage, work, home, and the shape of our lives.

If the psychologists are right, most of us count on marriage. For those of us who do, the importance of marriage in our lives is both conscious and un-conscious. It goes beyond media, beyond conduct literature. Marriage reaches deep into a girl's life, deep into her psychological preparation and develop-ment. It may well involve the very formation of the female self.

In the male world, the difference between expecting a role and staking one's whole self on it would be obvious: a young boy might expect to be a leader, but only the exceptional case stakes everything he is, everything he can be, every connection he makes, every picture he has of himself, on becoming a CEO. Similarly, he could expect to be a father, but in a society that emphasizes male autonomy, initiative, and competitiveness, only an exceptional case would stake his whole self-concept on his potential fatherhood. In fact, educators typically cringe when they see young boys stake their identities on a narrow precipice—say, becoming a basketball star.

In the female world, the difference between expecting a role—a traditional role—and staking one's identity on it isn't nearly as public or as clear. One reason is that the narrow precipice a girl counts on is traditionally sanctioned. A second reason is more subtle, and it relates to what goes into achieving the traditional female role.

What goes into achieving the traditional female role is very different from what goes into preparing for the traditional male role. The skills that life as a wife requires are different in character from the skills required for a man to become, say, a corporate executive. The boy's success relies on volition and autonomy; the girl's success relies on flexibility and relatedness. The boy, especially if he marries and has children, appears to achieve the mature adult identity that psychologists such as Sigmund Freud and Erik Erikson highlighted; the boy is able to have relationships—including a marriage—but he's also able to compete in the business world, be productive and decisive in his work, and make sound choices about where he lives and dies.

In contrast, the girl seems to get off the developmental escalator at some point and lose herself in the giftware department: she is less likely to make independent assessments and competitive choices, and she is more likely to rely on her relationships for her sense of direction and identity. She doesn't know which movie she wants to see Saturday night ("Anything's fine with me"); she can't imagine buying herself flowers on the way home from work (that's what a suitor is supposed to do for her). In fact, Freud believed that a woman never develops a full superego, the part of the "I" that we call the conscience, the part of the "I" that regulates morality and the self. He understood that in fulfilling the traditional role, in being the nurturing, dedicated helpmate, a woman has to focus on the "other" rather than the "I," and that she demonstrates this mind-set early on—well before courtship. According to Freud, it is probably her organic and psychological nature to form a self dependent on others (on men) for sustenance and direction. The Freudian woman has a kind of half-self. She's like a romantic heroine in a novel who needs a reader to bring her alive.

Instinctively, women recoil: *Of course I have an "I,"* we say. *Of course I have an identity and a conscience. Of course I have a self. I can feel it, hear it speak, watch it dance; and I can feel it writhe when it's mistreated, underestimated, ignored.* After all, a great body of work, from published diaries to "Dear Abby" columns, from literary masterpieces to clinical studies of depression, tells us that many women have struggled with identity, especially in the context of marriage. Writers as diverse as Henrik Ibsen, Edna St. Vincent Millay, and Doris Lessing have all portrayed married and unmarried women poised on a precipice of identity, the painful loss of self well within their sights, like a threat mounting the horizon. To feel these things, to rebel against constraints, even to tumble into depression, these female characters and their living sisters have to have selves. *Don't they?*

Maybe not. Like Freud, feminist psychologists Carol Gilligan and Jean Baker Miller believe that the whole question of the self is different for women. They believe that a girl does not define her "self" through increasing levels of autonomy the way a boy does. Instead, she defines her "self" through her relations to others. In Miller's view, this is a complicated adjustment in which a girl learns that her perceptions are not central to her survival. She doesn't develop by adjusting to "reality" the way a boy does; instead, she learns to perceive and adjust to the realities of others, thereby assuring connection. This is a profound thing: it suggests that as little girls we see through other people's eyes—our fathers', our teachers', our mothers'—and that we make connections and create our selves accordingly. We don't learn to choose movies; we learn to enjoy other people's choices. We don't learn to take care of our own needs; we learn to take of others' emotional needs so that they'll take care of our physical ones. "Indeed, women's sense of self becomes very much organized around being able to make and then maintain . . . relationships," writes Miller. "Eventually, for many women the threat of disruption of connections is perceived not as just a loss of a relationship but as something closer to a loss of the self." In Miller's model, the end of a relationship may threaten a woman's very notion of being a person.

No matter which model you choose—Freud's superego-interruptus or the feminist relation-as-self—the reasons why so many of us grow up *counting on* marriage are clear. So are the reasons why someone who grows up counting on relationships for a sense of self might have difficulties living without a marital connection: it's as if many of the things that make girls into excellent traditional wives also make life difficult for girls who don't marry.

In fact, that's very close to the point that Mary Pipher makes in her profile of female adolescence, *Reviving Ophelia*. Pipher is a psychologist who works with young girls in Lincoln, Nebraska, and she says that adolescence for a girl is a kind of personal Armageddon, a time when a girl must choose what self actually means. According to Pipher, the adolescent girl faces an unpleasant choice: she can continue to be herself and be unpopular, criticized for being too fat, too plain, too different, too self-sufficient, too outspoken, or too smart—or she can abandon the identity she's had for twelve years and become someone else, someone thin, someone painstakingly well-dressed and well-coiffed, someone quiet, group-oriented, uncertain, and unthreatening. Pipher believes that this painful, media-driven hazing process—the "crucible," she calls it—forces many young girls to their emotional and psychological knees as they prepare for the adult female role. In order to be feminine, to be liked, loved, included in the group, accepted as a woman, chosen by boyfriends, and courted by potential husbands, the young girl splits into two pieces. The first piece is the *real self* she grew up with, which may eventually disappear; the second piece is the *false self*, which she needs in order to achieve the things that girls are supposed to achieve. And a primary achievement is, of course, a fairy-tale wedding and a happily-ever-after marriage.

For the girl who signs on to a false self, who begins to see herself in light of *Seventeen* magazine images and *Beverly Hills 90210* values, life as a single woman can be extraordinarily difficult. That's because the girl who has been thoroughly hazed doesn't have much to fall back on: she has deserted her own self and some part of her human potential, and she lacks the inner skills and long-term dreams that are necessary to pursue an alternative life course. "I never go out with women," one such woman told me over the phone. "I just can't stand that. I think it's terrible. They just get so competitive." The unhappy alumna of two or three dating services, she loved *Sleepless in Seattle* and is sure that if she sits alone in the right places, looking the right way long enough, someone will find her and make her life happy.

"How old are you?" I asked.

"Fifty-eight," she answered.

Listening to such painful stories, reading Freud, reading Miller, reading

Pipher, you begin to wonder how any little girls—after the fairy tales, the copies of *Seventeen*, the developmental processes, and the adolescent crucible—end up single and reasonably well adjusted. How do they do it?

For all their esoteric, mind-twisting work, the theorists don't know. Developmental theory doesn't have much to say about the young woman who accepted an engagement ring and then gave it back, or the one who laughed at me over the phone and said, "Why didn't I get married? You wouldn't ask that question if you'd seen what marriage looked like in 1952." As researcher Pat Keith has noted, developmental theory has a tendency to assume a specific, cumulative life course, and it tends to discard anyone who has strayed from that course—including single people.

In contrast, singular women, women who have created satisfying lives in the absence of marriage, do have something to say about it. Nearly everyone has a childhood story, an image that she has settled on as some kind of explanation of her developing identity and her adult strength. And many of them involve a vague sense of being supported for their real, emerging selves.

Growing up in Cuba, Teresa Sanchez felt different from her mother. "My mother was a very traditional mother, very dedicated to us; she worked very hard," she recalls. "Monday was the wash day. Tuesday was the day you prepared the clothes to iron on Wednesday, because they had to have a special preparation, and you know Friday was a cleaning day, that you had to clean the house. . . . So we talked about that and she said, 'Think about it very carefully. It's a lot of responsibility. You shouldn't rush into getting married.'"

Teresa thought about it, and sometimes she escaped the chores by hiding behind the house and reading back issues of *Reader's Digest*. "I noticed her working day after day and I guess I had the feeling that there was a contradiction between being a good housewife and reading," Teresa says, laughing at her adolescent logic. But in fact, her mother had given her a great gift—the permission to be herself, to take her time, to come into her own.

When the political situation heated up in Cuba, Teresa's family sent her to Spain alone. From there she emigrated to the U.S., where she joined an uncle and took a job in a bottling factory. Her family reunited some years later in Miami—with one exception: her sister's fiancé was stuck back in Cuba. For many years her sister waited, worried, and languished, and Teresa became impatient. "That's one of the reasons I left home," Teresa recalls now, apparently without remorse. "Because she was depressed all the time because she was waiting for him. She would come home from work and go to sleep. I said, 'I can't take it.'"

The waiting did pay off: Maria's fiancé appeared ten years later, and they married. Meanwhile, Teresa had moved on to become a graduate student in Spanish and a professor of comparative literature.

She still *expected* to marry. But the expectation lived beside other expectations—especially educational ones—that seemed to claim equal weight. In some ineffable way she knew that she was a woman, that she was feminine, that she was loved and competent and lovable without marriage. And she has lived accordingly.

Like Teresa, Kate O'Connor, sixty-two, seems to have gotten a show of family support. Among her peers, she had all the markings of a girl destined to be dateless, she says: "I am very nearsighted, so I couldn't really participate in sports: I couldn't see the ball. I was very klutzy . . . and I was considered a brain, supersmart. Those were two kisses of death in those days." Meanwhile, she incurred her mother's wrath by correcting adults' mistakes whenever possible, and she was once exiled from a family outing for just such a crime. But fundamentally, her family accepted her and her potential: "I don't know whether I expected to marry or not," she says. "I think I knew that other people expected me to do *something*." As a result, Kate was the first in her family to go to college.

Many women say they went through the adolescent crucible in a kind of daze. "I was timid," says Lillian Salinger, seventy-four, who blushes when I ask her if she dated in high school. "I read my way through high school," says Katrina Baker, the woman who argued with her mechanic over the term "old maid." "I just was there at the wrong time." Many suffered a nagging sense that they just weren't in step with the girls who read *Seventeen*, giggled at appropriate moments, or knew how to talk to boys. They wanted to participate on some level—but couldn't quite do it. Roxanne Walters remembers doing what she thought was necessary—playing it sweet and submissive—and then suddenly letting loose with her real personality, a spontaneous, assertive personality that had a tendency to blow boys out of the water. As a result, a seventh-grade boyfriend once told her that the reason he deserted her during her many extracurricular projects was that she was too competent. "I get jealous," he said, "because you're in charge and no one comes to me."

"I always felt slower than the rest of the girls," soft-spoken, multitalented

Rachel Jacobs says of those adolescent years. She doesn't mean that she was slow intellectually (she has a Ph.D.); she means socially, emotionally, sexually. "I don't think I was in the mainstream of what was going on; it's just how I felt." She was overweight and shy. Meanwhile, the boys in her south Texas town were downright speedy in the early 1970s—they got their sex early from prostitutes across the border—which added to Rachel's inhibitions. Eventually Rachel stumbled onto a partial solution: life was less painful, she found, when she concentrated on things that came easily to her; in math class, in science clubs, she could do what she loved—and she could talk comfortably with boys who shared her interests.

But among the adolescent stories, Marguerite Ramanis's stands out. Reaching high school in the early seventies, she felt behind the sexual and social curve in her small town near the Berkshires, but she was also schooled in the strong immigrant values of her Latvian family, who sang together after holiday dinners and emphasized hard work. So when she wasn't invited to the senior prom, Marguerite simply took herself. The way she saw it, if she was good enough to be a class officer, she was good enough to go to the prom, despite the fact that she hadn't caught the approving eye of a young man. "I thought, damn it, I don't have to go with a date," she remembers, looking back nearly twenty years. "I don't know where I came up with the idea, but I was going to be damned if I stayed away from the prom because it was a couple deal." But what about the validation that goes with dating, with being chosen, with having someone who thought she was pretty? She shrugs. She had another kind of validation. She was good enough. Period.

✺

So little is known about female development, and so little is understood about single life, that it's impossible to fully understand how our early expectations inform our later lives. The study of adolescent girls is in its infancy, and some of the work has met with severe criticism for its methodology. The traditional studies of ever-single women aren't much help either: they tend to focus on elderly women and they rarely address early experiences.

One important pattern does appear, and it may relate to the strength of Pipher's so-called "real self." In Barbara Levy Simon's study, as in nearly every other study conducted in the U.S. and Britain, ever-single women achieved high levels of education, higher on average than their married peers. This overarching pattern among ever-single women with high life satisfaction rates has led researchers to conclude that education is a major determinant of life satisfaction among single women.

This doesn't mean that education makes spinsters, at least in contemporary times: plenty of women who marry are extremely well educated and recent evidence indicates that the negative correlation between marriage and education is fast diminishing. It's more likely that education—as well as the kind of support that Teresa Sanchez got from her mother—sometimes acts as a prophylactic against making an obviously bad marriage, a marriage for the sake of marriage, or a marriage based on a false self. With an education that has taught her to develop and trust her own perceptions, and with additional support for being a worthy person in and of herself, a young woman might choose not to hitch her wagon to a faulty star—even if it's the only star around.

More concretely, once a woman has passed the common age of marriage, her education probably makes adjusting her expectations and adapting her behavior to an alternative life course easier. It also makes supporting herself easier, and researchers tell us that financial security is another major indicator of a satisfying single life.

But of course it's more complicated than that. The making of an identity is profound, and it may continue well past high school. The pressures and expectations around marriage are enormous, and they continue until well into our thirties.

As a result, even if she grows up just expecting, not counting on, marriage, even if she has education and emotional support behind her, the woman who finds herself single at thirty and forty-five and fifty finds herself on an unexpected, ungroomed trail. It's unmapped; it's uncleared; it's uncelebrated. It's a trail often taken, but rarely by choice and never with a full understanding of what's ahead.

And the first part of the trip seems to be the roughest.

CHAPTER THREE

Scriptless

The tears came in a sudden, convulsive wave, and she was not ready for it. It was morning, and the sun had not fully cleared the canyon rim above her; friends were breaking camp, and she was falling apart.

Back home in New York, there was a man who wanted to marry her. He told her, just do it, stop thinking about it. He told her, I'm a doing person; I don't just read about life, I do it. She loved him, loved his sense of adventure, his Peace Corps background, his confident grasp of life, but she knew she would probably not marry him.

And so here she was, twenty-eight and single, sitting on a rock at the bottom of the Grand Canyon. Everything that had ever burdened her came rushing out; every love she'd had, every question she'd never answered took a seat beside her; every doubt she'd never shared, every time she'd wanted help, every job she hadn't taken, every decision she'd ever made alone and wondered about later—everything appeared and filled the canyon around her.

A friend stayed behind to sit with her. "He did exactly the right thing," Christi Wagner says now. "He let me cry."

"She's unhappy," people say, "because she isn't married." That sounds right, I guess, if you're married and have never really thought about it, or if for some reason you've never faced the challenge of creating a life all by yourself, or if you have difficulty breaking down a big lump—"unmarried"—into its smaller constituent lumps.

It sounds right but it isn't. It's a simplification, a myth; it's a cliché that keeps us from recognizing the real causes of pain and the real people who prevail over them. It's a cliché that scares young women, scares them away from important challenges and questions that all women would do well to consider as they approach marriage.

It sounds right, but a number of statistics tell us that it probably isn't. Being unmarried isn't a recipe for individual unhappiness any more than being married is a recipe for individual bliss: one half of American marriages dissolve, a great portion of them before the tenth year; and while marriage seems to ensure men some degree of psychological comfort, the jury is still out on women. Meanwhile, there's evidence that a bad marriage may be worse than no marriage at all: a series of surveys on the happiness of Americans shows that married people who do not characterize their marriage as "very happy" report the lowest overall happiness of any category of people, including the ever-single.

That could be why women today seem less eager to go to the altar: in 1987, when the *Los Angeles Times* asked 1,635 southern California women what their primary goals were, a mere 37 percent said marriage. In a 1993 survey of 1,057 adults, about 51 percent of the unmarried women said they wanted to get married (60 percent of the unmarried men said they wanted to). More revealing, a 1987 survey of sixteen thousand divorced and ever-single *New Woman* readers suggests that many women make a distinction between wanting marriage and wanting it at all costs: 65 percent of the women in the survey said they wanted to marry, but 67 percent said they would not marry someone they didn't consider Mr. Right. Seventy-four percent said that personal fulfillment was more important than a good marriage.

Still, to say *she's unhappy because she's unmarried* sounds right—especially if you know a single woman in her late twenties to late thirties. It is, as researchers have noted, simply not a good time of life for the single woman. If ever there's a time when unhappiness seems to be linked to singleness, it's during this decade, because it's during this decade that a young woman discovers that her expectations may not pan out and that her identity—centered as it has been on the expectation of marriage—is back in flux. Having expected a certain script, she finds herself on a movie set with no script at all. But the movie must go on, and so she faces an extraordinary challenge and a series of unanticipated questions, the kinds of questions girls in fairy tales never face.

The challenge is making an identity without the usual script and the usual structures. The first, nearly inevitable question is *What's wrong with me?* The succeeding questions are: *So, can I do this? And if I did this, what would it look like? How would it work? And who would I be? And who would love and support me? And how would I feel?*

In the mid-1800s, the ever-single poet Alice Cary described the juncture this way: "Her wild fears are more than she can bear."

"It's an abyss," a colleague of mine said recently as she sat in the part-time faculty office of a Chicago college. She is thinking of moving in with her boyfriend; she is also thinking of taking off on her own and getting a Ph.D. Bright and funny, she once moved from the East Coast to the Midwest for a relationship that later dissolved. Now she is wondering how to make her own choices if she leaves this second relationship: "I don't know where to start."

The self-help books and women's magazines aren't much help. Most self-help books avoid the challenges posed by the scriptless life; instead, they get stuck on that first question (*What's wrong with me?*) and formulate answers designed to get us all back on script. As a result, too often self-help really means self-flagellation; in *No More Lonely Nights*, for instance, the authors, a husband-and-wife team, exhume every possible female fault, including fear of love, fear of ending up like our mothers, and compulsive nurturing. By page 79, it's clear that getting married requires skills closer to mastering the inner game of tennis than skills we typically associate with social intercourse and emotional commitment: "Fantasize about being married," advises the book, and in the margin the ghost woman who borrowed the book from the Chicago Public Library before I did has written, "Picture myself married." In courtship, as in tennis, flaws can be corrected and imagery can be powerful: apply the right amount of practice and you'll win (6–Love). Indeed, the last chapter is entitled, "It's Up to You to Get Married."

Some books go so far as to suggest that women are products and that they should sell themselves in the marriage market, package themselves like a microwave dinner or a box of cereal. These books deal in the false self, and they mirror the women's magazines, which tout "Never Meet Any Decent Men? Stop Making It So Difficult on Yourself," "How Intelligent Women Flirt," and

"How to Get Him to Commit" on their covers. Racy as they sound, these media messages are just part of the conduct tradition. They subscribe to the same basic ethic that Wendell Wilkes did back in the eighteenth century: they believe that women can be packaged, that a woman's self, her mind and her soul, are infinitely mutable and ultimately inconsequential. They tell us that if a woman makes herself quiet enough, pretty enough, thin enough, or wily enough, then she will be both acceptable and accepted—and she'll be content to stay that way. In other words, they presume that if ketchup is packaged as mustard, somehow, miraculously, when the package is opened, the ketchup will indeed have changed into mustard—happily and forever. But for some of us (maybe for many of us, if the divorce rate is any indication), this self-transformation through packaging doesn't work, and some women find turning into mustard (or relish or German chocolate cake) uncomfortable. And when they don't succeed, they feel awful (*What's wrong with me?*).

"He wanted me to cook," remembers Roxanne, who, having failed to fit a predetermined mold in high school, was still trying to do it in her late twenties, "and I was cooking and I was cooking—and I *hate* to cook!" She laughs, shakes her head, and shrugs.

"We had this huge fight because he came to take me to a party one day and my nails weren't done," recalls Katrina Baker. "I thought, what planet are you on?" Katrina is an exotic-looking black woman with a formal bearing and an unremittingly direct manner. Today, she's wearing red lipstick and diamond earrings. Her nails are done. "I like to have my nails painted," she says, "but it's not a priority in my life. If they are, fine. But if they're not, that's fine too."

Katrina's complaint recalls the story of *The Paper Bag Princess*, a recent fairy tale that actually touches on this issue. In the story, a beautiful princess named Elizabeth is engaged to marry a prince named Ronald, but a dragon burns down the castle and kidnaps Ronald. Every stitch of clothing Elizabeth owns is destroyed, so she dons a paper bag and pursues the kidnapper. She tricks the dragon and saves Ronald, but Ronald is ungrateful. "Elizabeth," he says, "you are a mess. You smell like ashes, your hair is all tangled and you are wearing a paper bag. Come back when you are dressed like a real princess." Elizabeth responds coolly. She tells Ronald that although he *looks* like a prince, he's really a bum. The last picture shows her dancing off into the sunset alone, her arms flung wide and happily.

The less spirited, less confident woman (say, someone like me) may not have such a gutsy response. She can spend years thumbing through those self-help pages trying to turn into mustard, correcting her dress or her laughter, learning to eat at the right places or vacation in the popular spots, haunted always by that underlying query whenever she goes back to her ketchup ways: *What's wrong with me?*

"Why don't you read *Vogue?*" a long-standing lover who disliked my taste in clothes once demanded.

I sputtered. I blinked. There were so many things to say. The way it felt, like a sugar rush, to look at those slender, long-legged models dressed to the teeth; the way it felt, like a sugar crash, to consider putting those bathing suits on my short little body. The painful implication of not being good enough as I was; the dispiriting sense of manipulation that seemed to pervade the articles on marrying men for money or learning to shoot pool because men shoot pool. Why didn't I read *Vogue?* I couldn't come up with a succinct answer, one that fully captured the crisis in self-esteem that was mounting within me. I resorted to humor. "I don't have enough years left to explain it to you," I said.

But I felt awful. Somehow I'd misplaced the original script, the one where I finished college and fell in love and had a marriage and a terrific career by thirty, and now I was throwing out the self-help script, the one that made me feel worse about myself every time I read it. But at least with the self-help script, I'd known what someone else thought I should be doing. Now what? Now I was really alone.

It would be years before I understood that I wasn't alone; it would be years before I knew that this crisis is as common as a credit card bill, that Susan B. Anthony had felt it, that nearly every women who had stood at a wedding alone had experienced it, and that it would pass. It would pass when I learned what others had learned before me—how to write my own script.

꙳

Strangely, this crisis of the scriptless life, which seems so common among women who delay or forgo marriage, has gone basically unexplored. That's because most of the popular explorers of adult life have allowed women, particularly ever-single women, to be squeezed out of the discussion.

In the mid-1970s Gail Sheehy, perhaps the most well-known explorer, wrote an immensely popular book called *Passages*. She based it on the work of a psychologist named Daniel Levinson, who relied heavily on the theoretical framework of psychologist Erik Erikson. Somewhere in this handoff, women were ignored, or worse, presumed to be exactly like men—even in that most specific of events, the marriage decision.

This exclusion was inevitable, in part because of Erikson's original framework, which was based on the lives of boys. Erikson's ideas are brilliant and conventional both; the schematic he created seems to confirm the purpose and course of the normal life. He believed that psychological growth was based on a series of eight tasks, each heralded by a crisis. At each crisis, the person achieves the task or fails it, and either moves on to the next task or gets stuck. It's in the early twenties that a young adult faces the sixth crisis, called intimacy versus isolation; the task is to choose intimacy and achieve partnership.

But Erikson didn't notice that the crisis of intimacy versus isolation might be different for women, and that the task of achieving marriage might rest on something quite different from the autonomous self he saw in young men. He didn't consider the possibility—as more recent psychologists have— that the feminine self at twenty is different, more fluid and more relational. If psychologists Jean Baker Miller and Dana Crowley Jack are right, marriage may present a difficult paradox for a woman.

The paradox looks like this. Because achieving marriage often means presenting a false self, and because maintaining marriage often means living within a partnership in which she has less economic and social power than her partner does, the married woman may be required to engage in self-denial. This self-denial is a kind of wholesale grooming, as she hones her identity, appearance, and behavior to meet the needs of her partner and the family they create together. It goes a long way in keeping the unequal marriage running and the household humming as the woman manages most of the emotional and domestic work in return for financial and social security. But it also simultaneously isolates her from both her self and her partner as she buries her real self, the space where her real needs and feelings reside. In other words, the process she uses to make and preserve her primary relationship may ultimately lead to her own isolation. One woman told Dana Crowley Jack: "I was absolutely stymied. . . . I could not be myself—I didn't think— because he would find my rough edges and leave . . . so I was trying to be someone that I wished I could be, I knew damn well I couldn't be or would not be happy being." Paradoxically, she is profoundly alone in an intimate relationship.

Oddly, the influential Erikson missed the paradox. He understood that unequal relationships in society affected the development of identity for African Americans. He described how the black child creates a false identity in order to survive alongside those more powerful than he; and he speculated that the need for this false identity made full ego development difficult. But unlike Pipher, he did not see the corollary structures that might impede intimate partnership in a woman's life—the media-driven hazing process, the early lessons in self-packaging, the impact of economic dependence, and the extraordinary demands of the traditional marital role.

Women in their twenties and thirties often do see it, though. They don't use terms like "ego development" and "false self," but they talk explicitly and thoughtfully about wanting marriage and fearing it, about forming an identity and guarding it, about pursuing connections and feeling isolated within those connections.

Caitlin McKuen talks about it. Leaving college at nineteen, she got involved with a commercial airline pilot; they lived together, and she became a flight attendant. But the relationship was stormy: he had affairs and lied about them; she was unsure about what she wanted. She changed locations and continued to see him, struggling to sort it all out. After five years, she had her sister move her stuff out of the apartment under the cover of darkness and went home to her parents in Michigan.

"It wasn't as bad as some women have it," she says. "It was a good thing because it made me very, very strong. I think . . . it made me really sure about what I want and don't want in a relationship in the future." But she was still confused about her own life and her own direction, and she did have a quirky habit of referring to her ex-boyfriend as "pond scum." Then she went back to college at twenty-eight, finished at thirty, and moved to India to get a master's in painting, where she dodged unwelcome invitations from local men and worked in a tiny studio not far from Calcutta. Along the way, living in a two-room house, cooking on a hot plate on the back porch, delving deep into her art and her assumptions about life, she discovered herself. "I'm happy now," she says, looking around the rock patio she has built between her match-box house and unheated studio on a woodsy street in Saugatauk, Michigan, where she waitresses five months a year and paints the other seven. "My work is central to my life."

After six years of social and sexual celibacy, she's thirty-three and dating a twenty-seven-year-old man who respects her independence and is wary of intruding on her painting time. Sometimes he stands at the door of her studio, cautious about entering, offering an invitation to share dinner. "It's really nice," she says. "It's kind of perfect, because he's really undemanding."

Lindsay Cordell, a thirty-year-old blond-haired beauty who runs white-water rapids and teaches Bible school at 6 A.M. every weekday, is more conceptual in the way she describes the struggle to find oneself: "Anyone who tries to get intimacy without having their identity first won't get it. Period." A second-grade teacher in a small suburban school, Lindsay is blunt, spirited, contemplative, and consciously in pursuit of her own identity. But, like Caitlin, she didn't start out that way.

She grew up in a Mormon household in Salt Lake City, and whenever she encountered a twenty-two-year-old single woman she wondered what was wrong with her. But gradually, silently, something shifted. She decided to go to college. Her father cried when she told him. "It was just beyond his notion of what women did and what he had envisioned my life to be," she remembers. Within a few years, she had left the traditional script completely. She broke off an engagement and began to date again. She went to Japan to teach English and to L.A. to teach elementary school. But it was never easy. She struggled with profound questions of faith and identity: How many of her life choices belonged to her? How many to her parents? Was Mormonism her choice? Was celibacy?

Today she leads an intimacy support group for single Latter Day Saints. "There are a lot of people who get married and then they ask why they have problems—because they haven't figured out their identity yet," she says. "And then they have to go through that in their marriage. *With* somebody. Where, if you figure it out first, and then two people with whole identities join, you're going to be much happier."

Even so, to leave the traditional script as she has, to deviate from the developmental schematics of Erikson or Sheehy, is a scary thing. Theoretically, it condemns the perpetrator to stagnation—or lopsided growth at best. We imagine thwarted women, isolated and timorous, unable to get to the next step in maturity; they're lopsided types who are overdeveloped in some

unimportant area, the care of canaries for instance. No wonder no one both-
ers to write a script for a movie like that. What would be the point? How
would it end?

There's no doubt it would open with that cheery line, *What's wrong
with me?*

No one at twenty-eight or thirty or thirty-eight decides to put herself in this
scriptless place.

"It just happened," Ellen Adams says. "It's a case of just not meeting the
right man."

It's an incremental thing, a shadowy thing, indefinable, unchartable until
later, much later: it is the result of a series of decisions, none of them obviously critical. "The truth is that for some reason what set my hormones hop-
ping didn't take to me, and what took to me did not set my hormones hop-
ping," laughs Maureen Cabot. Back in the 1940s, when Maureen's boss gave
her a five-year pin, she told him that he wouldn't be giving her another: she'd
be married by then. But one decision led to another, and she retired from the
electric company at age fifty-seven without identifying a turning point that
made her singular. She is typical. Occasionally, a woman will say, "I could
have married Harold. I should have married Harold." But rarely.

Allie Ackerman, who is still caught in a mire of self-accusation and
doubt, is one who does. Back in the late sixties she was driving across Ohio to
her home in Cincinnati when she came to a tollbooth and her fiancé failed to
fork over the fare. "That's it," she told Peter with characteristic flipness,
"You're too cheap to marry." Peter's now a CEO, a millionaire with two grown
children and houses in two states. Allie is still a firebrand, an ever-single
mother who supports her two beautiful adolescent children on real estate
holdings. Every once in a while she gives herself the third degree for not
marrying Peter.

But for the most part, in these first scriptless days of the twenties and thirties, the forces, the choices, and the pivotal moments are indistinguishable
from one another. Even singular women who have turned down proposals
typically see those events in contexts packed with circumstances. For Rachel
Jacobs, once an intimidated teen growing up in a Texas border town, the de-

cision in her late twenties seemed to be: Am I going to use this fancy Ph.D. or hang out unemployed with my unemployed boyfriend? For confident, pragmatic Marguerite Ramanis, the decision in her mid-twenties seemed to be: Am I going to give up my job to move to a place I dislike to be with someone I'm not quite sure about right now? Even now, Rachel cannot say that leaving Austin, Texas, is the reason she hasn't married yet; although she is sometimes tempted to, Marguerite still cannot say that Martin really was the only man she'll ever love and want to live with.

Although there's no single choice, no transforming life event that typically marks these years, there *is* an emotional gristmill. Ever-single women say—almost to a woman—that the hardest time in their lives was the time when they inarguably passed the common age of marriage. For women who came of age in the late 1950s, the worst time occurred in their late twenties or early thirties. For women who came of age in the seventies and eighties, when the common age of marriage was later, the worst time occurred during their early to late thirties. It's a time when the capacity to deny fails, the pressures peak, and a realization occurs: *Things are not as I expected them to be.*

"I cried for days," says Roxanne of turning thirty.

"I felt pretty bad for myself," Christi says of attending her younger sister's wedding.

"The year my sister got married I always rank as the worst year of my life," observes Kate O'Connor, who still lives in the same small town where she walked to grade school with her nose in a book and excused herself from sports. "I was just turning thirty, and everyone would say, 'Why have you not been married?' Even her friends were saying, 'What about you, Kate?'" Kate pauses. "You think of remarks you would like to say, and there is no answer. People would say, 'Well, she doesn't want to get married.' But that isn't comfortable, because you truly do not choose not to be [married] at that age. I didn't, at least."

When they talk about these times, most women mention the outside pressures first, the questions and the silent judgments, some of which they felt themselves internalizing. Ellen Adams, the independent-minded environmentalist, recalls a drive up the eastern seaboard on the way to her sister's wedding in the mid-eighties. In the car she and a single friend spent hours coming up with answers to the inevitable question Ellen would face: *Why aren't you married?* Well, I'm living with someone, she planned to answer before she proceeded to describe her pet carp (quiet, big eyes, great swimmer, enthusiastic eater . . .). She was laughing as she drove, but under the laughter was a quiet irritation insistently whispering, *How do I prove there's nothing wrong with me?*

One of the most common outside pressures is the pressure to compromise. At least a dozen women recall being accused of being too selfish, too picky, too independent, or too strong-willed to be marriageable, or, more critically, to be worthy of happiness. But compromise is situational: children don't compromise on the use of the family computer unless they've been compelled to; married partners don't compromise on where they will live unless there are two competing needs. The ever-single woman hasn't compromised because there hasn't been a perceived need to compromise—or a compelling context: a relationship that is worth compromising for. Someday, there may be a perceived need—although most of these women recoil from a compromise of the self. To a woman raised in a culture soaked in the rhetoric of independence, in a century marked by an increasing emphasis on individual rights, this logic makes sense. Karen King articulates it; Roxanne Walters struggles to hold on to it. Yet the pressure persists, and women often find it painful and confusing, especially during this tumultuous time.

A worse feeling at thirty and thirty-five is the unmistakable impression that while half the world is squirming with discomfort over dealing with a budding "spinster," the other half of the world is simply looking down on her. There is a status in marriage, a mark of achievement, and unmarried women feel it being wielded over them. Felicia Collinet, the young fund-raiser, still feels these pressures, and they invade her sense of self and her sense of direction. "I get to the point where I can't listen to them sometimes," she says of her colleagues, who are predominantly married women. "There are certainly some times when people feel sorry for me, like *this poor woman who has no life,* and that's not completely untrue."

An energetic black woman with an M.B.A. that she paid for herself, Felicia believes that her coworkers' attitudes come from the media around them, and she is haunted by the hints and judgments, and by her own self-accusation. "I think of shows like *thirtysomething,*" she says. "I used to watch it all the time. And the single women were really unstable. I guess I'm afraid that I seem like that, or like this woman who all she thinks about is her job."

Inevitably, she says, the *thirtysomething* stereotype affects her relationships, especially at work. "I've been thought of as not very kind. I've been thought of as a complete bitch," she says unhappily. "I'm angry because I'm not married and I don't have children and I don't have all this other . . . So I do have all this pent-up hostility, so maybe sometimes it's true." She pauses and shakes her head. "But I *don't* really think so," she says. "I think the person is making me angry or not being fair, and I'm reacting to it."

She is not being paranoid. There's a long history of suspicion and dis-crimination aimed at unmarried women. Back in 1851 poor ever-single Rebecca Ketchum, who traveled unescorted from New York to Oregon on a wagon train, got a dose of both. She was charged more for her trip, required to work, excluded socially by the married women, and made to ride horseback while the other women rode in wagons. The exclusion was so complete that she once endured a rainstorm outside, alone in the dark, with only a donated raincoat for protection.

One hundred forty years later the treatment was a little gentler, but still riddled with misunderstanding and prejudice—as evidenced by a 1991 *Wash-ington Post* essay about a fictional thirty-year-old woman named Alice. In writer Richard Cohen's imagination, Alice is ever-single, a successful lawyer and a loyal friend. But Alice is tired of being unmarried and Alice hates going to weddings (every invitation to a shower or wedding is like getting "a flunk-ing report card," writes Cohen). Worst of all, Alice doesn't get as many pre-sents from her friends as she gives. Alice's friends get shower and wedding and baby presents, none of which Alice qualifies for. Alice is always on the giving end, attending her friends' celebrations (we never hear about birthdays, housewarmings, and Christmas, which Alice probably does qualify for). So, solitary, depleted Alice is pitiable. Indeed, the last line of the essay is, "Alice, my heart goes out to you."

For a woman struggling to create a life in the absence of the structures she expected, for a woman trying to understand what a feminine identity is before or in the absence of marriage, having Cohen pity her is confounding; even more confounding is the way he reduces the serious issue of how to live with-out a script to a question of booty.

This is just the kind of pity that resonates. And for a woman of thirty, the resonance is powerful and nearly impossible to ignore.

To Felicia it feels like one big lump. It feels like a mounting emotional pain, a loneliness compounded daily by outside imagery, like a credit-card account gone berserk. But when ever-single women really talk about their lives, it's clear that the unhappiness doesn't originate from one big lump—the lack of a partner in marriage—but from many constituent lumps that have all been piled together under the banner *not married*.

Each lump is a part of everyday life, an area where the script has been erased and the movie set has changed.

The set changes are subtle and unexpected. As the ever-single woman traverses her twenties and thirties without a script, the props and structures that usually help to define a life course transform and sometimes even disappear. Adults use the structures of marriage, family, friends, work, and community to write the basic outlines of their lives: where to live, how to live, whom to live with, whether to change careers, what to do with their free time, their holidays, their vacations, even their assets. As the unmarried woman drifts away from the traditional script and past the common age of marriage, these structures shift too. Deep in the murk of uncertainty at twenty-eight or thirty-five, the ever-single woman says, *I'm unhappy because I don't have a husband*, but in fact there are lots of other things she doesn't have. The guideposts around her have changed.

Family relationships have changed because some families value their married members more and they don't quite know what to do with a daughter who has not formed her own family. Friends have changed because their marriages have changed them, or many have come to look on unmarried friends as inherently less mature and no longer relevant. The connection with the community has changed because the community—including many churches and certainly many workplaces—make no room for the unmarried adult. "I'm shut out," a woman, forty-two, told me over the phone. "My church doesn't even know I'm here."

Women feel the attrition of these structures in varying degrees, and they react in various ways. Some have had enough support in one area to ignore the attrition in other areas. Roxanne has had that; pained as she is by the loss of her closest friend, she's comforted by a mother who has become her best friend and supporter.

Some ever-single women noted the absence of traditional guideposts, trembled a little at assorted weddings and family gatherings, and simply struck out on their own without looking back. Ellen Adams, the mischievous owner of the pet carp, seems to have done that.

But most of us drifted along in our twenties and thirties, making adjustments only as we absolutely had to, watching people disappear from our movies, coping with strange messages from family, dipping periodically into panic or sadness, passively delaying our full adult identities as long as we could, hoping always for that preeminent rite of passage that would tie up all those loose ends. Still others of us grasped instinctively toward structures we wanted to keep in place; we hastily wrote substitute scripts and lived for a time, biding time, never really confronting singularity, never recognizing the attrition.

By all accounts, these last two approaches—the passive approach and the substitute script approach—both have serious drawbacks. The first is incrementally, inarguably painful. It's invisible, it's a kind of slow bleed, and it's isolating. To talk about the scriptless life, to take the hard questions and challenges head-on, feels like making an admission that yes, I'll always be alone. So the single woman doesn't do it, and the people around her conspire in that silence and discomfort, which doubles that murky under-mud feeling of shame, sadness, and fear. "We're very close," Felicia says of her relationship with her unmarried sister, "but we don't talk about it too much." Christi's father, Lindsay's parents, some of my oldest friends, dance around in the margins of silence, embarrassed perhaps to ask, afraid perhaps of the feelings we might express—saved by the proverbial bell of denial. Some even giggle nervously when the subject comes up, as if the notion of being alone is threatening to *their* sense of security.

"My father never discussed it with me," Rachel Jacobs recalls. "But he talked to my cousin about me." Her father died sometime later, probably concerned that she was unhappy and never knowing how she actually felt. For many women, the hallmark of this passive approach is a kind of nagging half-intimacy: "I'm intimate with *your* life," the single woman can say to her friends and family, "but you don't know a thing about *mine*."

The substitute script approach is more active, but still confusing; it's like one of those shell games where the pea keeps moving from spot to spot, escaping discovery. The issue—how to be an adult woman outside marriage—is the pea, and the mistress of the game is perfectly capable of hiding it under substitute shells for a very long time.

It works for a while. Pat McDonald recalls rewarding years packed with a series of families whose worlds she joined as a kind of adjunct mother-friend in the Midwestern town where she grew up, went to church, and taught. She was an honorary member of these families, she felt; she was a welcome guest at birthday parties and an important addition on trips to the park. But as the children aged and the marriages changed, the friendships drifted, and at some point in her forties, Pat realized that she'd mimicked the life she'd expected rather than build a life of her own with friends who shared her interests. Suddenly she realized that there was an entire person still waiting to be created: a woman who sang, who had an interest in theater, who wanted to date and go dancing. At fifty, she is still traversing this passage, reading voraciously, singing to her students, working in a local theater, joining a singles group. In her pale blue eyes there's a gentle light of self-celebration and discovery; but occasionally you can glimpse the sadness for so much time passed.

For Jillian Goodman, an obstetric nurse living in a suburb of Washington, D.C., the discovery was wrenching. Jillian is an expert nurse; in her early career, she was one of a half dozen nurses chosen from her native England to set up clinics in isolated spots in the Caribbean. From there, she zigzagged between Britain and the U.S., where she finally took a job in New Orleans, not far from an uncle who is a Catholic priest. In the absence of marriage, she spent her weekends in her uncle's parish, fulfilling a role she was familiar with: "I am the perfect daughter," she says. When she left New Orleans for a better job in D.C., she joined another parish where she continued to be a substitute daughter, this time to older couples whose children had grown. She planned church functions with them and had Sunday dinners with them; she thoroughly enjoyed their company and they enjoyed hers. Meanwhile, she delivered other people's high-risk babies late at night in a university hospital deep in the city; in the mornings, she drove home to a silent house in a suburb full of families.

And then she turned forty and she hit the wall. She stopped sleeping. She cried all the time, although she didn't know what was wrong—after all, she'd just finished her B.A. and she'd just gotten a promotion. One night she burst into tears when a colleague asked her how her vacation was. "My whole world fell apart," she recalls.

She went to a therapist, took off three months from work, and began to face the loss she'd suffered. "I think it was because I hadn't realized that life was passing by and that I wasn't married. . . . I had decided in my head that unless I was married by forty, that was not going to be. So when I hit forty, I had to grieve the loss of a dream, and that dream was to be married and have children."

A year later, she is in a master's program, she works days, and she understands her unproclaimed role in substitute families. She has cultivated younger friends through her studies and she is considering joining a singles group. Snacking on tea and cookies on a Sunday afternoon, she makes plans to meet friends at a foreign movie. Her British accent drifts across the dusky living room in her tidy apartment, she laughs easily, and then she looks down, quiet and intent. It's been hard, she says, and it's still hard, but she is happy to have emerged, stronger and more comfortable: "I feel that I was very, very fortunate."

In the lives of singular women, as acute as the pain of delayed or unfulfilled expectations seems, it passes; as confounding as the idea of building a life without the usual structures seems, it happens.

I'm not sure exactly how. Among the singular women I met, few were able to define the time or the cause of the actual turning point, but all were able to say, "It was hard, and it got better." Sometimes the turning point came after a crisis; more often it happened gradually—action first, realization second, the way a kid pedals her two-wheeler for a hundred yards before she realizes she's riding a bike all by herself. I'm doing it, the singular woman notes to herself, I'm writing a script I can live with.

"Do you know what I think started to happen?" asks Christi some fifteen years after her crisis at the bottom of the Grand Canyon. "My perception of myself changed in my life. I don't think I stopped feeling anything so much as I stopped feeling patronized."

"It was so liberating for some reason," says Lindsay, who spent her thirtieth birthday ceremonially writing down her disappointments and throwing them away. "This dam burst from having to look a certain way. . . . I say, 'Damn it, if I'm ten pounds overweight, who cares?' And I don't know why it happened so much, but it really freed me up." Later, she does offer a theory about what happens to women at this unmarked turning point: "I think there's a paradigm shift," she says. "They've had their vision, and it didn't happen. Then you have a choice—whether to be happy or not."

For Katrina Baker, with her exotic looks and her crisp manner, the change happened early, at twenty-five. "I knew that my expectations were not going to be met," she says. "I came to realize that." At first she felt angry: "That was hard for me to take. It was because I thought, I've done all the right things. I've been a nice girl. I don't hang out on street corners." But Katrina decided to move on; she'd seen her divorced mother turn bitter and she herself had struggled with the constant assault of racism. She was not going to dwell on it: "Because I think that if you dwell on something so negative it consumes you. And I didn't want this to happen to me." She knew there must be an alternative: "I could still be a fulfilled person and have a career and have a life and have some happiness without being married and I was going to do that." Her grandmother, who married at fourteen, continues to inquire about what's wrong, and her mother continues to worry that she is the cause of Katrina's singleness, but Katrina has forged ahead through the disappointment and disapproval. "I had to do something. I had to enjoy myself and have some fun," she says. "And I had to be in a position to do something that's rewarding." Eventually Katrina stumbled onto something that sociologists have noted in the lives of the happiest single women: she found work that pleased her. She became a kindergarten teacher.

Still uncertain about how to create a life, Felicia feels herself on the brink of a similar change. "It's hard to—it's hard to live this way," she says. "It's hard to live like, like you're just waiting for something. . . . You wait and you wait and you wait, and what if it doesn't happen? You know, what do you do? And you just have to start, I don't know, living for the moment or . . . looking at the moment in a different way."

It's confounding to look at the moment in a different way, and for those who haven't tried it, it appears to be a form of giving up. Years ago, when that therapist in her beige-walled office looked up from her notes and told me, "You should learn to live as if you'll always be alone," I was sure that she was telling me to give up, turn off my phone, and buy a Miss Gulch wardrobe. Part of the problem was that she used the phrase "as if you'll always be alone," when she meant "as if you'll never marry." But part of the problem was the enormity of the task, the size of the lump, the unspeakable superstition that living as a single woman would doom me to everlasting solitude, and the un-shakable certainty that it was going to hurt. Ironically, in the end it wasn't the turning point that hurt, but the fear and self-accusation that preceded it. And like most of the singular women I met, I still consider marriage a possibility.

For most of the women I met, as well as the women in Barbara Levy Simon's study, the transition to singularity seems to have happened in the late thirties, although there's certainly no schedule. At fifty, feisty Allie Acker-man is still in conflict, still sure that her life would be better if she were mar-ried, still half-convinced that something is wrong with her. As proof she pulls out the eight or ten men she has dated who have gone on to marry. "It's gotta be us!" she tells me. "Who are we kidding?" In her unhappy moments, she takes the fact that she has not married as a kind of testimony against her. But in a calmer moment she reflects on what a singular woman is: if she were to write a children's book about a single woman, the main character would be athletic and healthy. She would have rosy cheeks and a long braid. "Men love her, women love her, children love her," Allie says. "She's comfortable any-where in the world. . . . She fits in everywhere, and I don't know how she makes a living; she just does."

"And what about you?" I ask. "Would that be enough?" I am thinking of Allie as I saw her last night, sitting comfortably in the stands at a Triple-A baseball game, eating peanuts, cheering the best players by name, yelling when the scoreboard cued us to yell, and helping her son cruise for foul balls. I can see Allie becoming a rosy-cheeked traveler.

"I would be happy with that," she answers.

Some women never face the scriptlessness in their lives, and some con-tinue to internalize the prejudices of the culture. A casebook example is Catharine Beecher, sister of Harriet Beecher Stowe. At an early age, Catha-rine struggled against the power of her dominating minister father and the image of her nearly invisible mother: she understood that if she married within her Calvinist religion she would have to bury her real self, just as her mother had. Reluctantly, she agreed to marry—but then her fiancé died in a shipwreck.

Freed of both the stigma of being undesirable and the subjugation she feared, Beecher embarked on a strange career that served to discount the status of unmarried women. As a single woman, she argued that single women should be able to teach so that they could support themselves; but as a defender of the status quo, she argued that school boards should hire women because they wouldn't have to pay them as much as they paid men. As an educator and activist, she traveled widely, established schools, and lectured; but as a writer, she wrote good-housekeeping books for married women and opposed the female vote because she believed that a woman's real sphere was her marriage, home, and family. As an ever-single woman, she avoided the script that she feared would enslave her, but as a conservative, she promoted the very attitudes that made the script so overpowering. Sadly, she looked into the cultural mirror and resisted the image she saw, then spent her whole life bolstering the social mechanisms that made that image so virulent. She was, in a sense, the Phyllis Schafly of her day: a woman who made the most of her privileges but whose work effectively inhibited the spread of those privileges to other women.

Probably sensing this contradiction, Susan B. Anthony once watched a Beecher-led conference break up and remarked, "Isn't it strange that women such as these—are so stupid?" But in fact, if Anthony had not found the civil rights movement she might have landed in the same predicament: scriptless and in self-doubt; motivated, creative, powerful, but unable to believe fully that hers was truly a legitimate and feminine life course. The explorer Mary Kingsley lived and died in that predicament. So did Florence Nightingale.

In the 1970s researcher Peter Stein predicted that increased social fluidity—caused by late marriage, divorce, remarriage, and economic independence among women—would make the prevailing social script less rigid and the guideposts more accessible to single people. Similarly, in 1981 researcher Nancy Peterson predicted that the younger ever-single women in her study would "blaze ahead" unaffected by the pressure to uphold social norms. In retrospect, both failed to anticipate the social rigidity of the 1980s, but they were probably onto something: a more fluid society can only be more accepting of singular women, more helpful and less accusatory. But when we'll achieve such fluidity is uncertain.

One thing is certain. An ever-single woman can live a lifetime starting her script with that cheery line *What's wrong with me?* But the singular woman eventually dumps it. ("Why does something have to be wrong with me because I'm not married?" demands Katrina.) In place of that loaded line, the singular script begins, *What am I going to do?*

What am I going to do about making a family? How am I going to handle the loneliness? What am I going to do to make intimacy in my life? Friendships? A comfortable home? Work? A safe future?

How can I make a full and satisfying life?

CHAPTER FOUR

Making Family

Clearly the doctor doesn't think much of midwives, and the midwife doesn't think about doctors at all.

"If she's not progressing in fifteen minutes, I'm going in," the doctor announces, and leaves the room abruptly, trailed by five respectful residents.

No one wants to hear that. Her sister, on her back now, has cramped and pushed for hours in a heroic attempt to have a vaginal delivery four years after a cesarean. Her brother-in-law has coached. The midwife has administered Pitocin. It's well past midnight.

She reverts to cheerleading. Standing at the foot of the bed, holding her sister's thigh, she tells her sister that it's going well, that she can see the baby's head. Her sister pushes, the midwife prods. And she cheers: "You're doing great, I can see the baby, you're doing great!"

It all works. It all comes together, and she feels grateful and proud that she has had a small role in the birth of her nephew.

But the next afternoon, after she has baby-sat her niece for the day, her brother-in-law arrives. He describes the first-day birthday party they're going to have in her sister's hospital room: hats, presents, those little whistles that stream out and curl back like candy-striped paper snails. She starts to get her purse, but there's an awkward pause while her brother-in-law explains that she's staying behind. She's not invited to the party.

"It's just for family," he says.

"Sure. Okay. No problem," she says as she helps the family—father and child—out the door.
This is a problem, she thinks, standing alone in the empty house.
This is a problem if this is what single means.

※

Do you have a family? people ask. It's an innocent question, but it's also a loaded one. It's loaded with cultural norms and presumptions. Of course the ever-single woman has a family, but not the kind people mean, the kind that inevitably involves marriage and babies. So the ever-single woman hesitates.

She hesitates because she understands the import of the question and she knows what's likely to happen when she starts her winding, unconventional answer. Americans value the institution of family and they often feel sorry for those who don't have one that they can pull out of their wallets with ease. If politicians are any indication, Americans still believe that the average wallet photo portrays a two-parent, biologically linked nuclear family; they're not prepared for the complex answer an ever-single woman might present. On the woman's side, no matter how much the American family has changed (and it has: the percentage of single-parent families doubled between 1960 and 1990), she may actually be confused by her own experience. The fact is, an ever-single woman may very well have many families.

She has a family of origin, where she is primarily a daughter and often a sister. She has an extended family, where she is a sister-in-law and probably an aunt. In some cases, she may form her own nuclear family by raising children. In other cases, she may well have an honorary family, where she is a major character and a welcome presence.

Laid out this way, her experience sounds simple, clear, even rich. But that's just part of the story. In part because of her status as a single woman, in part because of America's cultural confusion over its commitment to and definition of family, family is a sensitive area in the life of a single woman—it's emotionally charged and emotionally rich, barren and painful; it's a confusing area of life that she may have little control over, particularly during that challenging time of life when she seeks definition, when she tries to place herself in a world of conventional, wallet-photo lives, politics, and expectations.

Looking to her family of origin, she may find rigidity where she needs flexibility; she may find criticism from her parents ("Maybe you're just too picky, dear") when she needs support. Looking to her extended family, she may find that her married siblings have no room for her in their families. Forming her own family, she may find stigma and economic hardship. Looking to other, honorary families, she may get a lukewarm, even a suspicious response. Laid out this way, her early experience looks pretty dismal.

But when she finds family support—and most ever-single women eventually do find some form of family that works—it's wonderful. Indeed, having or creating a family can make a singular life sing. "I know I can rely on my family one hundred percent," says Caitlin McKuen, the artist, who recently mounted a joint exhibition with her mother. "They're always going to be there for me, and they'll never hurt me."

"My family?" asks Janice Patinkin, who recently stayed with her parents while she recovered from major surgery. "My family's great."

Not long after she retired from her teaching job, Kate O'Connor gave her niece a special Christmas gift: five hundred hours of baby-sitting, available on demand. It was well timed. Her niece was young, unmarried, newly a mother, and not making much money. So for the next two years, Kate cared for her grand-nephew as much as forty hours a week.

In her own independent style, Kate was fulfilling a time-honored role, the role of the spinster-aunt—with one difference. She *chose* it.

A hundred years before, she probably wouldn't have had a choice. Unable to demonstrate her use by fulfilling the whole adult female role—wife and mother—the ever-single woman in Britain and the U.S. was compelled to fulfill parts of it. Often, she stuck with her family of origin, staying at home to help her mother or run her widowed father's house. Alternatively, she turned to her extended family, traveling from house to house to house, raising a brother's children one year, nursing a sick sister the next, helping a grieving cousin the next. Even for women who had their own work, this was the role and the cultural expectation. The poet Emily Dickinson spent seven years nursing her mother, and the educator Catharine Beecher ran her sister Harriet Beecher Stowe's household while Harriet wrote *Uncle Tom's Cabin*. Similarly, teacher and activist Susan B. Anthony spent many months nursing a cousin through a difficult pregnancy, and she never established her own home.

At best, the spinster-aunt role was an established custom that gave ever-single women a place in the world and a family to rely on. And that place was sometimes revered: in the early 1800s, during the heyday of what was called "the cult of single blessedness," ever-single women became the heroines of pop literature, saving nieces from their weak-willed mothers, whipping relatives' households into shape, and generally demonstrating that the childless woman was a better mother than her married sister. The spinster-aunt was a kind of one-woman moral SWAT team, always ready to infiltrate, correct, and then leave, no thanks necessary.

At worst, the family role of the ever-single woman was akin to servitude. Poor Mary Kingsley knew that. Having nursed her parents until they died in the 1890s, Mary then became the housekeeper to her underachiever brother, who seems to have spent more money than he made. She did this because this is what was done. "I came home to look after him domestically as long as he wants me to do so," she wrote. "I must do it—it is duty—the religion I was brought up in." In this religion, Mary could launch her biological expeditions only when Charley decided that he didn't need her; and, in this religion, when Charley failed to meet his commitment to write their father's biography, she did it. Mary was the ultimate cleaning lady.

Historically, the woman most angered by this spinster role was probably Florence Nightingale. An ever-single woman who might have been homosexual if she'd expressed her sexuality at all, Nightingale railed against the half-adult role she was assigned in her socially rigid, relentlessly needy family, which refused to let her work outside the house for fourteen tumultuous years. "This system dooms some minds to incurable infancy, others to silent misery," she wrote. Breaking free, she eventually went to the Crimea, where she vanquished competitive nurses and saved the British Army from disease. But once she returned home to London, Nightingale was unable to break out of the static, home-bound spinster role a second time. So she chose not-so-silent misery—and officially took to her deathbed for the next fifty-three years.

Although few were probably tortured quite the way Nightingale was, most spinster-aunts seem to have encountered public shame. In the early twentieth century, the supposedly liberal Ellen Key talked about envious, "ill-natured" aunts who were the "laughing stock" of their communities. Twenty years later, Edith Wharton created exactly that kind of aunt in her story "The Old Maid." In the story, young Charlotte Lovell lets passion run away with her and secretly has a baby out of wedlock. But after Charlotte delivers her baby, she sheds her femininity and her charm and descends into the role of spinster-aunt, complete with pinched lips and a straight-backed chair. Although she gets to live in the house where her baby is raised, she never achieves the public validation of motherhood. Instead, she is repeatedly humiliated by her own daughter, who calls her "aunt" and thinks of her as a sour, shrunken, jealous, and rigid old woman—*which she is*. In the end, it's hard to know whether Wharton is telling us that humiliation creates the spinster or the spinster creates the humiliation. She doesn't seem to know.

Good and bad, the spinster-aunt role continued well into the twentieth century. It began to disappear only in the fifties and sixties as the American family became increasingly suburbanized, nuclear, and self-contained, and as more women left home to go to college. By the 1970s, the serving, supporting, subordinate (presumably bitter, dependent, deformed) live-in spinster had virtually disappeared among young women. The spinster-aunt had become independent; she'd also fallen victim to the entropy that stalked American family life in the twentieth century. The ever-single woman had gained, gained independence—but she'd also lost, lost position.

❦

The idea of being a spinster-aunt never occurred to Mary Stendahl, who teaches first grade in a New England town not far from where she grew up and went to college. She lived with her parents for a short time after college, and she roomed for a while with her sister, but she created her own role as she developed a circle of close friends, bought her dog, bought her house, and planted her garden; she's not a twentieth-century Mary Kingsley.

Yet some themes and feelings have survived the demise of the traditional, rigid spinster-aunt role, and they sometimes reside in the lives of ever-single women like Mary.

One feeling is the disconcerting sense that the aging family has dissolved and reconvened in some other, uncomfortable form. Siblings marry and their families take center stage; sisters shift their focus and drift off into another identity, less accessible and less conversant. Susan B. Anthony experienced such a shift, suffering a tremendous loss when her sister Guelma became engaged. Almost immediately, Susan felt Guelma's change in identity, and she dreaded the loss of intimacy between them so profoundly that she nearly skipped the wedding. A century later, Mary's experience was less dramatic, but still poignant: marriage took her sister far away from New England and transformed their friendship into a visiting, telephoning relationship. "It changed a little bit too because she talks about the kids all the time now. Not that I don't want to talk about the kids," Mary says quickly. "And she still talks about me and wants to know what is happening to me too—but she doesn't take good care of herself." Mary pauses, reaching for a better explanation of the gap that has appeared. "The Barbara that I used to know seems like it's gone," she says. "I think that her identity is just different now."

Another consequence of the aging family is a subtle form of isolation. In some cases, as the family of origin revels in its expansion, as members take off and form their own families, they inadvertently leave single family members behind. "I look at it that they close the door. They close the door to family. They create this tight little unit inside so no one can join; anyone who tries is an intruder," observes Allie Ackerman. Still the feisty woman who once dumped a fiancé over an unpaid toll, Allie has formed her own nuclear family and yearns for the comfort and coverage of an extended family. A few years ago, she confronted her older sister about being excluded from holidays and vacations—to no avail. "She said, 'It's just for *family*,'" Allie recalls bitterly. "And I said, 'What are we . . . *chopped liver?*'" Not surprisingly, her sister's recent divorce seems to have changed things. Allie and her children are more welcome now, and her sister's wallet-photo definition of family has become more inclusive: "Now the door is open," Allie says.

Usually the exclusion goes unchallenged. Not long ago, Juillissa Rivera's otherwise supportive family—brothers, sisters, nieces, and nephews—left her standing in front of a church alone after a family wedding. Thinking in tight, nuclear units, they all jumped into their cars and headed off for the reception. No one had thought about her, the "extra" person who didn't fit into the standard family structure.

But this exclusion is deeper and more subtle than it looks, according to Juillissa, who, in her fifties, is a public school teacher, administrator, and grief counselor with a couple of master's degrees. Because she hasn't made that rite of passage, because she doesn't meet the unstated definition of adulthood, she is minister without portfolio, an adult without credentials, a perpetual daughter. "It's something like being a grown-up child," Juillissa observes. On visits, she's been told to share a room with the kids; and one sister sends a clear message that allows for little negotiation. The message, according to Juillissa, goes: "This is my family and everyone in it, and you're the aunt. You're not a parent." The rigidity makes Juillissa hesitate. "I'm very uncomfortable because I'm an aunt, and that's somewhere between a guest and a stranger. I'm not sure what the definition of aunt is," she muses, and then concludes, "It's not part of the family with a capital F."

One by-product of not being seen as a fully vested adult is the idea that a single woman has no other obligations claiming her time. For many women, this idea leads to being assigned the care of an aging parent, as it once did for Kate O'Connor. For others, the idea leads to more subtle experiences. Most of the women that I met do most of the visiting—their families expect it—and many find that their families presume that their time is unscheduled and just a little less important. "You know, I'll get over to my parents' place expecting dinner and I find things have changed," says Mary, who has found herself arriving at family events at the wrong time. "No one thought to tell me."

Even younger members of the family indulge in this notion of the ever-single aunt as somehow not quite adult. Years ago I heard two thirtyish brothers talk about their aging family. "I worry about how they're going to make it," one brother said of his frail, eighty-plus grandparents, who were living alone in a sizable house. "I worry about how our *crazy, spacy aunt* is going to make it without them," said the other. He was referring to a shy sixty-four-year-old woman who had survived cancer, traveled extensively with friends, and held a job as an executive secretary in a prestigious law firm for more than forty years. She had lived independently all her life, supporting herself and helping her parents with household chores; she was by every definition an adult, except that she hadn't married. I was stunned.

But he was expressing the same perception that Nightingale so hated: never ceremonially given away by her father to another man, the ever-single woman is a half-adult, not quite launched in the eyes of her rigid family. The key word here is *rigid:* a *flexible* family, an *adaptive* family that dealt in *real* people—not expected roles—would have adjusted to her unconventional life and valued her achievement. Indeed, this is an important, lifelong task of the family of origin: the family of origin is the place where a child first tests and

74

confirms her worth; they're the people she comes home to during the adolescent crucible. And although it's the structure that a young woman is often expected to duplicate as she becomes an adult, it's also a structure capable of helping her feel good about living differently, about taking off on her own path at her own pace. In a profound way, some families, families like the one Allie grew up in or the one Mary Kingsley suffered, fail in that task. But others succeed brilliantly.

🦅

Being single in an adaptive family of origin is far more comfortable, far more rewarding and reassuring than being single in an unadaptive one. And there are many adaptive families: there are families in which a daughter grows up, lives a singular life, maintains a close and abiding relationship with her parents, siblings, nieces, and nephews, and achieves an adult identity all her own. These adaptive families adjust to their members' real selves and unscripted lives. They value their members as individuals with individual worth.

To adapt is a significant achievement. To do it, everyone in the family must adjust his and her idea of what a grown-up female is. Everyone must adjust to a new, less nuclear definition of family. It takes patience as this new definition is worked out. It takes genuine interest and it takes communication. Early in her thirties, Janice Patinkin made it clear that being told she was too picky was contributing to her discomfort—and her family has begun to understand. "They used to talk about it more, but now they know they can't because I'll jump on them," she says. "*'Just leave me alone,'*" she mimics herself. "*'I can't pick them [men] out of thin air, you know.'*"

When Ellen Adams's mother told her that her problem was that she was too strong to attract a man, Ellen reacted angrily and then let it go. In turn, Mrs. Adams continued to watch as Ellen lived her life, joining the Peace Corps, setting up her own household, dating men and introducing them to her mother as she went. In time she came to accept that Ellen is not going to change who she is in order to marry and that Ellen may not need marriage the way Mrs. Adams once thought. "I don't think she's worried about me anymore," Ellen says. "At this point, she knows that I'm taken care of. I'm taking care of myself."

Remarkably, in many cases this adaptation seems to happen naturally. Some women, like Rosalie Morgan, seventy-six, and Lillian Salinger, seventy-four, have extraordinarily close relationships with their siblings and they remember getting immediate support from their parents. Urbane, socially active Rosalie has lived with her ever-single sister all her life and says that their father always considered them "unclaimed treasures." Taciturn, hard-working Lillian, who lives with her ever-single brother Walter, says that their relationship is so close people who don't know the situation assume that they're married.

You can understand why. When Lillian and Walter talk, sitting side by side on a couch in the Illinois farmhouse they grew up in, their closeness is obvious and yet unstated. They have managed different tracts of the same land for nearly forty years; they share their working lives and their values, a large part of the their social lives, and all of their holidays (for Thanksgiving and Christmas, it's a major potluck with seventeen cousins who live on nearby farms).

"Actually," says Walter, "Lillian did a lot of work for me here after Mom passed away. That was way back in fifty-eight. There were a lot of things that she did. She'd drive a tractor to bale hay."

"I don't know about [that] now," Lillian interjects. She's a soft-spoken, slender woman who used to teach piano on the side. "I don't know how I did that."

"Then we'd have young guys help unload it and she would be busy with me, out—" Walter continues.

"Well," interrupts Lillian, "they would be out in the field loading and I would get lunch for those guys and I would get supper and still be out in the field." Walter is nodding proudly; Lillian pauses, glancing at Walter. He's a gentle man with a self-deprecating humor and a warmth that are immediately apparent. Then Lillian turns back to me, smiling. "Now, I could never do that anymore."

Maureen Cabot's family life has similar closeness. Never having found a man whose "hormones hopped" when hers did, she lived with her parents while her brother and sister married and moved out. After her father and then her mother died, Maureen found the freezer full of ready-made meals. Typical of the family humor, there were notes attached. One said, "You better learn to do this chicken yourself. The recipe is there." Another said, "This won't last forever. You better learn to cook." And another read rather cryptically, "Anyone can cook who can read English!"

"As I say, I was very lucky with my family," says Maureen. "I think they thought that some man was missing the biggest treasure in the world. But their attitude was—well, my father once said, 'If you want to be street cleaners, I'll go out and get you a broom, but make sure that's what you want to do.'" Her parents understood that Maureen was satisfied living her life as she saw it unfolding. "I was happy," she says simply.

Years after her mother's death, Maureen's family continues to be close. In fact, these days, scheduling meetings with Maureen, who is retired, is difficult. "I'm beginning to think that I'm being covered by my nieces and nephews," she explains as we struggle over the phone to find a clear day on her calendar. "You know, I think they confer with each other—'Who's going to see the old gal this week?'" she jokes.

Family adaptation comes both in small acts and in big ones. It's a kind of graciousness made normal. Marguerite Ramanis's family has come to her place for Thanksgiving for the last three years, and Pat McDonald is a regular overnight guest at her brother's place on Christmas Eve—the kids expect it. Roxanne Walters's four-year-old nephew takes his vacations at her house, and he had a tough time keeping up with her on roller-blades last summer. In her fifties, Ellen Adams's mother traveled in bumpy, crowded buses filled with live chickens and people seated four and five to a seat to see her daughter's Peace Corps site in Paraguay; Caitlin McKuen's parents visited her while she was studying art in India.

One evening over a glass of wine, I asked Caitlin's mother, who married when she was twenty, if she was disappointed at having three unmarried daughters in their thirties. She smiled. "No! No!" she said.

Immediately her daughters set up a chorus of laughter. "Oh, come on, I remember you used to sit there and talk about our weddings," one needled her. "'*Wouldn't it be nice to do this . . . ?*'" she mimicked.

"That's probably because I came from the old school," Mrs. McKuen admitted. Tanned and relaxed, an avid traveler and an expert gardener, she laughed at the kidding even as she mounted her defense. "So when you got out of college, I thought, okay, now they'll find a guy and they'll all settle down and that will be it." How could she have known her daughters would study in India, travel the world, and build a career on the other side of the continent instead? She turned to me. "But I could see that they're very happy and I certainly don't want them to get married because I thought they should get married."

In a scriptless life, this kind support is invaluable, and Caitlin knows it. "Mom and Dad were great because no matter what we wanted to do . . . they always supported us and never discouraged us," she tells me later, when we're out of earshot. "I mean, if they thought it was a bad idea, they expressed that opinion, but they never tried to stop us. And they were always there to help us out and support us when we realized it *was* a bad idea.

"We were lucky," she concludes, "that we were raised with the idea that we could do anything we wanted to do."

❦

As important as family is in the emotional lives of women, as central as the notion of motherhood is to the image of the fulfilled and feminine woman, having children does not seem important to the singular women I met. Most say that they don't miss having children, and none has considered marrying for the sole purpose of having children. Some don't like children much, but a greater number enjoy the opportunity to spend time with children—and then go home alone at the end of the day.

Evidently this group is more typical than it looks. According to a number of studies, motherhood doesn't have the cachet that it once had: in 1976, just 16 percent of women between thirty and thirty-four were childless; by 1990, 25 percent were childless. If trends continue, some 17 percent of the women born between 1956 and 1965 will not have kids, mostly by choice. In a 1991 *Self* magazine survey, a whopping 46 percent of single women said that marriage without children was "alluring." This is one reason why demographers believe that the fastest growing household type in the 1990s will be married couples with no children; the second fastest will be women who live alone.

It was toward the end of our acquaintance that Caitlin McKuen had a tubal ligation. Her father opposed the operation, but her mother and sisters supported it. Caitlin was absolutely sure she didn't want children and she felt that her mother's breast cancer had forced her hand. She was sexually active and she didn't want to be on the pill. "I started thinking about having my tubes tied in my early twenties," she says at thirty-three. "It was time."

She didn't feel any different after the operation. She didn't have a sense that an important door had closed. Although her current boyfriend may want children in the future, she knew she would never have had children solely to please her partner. "I mean, it's my body, it's my life; this is what I want for me," she says, sitting in a wire chair on the rocky terrace between her studio and her house. "So I made the decision based on me, not based on who I was with or who I might be with in the future."

"What about when you're older?" I ask. "A lot of people have children so that they'll have someone to care for them in old age."

Caitlin folds her long legs up against her body. She's barefoot, dressed in loose pants and a shirt, and she's holding a cup of strong (nearly solid) coffee. She has thought about this one too. "I think that's the wrong reason to have children," she says. "That [having children] doesn't mean they're going to take care of you; that doesn't automatically mean that they're going to be there when you're old. Look," she concludes iconoclastically, "I can put *my own self* in a nursing home."

Frankly, I was surprised by all of this. Motherhood is, after all, part of the script, part of the definition of feminine adulthood; in the cultural mirror, it's the primary experience that gives women shape to their identities and meaning to their lives. In her interviews with both straight and lesbian ever-single women in the late 1970s, author Nancy L. Peterson concluded that motherhood was a major issue for unmarried women. As a result, I thought I would find more biological tickings and quiet regrets. But among the older women, Jillian Goodman, Linda Schindler, and I seem to be the only ones who have felt bereft, who have suffered an invisible loss and approached menopause with regret.

In my life, this hidden loss has been isolating and painful, and for years as I sat in school auditoriums watching other people's children dance, as I helped other people's children learn to read, as I bought gifts, made runs to the school nurse when a parent was unavailable, and cheered my niece at soccer games, I grieved. It was the kind of grief that could make me cry on cue, when I saw a child grasp a mother's hand, when I passed a crowd of kids in Halloween costumes, when I realized that I was irreplaceable to no one. There's no forum for this grief; there's no support for it. When you talk about it, people generally start to squirm; others actually make jokes. So I have counted it as one of my most difficult, and most private, challenges.

In contrast, Jillian Goodman has been more forthright in her approach and, I think, more successful. As an obstetric nurse, for years she taught grief workshops for parents who had lost babies to miscarriages and stillbirths. Then, as she recovered from her fortieth-birthday crisis, she realized that she had something to learn too. Parents who had lost a child to miscarriage had told her that their child seemed invisible—just as hers was. They told her that their grief was hard to share—just as hers was. So she began to talk about her loss at her workshops. "I would verbalize my feelings," she says. "I would say, 'It hurts so badly, I feel such despair, that I just want to go to sleep and not wake up.' Or, 'I feel I'm in the bottom of a great big hole and people are saying, Come up! Come up! It's okay up here! And I'm going, No, no, it's all black and horrible.'" She continues, almost rushing through the blackness to reach the turning point for me. "And so I turned what I felt was my greatest misfortune around," she says. It has been a year since she first began to express her feelings, and she has allowed herself to grieve and backslide and grieve again. Not long ago, she came out of the hole, relieved and purposeful: "I believe that that experience . . . was to make me a better grief counselor and better at my workshops."

But such experiences are unusual in this crowd. Only the two youngest women and one woman in her mid-thirties feel as Jillian, Linda, and I did at thirty, thirty-five, and forty: caught between the desire to have children and the fear that doing it alone might be detrimental to the child, or morally wrong, or just plain difficult. Of the two youngest women, Roxanne has turned her energies toward her nephew and Felicia has turned her energies toward friends. But neither has come to resolution. "I think if I don't have children, it will be the most disappointing thing in my life," says Felicia. Her feelings are familiar, and a number of studies indicate that they may persist for a lifetime.

Janice, in turn, is still considering having a child outside of marriage. "There are days, right before my period mostly, that I just bawl my eyes out that I've never had a kid yet," she says. "I really do want one, and I've just started within the last six months thinking about having one on my own."

Six months ago, she began to answer the important questions: Where would she live? How would she ensure a male influence? Would she have enough practical and emotional support to pull it off? "I have worked all those out," she says. "I have a huge support system. I would move back to

Spokane and live with my sister . . . she has three boys now, and she has a nanny."

Then she talked to her parents, who, according to Janice, have a nearly perfect marriage and up until now have held fairly conventional expectations. At first, she says, her father, the owner of a large children's store, hesitated. But her mother's enthusiasm was immediate. "My parents have already said they love the idea," Janice says with evident pride. "They just think it would be wonderful for me."

🦋

A few of the women I met have already made their own families. They are part of a well-publicized trend that became a political football in the early 1990s. In 1970, 7 percent of single parents in the U.S. had never married. By 1990 a surprising 31 percent of single parents had never married; tragically, an estimated 29.7 percent of unwed mothers are teenagers. Yet the statistic is not the pure indicator of contemporary licentiousness that it seems to be. Shocking as it may seem, during the Revolutionary War era 33 percent of first births were conceived out of wedlock; the rate dipped to a little over 12 percent during the mid-nineteenth century, but it was up to nearly 25 percent during the turn of the twentieth century. Single women have always had sex, and they've always conceived. Until recently, though, they had a greater tendency to marry immediately or give up their babies. White women in particular no longer give up their children the way they once did: before 1973, 19 percent of single white mothers gave up their babies. Fifteen years later only 3 percent did. In contrast, African American women have traditionally held on to their babies—their so-called "relinquishment rate" has traditionally hovered around 2 percent. Meanwhile, since the 1973 Supreme Court decision legalizing abortion, unmarried (divorced, widowed, and ever-single) women have accounted for 53 percent of the abortions in the U.S. In the group I met, five women talked about having had abortions, most with a distant, lingering sadness and all with the caveat that they had made the decision at a time in their lives when they felt they could not handle a full-term pregnancy or a baby.

For those women who have had children, life as a single mother has not been easy, partly because raising children isn't easy and partly because raising children draws on existing structures—the family structure, the finances, the parameters and scheduling of one's job, the resources in the community—and to do it without a husband is to put increased pressure on all these structures. For one woman the structures were strong and reliable. For two others—Allie Ackerman and Victoria Mason—the structures around them often buckled under the pressure.

Both Allie and Victoria come from families that are unable or unwilling to provide healthy emotional support, and neither had the financial backing they needed. Although Allie planned ahead in a casual way, underneath she secretly expected the father of her first child to take more of an interest. She also expected her parents to warm up to the idea once her daughter was born. Neither happened: the father made it clear he was not responsible, and Allie's mother made it clear that such an event wasn't to happen again, especially in full view of their close-knit and watchful Methodist community. Therein began a journey that took Allie through a second pregnancy and a series of cramped living quarters in and out of her home town; fights with the schools and Little League victories; retrieved memories of sexual abuse and clinical depression; straight-A report cards and a condo literally lined with kids' drawings. In short, it has been rewarding and tough—and continues to be.

Victoria simply made a mistake: born out of wedlock herself, at nineteen Vicki bolted from her dysfunctional family, worked for the Black Panthers, got pregnant, and returned home to her also-pregnant mother. Unskilled and unable to support herself, Vicki never considered abortion. She wanted the child. She wanted a healthy connection.

But her choice was complicated by the fact that she had been sexually molested by her stepfather, the man her mother was still married to. And it was further complicated by the reality that her mother still had a houseful of children—including a baby nearly the same age as Vicki's baby. Vicki veered between welfare and low-paying jobs that bored her. She took courses in theater and film, she moved in and out of her mother's house, and she spent a night in a homeless shelter. She had a second child by another man and worked while her mother stayed with the children.

If it was hard financially, it was even harder emotionally. Always, Vicki was hounded by the disturbing symmetry of her life: "I'd become my mother!" she says dramatically, so that the schoolroom we're sitting in fills with her rich contralto voice. "And I didn't want to become my mother!" She was

determined to protect her daughter, but had trouble achieving full independence from her mother's household—and the stepfather who came and went.
Vicki strictly forbade her mother to leave the kids with her stepfather, but she
worried, and she wished she had more control.

Then came what she calls the "daddy questions." "The hardest time is
when the children go to school and the comparisons," she says now. " 'My
daddy so and so, my daddy'—you know that type of thing starts happening.
And you have to sit down and explain to your children what your explanation will be at that point. . . . And hopefully by that time you have been able
to kind of go over it in your own head and be really okay with it." It was some
time later that she finally came to terms with her situation and her choices:
"It was time for me to stop hiding my head in the sand . . . to recognize that I
didn't know what my life would have been like had they not been a part of it;
to recognize that they really taught me about love."

With a good job in the Milwaukee public schools, Victoria is on her own
again. Her daughter is an honor student in college, and, when her son leaves
for college in two years, Vicki may go back to school herself. She has never
considered marriage, but she says she will now that her children are virtually
launched. "I decided I would not—I would do everything, every single thing
I could do to make sure [my daughter] did not experience the difficulty of having a stepfather," she says. At thirty-eight, she has emerged from a personal
odyssey, from a task not well thought out, but a task well achieved.

In contrast, indomitable, forward-thinking Karen King, the high school
teacher who was born in Jamaica and educated in the U.S., had all her supports in place, particularly her family. When she was unable to pick up her
newly adopted daughter Michelle, her mother took care of the baby in
Jamaica. When she was scheduled to go to a teacher's conference, her mother
came to the U.S. to stay with Michelle. In addition, at forty-two, Karen had
the financial resources to provide good child care while she worked, and she
owned her own home.

Then Michelle got sick. At first she had a couple of flulike symptoms;
then she had a seizure. In March of 1985, at the age of five, Michelle was
diagnosed with a brain tumor, and Karen took a leave of absence from the
Sacramento school system. Michelle died in July, and for more than a year
Karen looked back and worried that she hadn't done enough, hadn't figured
out soon enough what was going on. "Initially I felt that there must have

been something I should have picked out. So I felt very bad about that. The other reason I felt guilty [was] I had taken this child to give her a better life, and now she is dead." In a brave and unusual move, she went to see Michelle's biological mother in Jamaica and brought pictures. Together, they looked at the pictures and talked about Michelle's life and death. "She was so sweet. She was so warm and had so much sorrow for me," Karen recalls. "Never did I see in her any kind of feeling that 'you took my child and look what happened.' She said, 'You know, I'm so glad she had that good life with you.'"

In Karen's description, Michelle was part of a huge, adaptive family, biological and emotional, that stretches across the U.S. and Jamaica; the funeral was packed with people who had traveled hundreds and thousands of miles, as well as children from Michelle's kindergarten class. Born in poverty, raised in a rural family that often ran out of food, Karen had learned her values from her divorced mother, who had raised her seven children alone. "We were very poor in all the material things that makes wealth for most people," she says. "We were extremely rich in family and love and in sharing and in the things that ultimately, I think, mattered and shaped who I am."

But even in the presence of such strong family connections, even with the backing of her religion, Karen suffered an isolating pain, the solitary pain of a mother who has watched her child die. So in November Karen went to Michelle's grave site, carrying a sweater. It was cold, and she wanted to keep her baby warm; she wanted to hold her and cover her and she remembered how hard she had tried to keep her little girl safe. She sat down at the site, held the sweater, and cried: she could not do what a mother is supposed to do.

In September a niece had told her that she knew of another young girl who needed adopting. Karen hesitated. In January she traveled to Jamaica to adopt Faith.

❧

Clearly it is easier to achieve singularity, a sense of individual worth and ease, in the presence of an adaptive family. Caitlin McKuen's confidence, Karen King's strength, Maureen Cabot's humor—while the qualities these women have seem exceptional, all three draw upon something conventional: loving, adaptive families.

In contrast, singularity comes hard to a woman whose family discounts her. It's no surprise that a woman whose father tells her that she could have been successful if she'd just married so-and-so might see marriage as a solution to what really is her father's problem, her father's failure to see his daughter as an individual with individual worth. This is a long and tragic dilemma, one that both Charlotte Brontë and Louisa May Alcott faced. Today it is such an accepted part of the culture that it is common fodder for TV routines and newspaper cartoons: in the early 1990s television daughters from *Ellen*, *Madman of the People*, and even *Star Trek: The Next Generation* squirmed under the scrutiny and pressure of mothers and grandmothers. In a series of "Cathy" cartoons, mother-pressure is a central theme, and even in the *New York Times*, you can catch a mother-pressure quip. Amusing as these quips may seem, in reality it's difficult for an ever-single daughter to sort through contradictory messages of parental love and disappointment. It's difficult to know your own worth when you catch your mother secretly answering personal ads for you, as Rachel Jacobs once did.

For many of these women, part of the journey through their late twenties and thirties is a search for family, for the profound and unwavering acceptance, for the access to the wonder of children that families traditionally provide. While some, like Allie Ackerman, create their own, others consciously write other, honorary families into their scripts, understanding their place and appreciating their function.

This is exactly the approach that the naturalist Sally Carrighar, who was a victim of extraordinary abuse (including strangulation and starvation at the hands of her mother), championed. In her childhood, Carrighar had been physically and emotionally saved through the intervention of two or three non-family adults. Later, as an adult working in the northern reaches of the continent in the late 1950s and 1960s, she encountered Eskimo culture, where parenting was shared and children were the sons and daughters of the whole community. Carrighar, an ever-single woman, saw this kind of shared family as ideal for children, parents, and the rest of the adult community.

But in mainstream culture, achieving an honorary family is a bit tricky. First, it takes an adaptive family to accept an unrelated member, and second, it takes a pioneering spirit to do what doesn't come naturally in the culture. Although Felicia Collinet, the fund-raiser who still feels scriptless, has found a family who enjoys her, her less adaptive friends are critical. "I think they think it's really odd," she says of her attachment to a certain two year old. "They're like, 'What's with you and this kid?'"

Third, families find trust hard to come by at a time when child abuse and molestation make weekly appearances on tabloid television. Even Allie, who instinctively builds small, tight-knit, neighborly communities wherever she lives, says that she ultimately keeps outsiders out.

In the end, the most obvious characteristic of the singular women I met was not that they came from adaptive or unadaptive families, but that they had examined their families. Each understood what she needed from her family and what she got; and those who needed more moved on.

They don't leave—exactly. But they learn to mitigate the impact of the rigidity that's there; they learn to shift their holidays elsewhere or come home after the presents are opened and the exclusivity of the more primary relationships is less visible. "It's fun," Juillissa says of Christmas with her extended family. "But in one way it's a little sad because everyone has their own family and so receive many gifts. . . . In that sense it's lonely for me." Not long ago she explained her feelings to one of her sisters. "She really understands that," says Juillissa, "and [she] always makes sure I receive a gift from her. . . . And what I've done a couple of times is arrive after all the gifts are opened."

Others learn to diffuse the sense of exclusion by creating their own events. And they learn to augment, to throw a Thanksgiving dinner that others will come to, to make friends who will remember their birthdays, to consciously include children in their lives. This kind of adaptation is a quiet process, largely unspoken and sometimes accidental—but necessary.

For me this silent, personal process culminated last year when my friend Anne asked me to attend the birth of her baby.

It was wonderful to be the third lay person at the birth of a baby, and it was initially awkward: in the midst of sudden preparations for a cesarean, as scrubs were distributed and nurses and doctors shot across the room like pinballs, it looked as if I might not be part of the birth after all. *How far does this honorary aunthood thing go?* I wondered, watching tubes and masks and caps appear. *I don't want to be too pushy, after all. After all, I'm not really related. . . .* But then Anne took control. She agitated for my inclusion in the operating room. She asked one doctor after another. They relented, and we all went in together.

Maggie was born at 2:22 P.M., and Joe and I described her wet, thin, purple-skinned beauty for Anne, whose view was blocked. Then Anne looked up at me. "Do you know we have known each other nineteen years?" she asked.

"Are you sure?" I said. "That many?"

"We want you to be her godmother."

This was new territory for me, an honorary family based on friendship, a place to come to when I wanted a shot of baby screams, the smell of crayons, the feel of child energy. It was new territory, without established roles, rules, expectations. It was something rare and something unwritten, something to be created as we went along.

Quite honestly, at another time in my life I might not have been ready. I might not have grasped the invitation as wholly as I grasped it that day at 2:22 P.M. At another time—a time when I was still asking *What's wrong with me?*—I might have delayed my response, confused it with my own desire to have children, worried that someone was taking pity on me, or felt strangely apart, like a hybrid with no natural place in the scheme of things.

But not now. I've changed since I first started my journey; I've stopped presuming that something is wrong with me. I've come to see that family is something bigger and more vague than the wallet-photo definition that once hounded me like a sitcom image duplicated and multiplied a hundred times over in a fun-house mirror. And so I grasped, wholly and happily, nervously and gratefully—and proudly.

I am proud that in the midst of this private and uncharted journey something I'd cultivated and cared for and believed in all my life had actually proved real and true. Not only was something not wrong with me, but I'd been doing something right all along.

I'd been making friends.

CHAPTER FIVE

Making Friends

~

Little Holly Hall stands up and proudly, formally introduces Kate O'Connor as her aunt.

"No, no, no, I'm not your aunt," *Kate tells her.*

Holly is perturbed at this news, but she thinks she's got it under control. Next time she introduces Kate as her mother's college roommate.

"Oh, no, no," *Kate tells her.* "I'm not your mother's college roommate."

Holly puts her hands on her hips, cranks up her six-year-old indignation, and demands, "Well, what are you?"

"I'm just a friend."

Holly had a right to be confused, Kate explains. Back in the fifties, Kate had met Holly's mother in junior college and watched her inspire half the boys in Kate's home town to undying love. "Clarissa was legendary," *Kate recalls.* "When she told her father that she was getting married, he asked, 'Who to?'"

A year after Clarissa married, Kate drove the seven hundred miles to Clarissa's new home. On the way she stopped to see Clarissa's mother, who gave her some advice. "Kate," *Mrs. Townsend told her,* "don't ever miss a summer going out there, because if you do, it's too easy to say, 'Well I didn't get there last summer and I am too busy and I can't get there this summer' . . . and the friendship fades."

Forty years later, Kate is very close to Clarissa's children—and their children. She is a regular part of their lives. But on a recent visit, one lit-

*tle four-year-old granddaughter just couldn't take her eyes off of her. She
stared and stared at Kate.*

*"She couldn't get it," Kate explains. "She'd been told, 'We're going
to visit Grandma's best friend.' So of course she expected a friend—say,
someone about four." Kate laughs and her tabby cat springs from her lap.
She repeats Mrs. Townsend's advice. And then, in a voice brimming with
certainty and fondness, she adds: "It was wise."*

🦋

For all the male buddy stories in the world, for all the profiles of Butch Cassidy and the Sundance Kid, Tom and Huckleberry, Rosencrantz and Guilden-
stern, Batman and Robin, Beavis and Butthead, there is nothing quite as deep
and abiding, as intense and voluntary, as rewarding and revealing as a friendship between women. The sentimental 1988 movie *Beaches* gives it a try; the
1991 revenge-adventure flick *Thelma and Louise* goes a part of the distance;
but no one has reached the emotional complexity of the friendship between
Susan B. Anthony and Elizabeth Cady Stanton, or the old-shoe comfort of
the friendship between Beatrix Potter and her novel-writing cousin, Margaret Harkness.

Friendship is an underestimated, underexplored part of women's lives—
as common as pantyhose, as regular as morning coffee, as deep and complex
as ten and twenty and forty years of mutual confidences can make it. In
a 1990 Gallup poll of 1,226 adults, 82 percent of the women reported having
a best friend, and 81 percent of these women said that their best friend was a
woman. In a revealing picture of marriage, only 13 percent of married women
said that their husband was their best friend.

"So what's the point?" one ever-single woman asked when I repeated
these statistics. "I mean, if he's not your best friend . . . ?"

"Actually, thirteen percent sounds high," said her sister, who has been divorced. "I would have said *five percent.*" They both laughed. But there was a
discomfort there, as if a fly had gotten into the pudding and no one wanted to
admit it. We seek friendship in marriage—and consequently we sometimes
underestimate it elsewhere in our lives.

It's no surprise, then, that in *New Woman's* 1987 survey of 16,000 divorced and ever-single readers, 60 percent said that *if they never marry* they

will pay more attention to their friends. Although studies differ, most seem to show that unmarried people—especially ever-single people—do rely more on friendships than married people do. They also seem to show that women's friendships are more intimate and more complex than men's.

Some single women say that friendship is as central to their lives as family is to the lives of married women. "I think true friendship has a tendency to help you grow," says Victoria Mason, who believes that her family of origin has at times inhibited her growth. "I always look at myself as someone who is trying to arrive. Now, I don't know what I'm trying to arrive at, but I think I'm trying to arrive at being the best human being I can be." She has looked for friendship with her sisters, but, given the family history of divorce, denial, and sexual abuse, it has never worked out. "We've had our moments of friendship," she says tentatively. But for consistent support, she has learned to look elsewhere. "I think that I have developed a circle outside that blood relationship," she says, "and my friends Penny and Jody are part of that *other* sister circle."

In a singular life, friendship can be everything, and—in a society that thinks that Connie Chung and Dan Rather are actually close friends (as CBS News's 1993 commercial campaign tried to contend, despite obvious evidence to the contrary)—it can be nothing. Friendship is the least defined, the most negotiable, and the most vulnerable relationship in our lives. Without formal sanction, without an established seal of approval or a specific code of behavior, friendship is a delicate thing, often tested and easily overwhelmed. In the lives of women who have not created their own families, that frequently makes friendship an unsteady guidepost, akin to an emotional mirage, half real and half not.

But it's probably that same negotiable quality, that inherent flexibility, that makes friendship so important in the lives of singular women. It may be that no other form of human connection has the flexibility to match the syncopated stride of a woman living an unconventional life while simultaneously cradling her sorrow, answering her shifting needs, enjoying her fluctuating rhythms, and remembering to send a card when she receives a promotion.

Friendship is two things: vulnerable and cherished both.

🦅

There was a time when I felt my life was shrinking. I remember the moment exactly. I was sitting in a restaurant waiting for an old friend, a male buddy, to meet me for brunch. I waited an hour while waiters served me coffee and asked me if I was in the right place. Meanwhile, fifteen miles away in an expensive suburb, my buddy's new wife was putting her foot down. She disapproved of our friendship, always had. I had my suspicions, of course, and on the fourth cup of coffee I began to count the friendships—with men and with women—that had survived marriage. I was two for five.

Few of the singular women I've talked with have close married friends, and most of those who do formed those predominantly same-sex friendships before the marriage. There are lots of reasons for this, and they start with the nature of the marriage script in women's lives.

In the archetypal script, an unformed girl embarks on a journey that ends in the arms of a man who will protect her and provide her with the social position that she cannot attain on her own. In the most popular marriage script, the fairy tale, this journey is extraordinarily lonely. Girls in fairy tales typically come from dysfunctional families (families that enslave them, for instance, or give them away for a head of cabbage). The first lesson of the fairy tale is abandonment.

The second is social isolation. Cinderella and Sleeping Beauty both have to rely on supernaturals for help. Rapunzel pretty much goes it alone. Snow White manages to cement one of the few friendships in a classic fairy tale— but it's basically a domestic, marital relationship between her and seven sloppy little men (one wonders what would have happened if Snow didn't like to clean or cook meals). A much more equal friendship occurs between Dorothy and her three male bodyguards (the Tin Man, the Scarecrow, and the Cowardly Lion), but it's truly rare, and it's strictly a twentieth-century phenomenon.

Where are the women in these stories? For the most part, they're feeling competitive and behaving abominably. In general, there are few good mothers and even fewer human friends for a girl in a fairy tale; her social identity can be confirmed only through marriage to a man. And once her social identity is confirmed, the story typically ends.

It ends at her marriage because there's no reason to go on: a literary critic would say that the abandonment plot and the isolation plot are both resolved. A new person—a person with social position—is born. And she'll live happily ever after.

In the past hundred years those powerful plots have been replayed over and over again in romance novels and theories of development, in smash-hit musicals and in pop songs like John Denver's "Follow Me" (which was a top choice of couples whose weddings I ran at the Stanford Memorial Chapel in the mid-seventies).

A quaint example of the updated marriage plot is Howard Chandler Christy's *The American Girl*, a 1906 portrait of American femininity that fairly drips with commercial interest (Christy himself acknowledged that the book had to end with a wedding or it wouldn't sell). Christy's American girl barely has female friends—except when they buzz around her at the wedding reception like a swarm of marriage-minded moths around a wedding candle. Mostly, Christy's American girl is a solo artist, desultorily waiting for a hero to cart her off into a new identity. Hit by Cupid's arrow, "she knows that she has received a new soul, a soul that *dominates* and *controls* her being" (emphasis mine). In this new identity the American girl is no longer responsible for her actions—if she ever was. And now she is swept into a world of social obligation: the girl and her beau "suddenly discover that alliances are the business not only of the parties most concerned but of all the world besides." Once she was an isolated schoolgirl. Now she is connected.

Some fifty years later, Alan Jay Lerner converted George Bernard Shaw's feminist play *Pygmalion* into a popular Broadway musical, *My Fair Lady*— and came up with a similar ending. In Shaw's 1913 play, Henry Higgins bets that he can teach a Cockney flower girl named Eliza Doolittle to look and act like a lady. He wins the bet, but at the end of the play Eliza declares her disgust at Henry's self-absorbed manipulation and leaves him. In the rewritten 1956 Broadway musical, Eliza joins Henry Higgins—in marriage, we assume—and we're actually happy about it, even though Henry's most articulate song on the subject of women is called "Why Can't a Woman Be More Like a Man?" One reason we're happy about the marriage is that Eliza is otherwise isolated. Motherless, she has a charming but apparently alcoholic father and no close friends (Henry, of course, does have a best friend). Now that she's a lady, she can't go back to her Cockney community. She's stuck. She might as well take the social identity that Higgins has to offer her. In this dilemma, mid-twentieth-century Eliza is not much different from her fairy tale ancestors.

Although Eliza's dilemma is extreme, this long-standing notion that a young woman finds a completely new identity in marriage does ring true in contemporary life, and it's a key to why single women and married women often have trouble connecting in true, lasting friendship. The key is something sociologists call "role discontinuity." For married women like Eliza, adult identity is characterized by schism—in the married woman's life, there's a "before" person and an "after" person. Traditionally, in big ways and in little ones, a woman is expected to discard the person she was before marriage and live only as the "after" person—which makes maintaining friendships, especially with single friends, very difficult.

You can see role discontinuity all around us. Until recently, in many states the married woman had to give up her maiden name, and often she not only took her husband's last name but his first name as well—hence the signature "Mrs. Donald M. Schultz," which offers no information about the woman who writes it. "We lose so many names in marriage," muses Diane Faverty, seventy-four, a retired Fortune 500 executive. "When they get married, they change their names; they've lost all identity."

She's right. The name change is often window dressing to a deeper process. Historically the married woman disappeared into her husband's movie; she followed his career and concerns and let her social associations form accordingly. In her study of women's diaries of the westward journey, Lillian Schlissel notes that few women wanted to make the move; they were often pregnant when they started the journey, and the journey meant leaving important connections just when they needed them. In a 1960s version of this same script, a woman who had moved her family six times in ten years during her executive husband's rise through corporate America once told me, "There's nothing lonelier than packing up." So ingrained is this before and after phenomenon that even in the 1970s social researchers seriously believed that women were psychologically incapable of forming real and lasting friendships—in part because researchers apparently saw so little evidence of long-lasting friendships among women. The researchers failed to consider the possibility that women's friendships were predicated on their marriages and that married women were often powerless to give friendship a primary spot in their lives.

In the popular understanding, this bifurcated script is regarded as normal and necessary. In *When Harry Met Sally* (1990), ever-single Sally and her best friend, Marie, contemplate the probability that marriage will end their friendship. It's only fifteen seconds before they revert to talking about Marie's unhappy affair with a married man. In the premiere of the 1995 sitcom *Almost Perfect*, beautiful, bubbly, ever-single Kim complains when her married friends leave a celebration for her promotion early. "I stayed for your baby showers," she reminds them. "You *owe* me!" In all fairness, they *do* owe her, but she's the one who looks foolish, sitting alone in a bar with a half-full bottle of champagne.

The happy side of the traditional, bifurcated movie is that marriage usually offers a community that is otherwise tough to attain in a highly mobile society. Marriage brings a nearly instant convergence of social contacts; marriage—especially a marriage with children—puts the wife in contact with a whole new community, the community of in-laws and car pools, of Little League games and after-school bake sales. The unhappy side of the movie is that it never recognizes that a woman does have a social identity before she marries. Unlike Cinderella and Rapunzel, girls usually do have empathetic mothers and interested siblings; they do have friendships and social roles that have meaning in their lives. But marriage often serves to discount that previous identity and discontinue those previous social roles.

For the single woman who lives outside this traditional script, watching this plot unfold can be confusing—and painful. "I don't hear from them. Sometimes all of a sudden they can't make simple decisions that they had made on their own," laments Felicia Collinet, who is just entering the age when most of her college and work friends are marrying. "They lose a lot of their individuality. It's very upsetting." For Rosalie Morgan, friends departed physically—and almost en masse. At the conclusion of World War II, as the men returned from war and the GI Bill made home ownership accessible, her friends married and left their jobs in the city. "They moved to the suburbs," she says gently. She never saw most of them again.

The experience is nearly archetypal. Firmly planted in the family homestead in Amherst, Massachusetts, in the 1850s, the ever-single Emily Dickinson watched her friendships dwindle as each childhood friend married and moved with her husband, and she thought about it and wrote about it frequently. "I know I can't be with you always . . . some day a 'brave dragoon' will

94

be stealing you away and I will have farther to go to discover you at all," she wrote to one friend, who would marry and move away two years later. In a letter to her future sister-in-law, Dickinson went further; she drew an image of a dragon who carries women off to his unscalable mountain where they live, unreachable. Alone at the bottom of the mountain, the unmarried Dickinson is in mourning, as if she has witnessed a death.

As intense as Emily Dickinson was, her picture expresses a common experience among contemporary single women. Just at the moment when they're facing the painful possibility that their own expectations may not be met, they see their friendships shrink away. For ever-single women, the role discontinuity that causes this shrinkage is often incomprehensible, and after a number of disappointments they're reluctant to find even a thread of continuity in their once-single friends. "You lose friends to men," says Marguerite Ramanis, the woman who took herself to the senior prom. When I ask her why, she shrugs and answers in her clipped, matter-of-fact way, "It's a time commitment."

Lindsay Cordell has encountered discontinuity too. In her socially active singles church in L.A., there's a spirited if cryptic term for friends who marry and move on. "Our terminology is that they've died," she says, laughing. Curiously, the notion of death also appears in a famous and frantic letter that Elizabeth Cady Stanton, who was married, once wrote to Susan B. Anthony, who was not. Unfettered by a husband and children, Anthony traveled continuously in support of women's rights and had fallen out of touch with Stanton, who had gone home to raise her children. Frustrated, Stanton wrote to Anthony: "Where are you Susan & what are you doing? Your silence is appalling. Are you dead or married?"—a surprising question coming from someone living in the married state.

"I don't think they [married women] realize how important their friendships are," summarizes Susan Ryerson, the forty-two-year-old L.A. fire fighter. "As I've gotten older, I've talked to a lot of women and I've realized that women don't get all their emotional needs met by men, that married women depend on women to get them through the day. And a lot of them don't realize it."

Sadly, premarital friendships that survive marriage sometimes fail to weather motherhood. Back at the turn of the twentieth century, one ever-single wit called the constant mother-talk of feedings and diapers, spit-up and poopie "the narrowing results of specialization." But wit can't cover the confusion that a single woman feels when her once-single friend changes identity yet again, this time from wife to mother. One singular woman recalls reading everything she could in an effort to bridge the gap between her and her best friend, who had just had a baby. She read about the self-absorption that comes with pregnancy; she learned about the new feelings and attitudes her mother-friend was likely to take on; she prepared herself for constant interruptions in phone calls and visits. In the end, though, there was still more to learn: there was the disconcerting truth that she would do most of the bridging, most of the preparing and connecting and compromising, to keep the friendship alive.

Eventually, in many friendships a kind of culture gap begins to yawn between the two women. For a woman who's writing her own script, waiting for another grown woman to confer with her husband before she agrees to see a play can be confounding. Not usually the feisty type, soft-spoken Pat McDonald admits, "I want to say, 'Get a life.'" Meanwhile, to a married woman this kind of impatience can come across as narcissistic and flighty. After all, she is the responsible, connected adult and she may wonder if she really needs another cast-member in her already crowded and demanding movie. Adding to the tension is the appearance of conflicting loyalties; the closeness between women friends is something many marriages are not prepared for. In one recent study, one third of married women maintained confidant relationships outside of their marriages and in most of these marriages this confidant relationship was considered puzzling or threatening by husbands.

Unfortunately, the culture gap between married and unmarried friends has its own circus barker: the media, which gave us poor, whiny Alice, Richard Cohen's imaginary unmarried lawyer who obsesses over wedding presents. In this case, it's Single White Female, a 1993 slasher movie that has a crazy, perpetually lonely wallflower terrorizing a sexually attractive, well-adjusted designer and her fiancé, or Beaches, which tries to portray a successful friendship but inevitably places the two women in direct competition over the same man. In these media portraits, jealousy is a major theme; maladjustment is a subplot. In the movies, in the pages of our magazines, the gap between women is uncrossable: ever-single women are just too weird, and three at the dinner table is just too awkward.

Take the inaugural issue of Married Woman, which claims to be the first magazine "to recognize that you're married." "Old friends, new friends," announces a caption that dances around a photograph of two young couples sharing a friendly dinner of pasta and wine. "After you marry, don't be surprised if you want to put your single friends on the back burner and reserve a table for four." Don't be surprised and don't feel guilty, says *MW.* "Your friendships change because you've changed. It's only natural to feel a strong urge to edit your address book."

As offensive as this line seems, I soon had to agree. The truth is, if my single friends were the nagging, insensitive gnats that *Married Woman* describes, I'd edit my address book too, but I wouldn't wait to marry before getting out the blue pencil. For in *MW*'s view, single people are too self-involved to see the Do Not Disturb sign hanging around the doorknob of an intimate relationship: "Most of us have had to suffer through at least one unwelcome visit early in the morning soon after our honeymoon."

It would be easy to ignore *Married Woman* if its message were rare. But it isn't. Even the *New York Times* has stooped to grapple with the issue of a single woman entertaining a married couple—stooped, grappled, and come up looking shortsighted. For the single woman who wants to entertain a couple, hosting at a restaurant is difficult, the paper explained in 1990, because surely the couple will want to pay. To avoid such awkwardness, the single woman can prepay. But the fact is, some women have just thrown in their social towels and chosen to give gifts (wine, videotapes), noted the paper approvingly.

This is a tragic and typical recommendation. It suggests that single women remain isolated, driven out of a normal social interaction because both parties are firmly planted in the nearly petrified social forests of bygone eras. The woman who gives a couple a bottle of wine instead of an invitation to her place for dinner is just an updated image of the ever-single woman in the movie *Rachel, Rachel* (1968)—a social misfit whose only friends are other social misfits: the town lesbian and the town undertaker. And the couple who pull the cork on the wine alone in their white-walled apartment is just an update of the much-ridiculed 1950s couples in their contiguous backyards, sharing cocktails with only like-looking and like-living folk.

This is just the kind of stuff that might make Peter Stein, the researcher who predicted that these social rigidities would relax as the divorce rate increased, wince. And it's the kind of the stuff that makes lasting friendships—

between a married and an unmarried woman, or between two unmarried women—that much more remarkable.

🖌

The package arrives a little tattered from its journey across the country. Inside is a novel, *Slow Dancing*, and a note from Ellen Adams, the environmentalist, saying "I thought you might find this interesting."

Ellen has sent the novel because one of its main characters is a single woman who's writing a book about single women. For me, reading the novel is a little like watching a production of a play I've already performed in myself; I keep wanting to skip to the scenes in which I appear.

But actually *Slow Dancing* (1985) isn't really about a woman who tries to write a book; it's about the friendship between two ever-single women in their late twenties and how that friendship fares as they approach marriage. Lexi and Nell are such close friends that Nell uprooted herself to follow Lexi to law school, and Lexi uprooted herself to follow Nell to L.A. Lexi's neighbor thinks they're lesbians, and indeed they dally with the idea. It's as if they feel that because they're intimate, they should also be sexual; but since they're not sexually attracted to each other, they sleep with strange men instead. The whole purpose of men is sex, they decide, so Lexi and Nell drink a lot, bounce from man to man, and use the F word a lot. And they talk about men constantly. "All the time," Lexi tells her new boyfriend.

Predictably, the friendship runs into trouble. Lexi gets involved with a man and then Nell does. Nell becomes jealous of Lexi's boyfriend, then decides to move away across the continent to be with her new boyfriend. In the end, the two women dance together and say good-bye, and it's clear that author Elizabeth Benedict wants us to believe that they will always be friends. But I doubt it.

It's not because the two friends will marry; it's because of the kind of friends they are. That's what introspective, articulate Christi Wagner believes. A solid friendship will survive and thrive because of its essential qualities, irrespective of marriage, divorce, or widowhood, she insists. "I know people say, 'Well, I got married and that's why the relationship changed.' But I don't think so," she says. She is sitting at her kitchen table, fingering a fresh-cut flower from a bouquet she bought this morning; her clear blue eyes search the room as if she'll find the answer there. "I think it's something else," she says finally. "I have single friends [and] the relationship is of a certain quality. If they got married, I don't think that the relationship would change." Although Christi has difficulty describing it and naming it, this distinguishing quality seems to have something to do with shared values and mutual commitment between real selves.

At least that's the experience of many singular women. In Maureen Cabot's life, for instance, friendships rest on shared activity. In a clear plastic box in her living room is a series of envelopes, each carefully marked: Paris, Beirut, Rome. From the one marked "Europe, 1955," Maureen pulls out a picture of herself with four other carefully dressed young women wearing red lipstick and high heels and leaning against the railing of a balcony in Switzerland. They're smiling, probably because Bridget Cassidy has just cracked a joke and Maureen has returned fire; clearly they're on top of the world in the middle of a trip that took two years to plan.

From another envelope, Maureen pulls out a picture of three of the same five women on an elephant in Thailand. From another, she pulls out a cliffhanger showing two women scaling the side of an Egyptian temple hundreds of head-spinning feet above the ground. In another is a quiet shot featuring two of the five women, now in their sixties, at a family party in Chicago. With each successive picture, the dresses change, the hair is grayer, the constellation shifts, but the sense of connection remains. At sixty-eight, Maureen is still in touch with three of the original women, two of whom have married; for many years she and her mother played bridge with Mary Moriarty and *her* mother. Maybe the glue of these friendships came from their Irish Catholic backgrounds or their jobs or their schooling; maybe it emanated from their sense of adventure; maybe their quick-shot, iconoclastic humor had a hand. In any case there was glue, and there still is.

In contrast, the friends in *Slow Dancing* share only one thing: the hunt for love. And when this hunt is over, there isn't much left for them to work with. Lexi and Nell never talk politics or art; they never go hiking together or discuss their work. In fact, you could say that their friendship is based on the idea that it will ultimately be replaced—by a marriage. In that way, it's a lot like the friendships Marguerite describes: casual, temporary groups that frequent bars together looking for men. When a member of the group marries, Marguerite's group closes in and fills the gap, like water. "We don't think about good or bad," she says. "It's just noticeable that so-and-so is not hanging around as much."

Another factor that's missing in the *Slow Dancing* friendship is commitment. In many of the best friendships singular women describe, the friends have tacitly agreed that their relationship is worth nurturing even though it isn't a marriage. Kate and Clarissa have done that—and maintained a relationship for forty years; Ellen Adams and her best friend have done that—and maintained a friendship for twenty-five.

Nan Hansen, a thirty-five-year-old marketing manager, describes the long and winding path a friendship of nineteen years has taken. "She and I have gone through a lot of different things—and there's almost a kind of bonding because of that," she says of a high school friend she roomed with after college and who, like Nan, is ever-single. "I feel like we've been close—really, really close sometimes—and then it will kind of ebb away." Nan used to worry that the changes she was making in her own life (going into therapy, switching jobs, going to school) would unseat the friendship, but no longer. The commitment remains. "I realize that we just go through phases," she says simply.

In contrast, the women in *Slow Dancing* are not quite sure how their friendship fits into their new lives. Lexi and Nell sense that things have changed and will change further, but neither is likely to address the changes—Lexi's pregnancy, Nell's new romance—head-on. In the end, as Nell quits writing her book on single women and moves across the country once more, it seems certain that she will slide into discontinuity and disappear into her new romance.

Of course, the uncertainty that Lexi and Nell feel as they approach these important changes is understandable. Maintaining a friendship between two women and committing to it is tricky business. There are no guidelines. We all know what you can reasonably expect from a marriage partner—but what can you expect from a friend? Can you expect to spend holidays together? Can you expect help when you're sick? Congratulations when you've succeeded? A birthday card on time? Is it appropriate to get angry when an expectation isn't fulfilled? *How* angry?

Soon enough, friendship starts to look pretty complicated. Family is so much simpler! Among relatives, certain obligations are presumed, but among friends, obligations, loyalties, and expectations are tacitly negotiated, one at a time. In fact, anthropologists suggest that the difference between the way we behave with family and the way we behave with friends can actually be mapped. Imagine a target you'd use in archery: at the bull's eye is the nuclear family and the axis of moral obligation; at each successive increasingly distant ring, the blood obligation decreases and the negotiation increases. At the bull's eye, a woman is expected to take care of her sick husband and she is obliged to care for her aging parents, who share close blood ties with her. But she is not obliged to take care of her great-aunt, who occupies a distant, outer ring where the blood tie is thin. She may indeed do so—but she does so out of personal feeling and loyalty, not out of an obligation based on blood ties. The care she offers is negotiated, not required.

Completely free of blood ties, friends live far away from the bull's eye on a distant ring. In this ring women do what they do because they want to. There are no obligations. That's the joy and wonder of friendship. That's also the problem with it. With each challenge—a change of location, a new child, a terrible sickness, an intimidating success—aspects of the friendship must be renegotiated, sometimes tacitly, sometimes openly. These negotiations are often touchy and difficult work; they get into values and perceptions, and in a world where women experience profound discontinuity as a matter of course, we often fail at it.

One of Roxanne Walters's great losses has been her best friendship. She grew up with Tonya, watched the Windsor wedding and wandered the bridal shops with her, and when she needed to find work, she took Tonya up on her invitation to stay with her in New York. But when Tonya got involved with a white man and Roxanne felt that he exhibited racial insensitivity, the friendship suffered and finally dissolved. To this day Roxanne misses the friendship. "I don't have a deep friendship with anybody," she says. "I have a girlfriend that I grew up with in high school and she's probably what you would call a best friend, but I don't have the same affection when I call her a best friend that I did with Tonya." Still, she is not looking for a replacement: a best friend is developed over time, she says; close friendship is a mixture of shared experiences and values. "I don't think it's just the immediacy of how you get along," she says. As a filmmaker Roxanne has plenty of acquaintances, people she works with under hothouse conditions that last twelve and fourteen hours a day, sometimes for months at a time; as a budding producer she gets along with most of them, prodding them, scheduling them, joking with them, eating three meals a day with them. But those aren't friendships. A half-grimace spreads across her face. She knows she counts on her parents for things that other single women turn to close friends for: "I just dread the day . . ."

The solution for some singular women has been to assume that friendships will not survive major life changes. Instead, they expect to have a series of social circles in their lives, much as married women do. When Rachel Jacobs left her boyfriend of four years in Texas to take a job in New Mexico, she arrived in Albuquerque sight unseen, knowing only the personnel manager and her new boss at the laboratory she'd joined. Undaunted, Rachel joined political and volunteer organizations, made friends, introduced them to one another, and created an extensive social community made up mostly of married couples. "In a way I just felt like it was a real creative experience just to bring these people together from all these different backgrounds, and they picked up on it," she recalls. "They enjoyed being together; it wasn't any favor they were doing for me."

They were close and comfortable friends, she says. "I could just drop over anybody's house anytime, call anytime. It was like having an extended family." But when Rachel was offered a job in the Midwest, she left. The extended family was about to change, and the ties were about to be tested: "This is another reason I left Albuquerque—because all of the women friends in that group started having children, and I just didn't want to be around." Duplicating that tight-knit community has been difficult in Libertyville, the wealthy, family-oriented Chicago suburb she lives in now. But she has developed a network in the past and she expects that she will someday develop yet another one—when she moves again or as she ages.

❧

For all that negotiation—or maybe because of it—friendship plays a unique role in the lives of singular women. But defining that role has proved a slippery task for researchers.

Barbara Levy Simon's experience is typical. In her study, she found that intimate friendships were key to the happiness of most ever-single women and that these friendships were often formed during that difficult decade when the women first passed the common age of marriage. However, Simon was unable to delineate the nature and scope of these friendships. She was summarily kicked out of one house when she asked if a same-sex friendship was sexual—and resolved never to push that social button again. Apparently, few researchers reach this crisis: they seem to assume automatically that their "never-married" subjects are heterosexual.

This oversight makes evaluating studies on the friendships of ever-single women difficult. If we don't know the nature of the friendships women are describing, we're not really sure which part of the target we're learning about— the bull's eye, where a nearly marital, highly committed lesbian relationship belongs, or the outer ring, where friendships between heterosexual women who may someday marry reside. Clearly, in the bull's eye issues of commitment, living arrangements, loyalty, obligation, and the handling of family members are very different than they are on the outer ring.

Still, working within this blind spot, most studies agree with Simon's conclusions. In Robert Rubinstein's study of thirty-one childless ever-single women over the age of sixty, the overwhelming majority counted their relationships with friends as among the most significant in their lives. Some of the women even argued that the voluntary quality of their friendships made them stronger and healthier than family relationships. Susan Ryerson, whose own family splintered after her mother's death, agrees. "I'm not family centered," she says. "I'm more centered on how people treat you. Just because you're my brother or sister, it doesn't mean that I love you more than someone who treats me better than you do."

This focus on friendship may be an edge that ever-single women have over ever-single men. In comparing the factors that influence life satisfaction in ever-single men with those that influence ever-single women, a 1985 study found that women benefited more from emotional attachments. Women tended to value and seek intimacy and they benefited from social integration—a network of people who shared activities and values. In contrast, attachment was less of a factor in men's lives. Their life satisfaction was much more influenced by self-esteem, by their feelings about themselves. While women used their emotional attachments and their work as buffers against the assault of social stigma, men found these buffers less effective. That's why, concluded the researchers, ever-single men seem to suffer much more from the stigma of "failing" to marry than ever-single women do—even though the stereotypes of ever-single men appear less denigrating than those of ever-single women.

So friendship is a gray area, a steady beacon for some women, a foggy, frustrating area for others. It works best when expectations match, mutual interests are shared, mutual needs are met, the timing is right, and a commitment is made. It falters when roles shift, when other obligations and claims intrude, when values change, when the negotiations break down.

As women gain greater social parity, as more women enter the work force and more return to the work force after having children, as more women divorce, as more women build social networks that reflect their multifaceted lives, this gray area may be validated more openly. But in the meantime it remains a place of contact, of support and love for those who are willing to work a bit, risk loss, and try again.

CHAPTER SIX

Making a Home

❧

". . . Or I could build out that way, out through the porch," she says,
crossing the well-kept living room, which a reasonably sized person can
cross in under five paces. "Or, and this is what my sister-in-law suggested, I could build up."

In her hand is a sketch her sister-in-law made; underfoot is Hershey,
the chocolate Labrador retriever who seems to take up more than a quarter of the living room. She turns. "Or I could just leave it the way it is."

Charmed by the view of Puget Sound, where seagulls swarm like
moths and the water changes color daily, Ellen Adams bought the place a
couple of years ago. Below her, sprawled across a lower part of the hill, a
neighbor's garage has spit out the carcass of a car, a truck, and some kind
of motor that once belonged to a refrigerator or maybe a boat. Below this
level is open space, and below that, a road that hangs above the waterline
like a bird of prey.

"The problem is, that guy"—she points to the open space—"has
asked for a variance. Six-story hotel."

The implication is clear. He'll break the low-rise character of this
sleepy harbor town. He'll stress the already stressed hillside. He'll bring
heavy traffic into a residential area, strain the sparse infrastructure, draw
more tourists with empty pop cans and recreational vehicles that need to
be parked. He'll block Ellen's view.

Piled around me on the glass kitchen table are appeals and ordinances, geological reports and letters to council members, hundreds of

*pages filled with tiny type. Ellen has been helping a landowner fight devel-
opment on a tiny spur that reaches out into the sound a few miles south
and she heads a volunteer watchdog group dedicated to protecting the
shoreline.*

*"They think I'm a pain in the ass now," she muses as she looks out
her window toward the water. "Just wait until they try it in my front
yard."*

Historically this wasn't a problem. Ever-single women didn't struggle with
architects, furniture, mortgages, ordinances, or even roommates. We didn't
face the challenge of finding a home that reflected our values, the difficulties
of decorating more than one room at a time, or the fear of scaring off potential husbands by owning real estate. We stayed in our fathers' homes until we
got married—or until we died. Before the vote, before property rights, before
education, we pretty much had to. There was generally nowhere to go and no
financial way to remain there.

Today in America most women leave their parents' households before
marriage, and many live alone. In this they are part of a vast and remarkable
trend in modern life. Between 1980 and 1990 the U.S. population grew by 10
percent, but the number of households grew 14 percent. A full one quarter of
American households consist of just one person, up from 13 percent in 1960.
Single women are currently the fastest growing group of first-home buyers in
the U.S.; nearly one third of ever-single women living alone own their own
homes. Many more than half of ever-single women over the age of thirty live
alone—clearly the largest percentage in the history of women.

So this is a strange and peculiarly modern thing for a woman to choose a
home, to make one, outside marriage. Culturally, home has always suggested
marriage: families with children and toys on the floor; couples with pets; new-
lyweds waving their first mortgage proudly; widows with their husbands' pictures on the mantel. And more: grocery lists that take everyone into account;
rules about the dishes, the phone, and the leftovers; sounds in the floorboards
and quirks in the faucet that the household has tacitly agreed to ignore. Only
when a woman marries does she become a home*maker*, star of the domestic

movie—and then the role sticks like Superglue. Even when she works outside the home, she is primarily responsible for home operations—the children's schedule, the dirty dishes, the faucet that leaks. She is by many reports exhausted by this; she is Super Woman or the Woman-with-No-Time-for-Herself, a kind of homemaking saint with rings under her eyes.

In contrast, choosing or making a home outside of marriage has no script. Worse, it has the reputation of a social black hole, the bottomless pothole of the permanently single: conventional wisdom has it that once an unmarried woman enters the housing market, she automatically leaves the marriage market. At one time, there was some truth to this. Back in the nineteenth century, it was generally understood that when Catharine Beecher set up her own household, she was declaring herself a permanent spinster, off limits to marriage offers. But more than a hundred years later, a friend of mine sounded the same alarm when I began house-shopping: "I would never marry a woman who owned a house," he told me. When I reversed the comment—I would never marry a *man* who owned a house—I recoiled. Here, suddenly, was the disturbing image of the unformed woman waiting for marriage to confer an identity, a home, even a tax break. Embedded in the image was a subtle double standard in which men who demonstrate their financial wherewithal and stability are considered good mates and women who do the same are considered irreparably independent. In a society in which nearly 90 percent of children who live with a single parent live in households headed by women, this notion must certainly be outdated, I thought. Yet a whisper of it still persists, women tell me, and so they stumble.

"I always expected to be married," forty-seven-year-old Linda Schindler says simply. She had lived with a man, left the relationship, and waited, renting an apartment, never buying furniture that she wanted, never quite acquiring the things a woman of her income would typically have. Then suddenly she bought a condo. "I bought a place and then I thought, 'What do I do with it?'"

Although the ever-single woman stumbles, staying in the house she was born in, watching roommates come and go ("I batted a thousand," says Marguerite wryly; "I had four different roommates and all of them married"), or renting a studio somewhere in a city—at some point it becomes uncomfortable to live in a state of suspension. Something must be done. Some rite of passage must be taken or at least acknowledged; she has to declare this "home" or create another one. Mary Stendahl, the New England school-teacher, remembers it well. "It was a very anxious time when I bought [the house] because I wasn't sure if I was doing the right thing," she says. "You know, there was this whole thing that I'm alone and what am I going to do? But looking back on it, I made the right decision."

Deciding to make a home is difficult and rewarding both. In the life of a woman, making a home outside marriage can be a disastrous tumble into emptiness or a rare opportunity to know and express herself. It is one of those rare individual acts that draws on a woman's values, her true concerns, her personal resources—and confirms them.

It's no wonder that women aren't prepared for this task. Everything in our history, everything in our upbringing, conspires against a woman choosing her own home.

Single women have long struggled with this issue. Back in the seventeenth century, a British woman named Mary Astell blazed the way. Astell believed marriage was a bad deal: if a woman were fool enough to marry, to sign away control of her life and her wealth, then so be it—Astell did not believe in divorce. But for the single woman who chose celibacy, Astell offered a women's community, a kind of secular convent where women could live and study together. As conservative as her proposal sounds today, it was positively flaky in its time, and critics warned of creeping popery. Five generations later, the more radical British feminist Mary Wollstonecraft took off in another direction: she grappled with the fact of her own social homelessness, lived with a man outside of marriage, and finally married.

Bolder yet, young Fanny Wright established a commune in 1826 along with her then ever-single sister and some colleagues on uncleared land in Tennessee. As a collective, the Nashoba community was dedicated to preparing slaves for life as free citizens. But it was poorly financed and it fell victim to charges of free love and unfair labor practices. It crumbled within a couple of years, and Wright went on to live a notorious and rootless life until she made a reluctant and loveless marriage at the late age of thirty-six.

The big wave finally happened forty years later, in the late 1800s, as single women left their fathers' homes and joined institutions—colleges and hospitals and settlement houses—that could assure both physical safety and social respectability. They were met with social dismay—and suspicions that they were examples of that dangerous phenomenon, the "New Woman." But this was no dribble of political radicals seeping slowly into the cities, wearing odd clothing, and demanding the vote; this was a major shift in the way women lived. In Italy, businesses recruited single women and set up dorms with special supervisors. In England and the U.S., women looking for jobs flooded the cities, and boardinghouses and clubs designated for single women proliferated. By the turn of the twentieth century, the demand for housing for single women was so great in New York City that one home for ladies turned away two out of three applicants.

For many, the act of moving out and making a separate place in the world proved traumatic; for others, it was socially and financially impossible. The era just didn't know what to do with headstrong or educated women and it continually reinforced the familiar edict that women should find identity in their relationships, whether or not those relationships nurtured their personal growth.

The experience of Wellesley College's early graduates is telling. Among those who graduated in 1897 and participated in a yearbook ten and thirteen years later, more than half returned to a single life at home, and in a series of letters remarkable for their lack of self-esteem and joy, many described cooking meals, accomplishing "nothing," and nursing ailing parents. A rare few, less than 6 percent, created their own homes, and these wrote some of the most intriguing and spirited letters. One graduate wrote about a singular classmate who lived in a "charming farmhouse [with] all the cares of home except the husband." Another singular graduate wrote playfully of herself, "Most things have come to me since college except invalidism and marriage." She went on to describe an extraordinary life of mountain climbing and teaching, constant dinner guests, mismatched china, and a house filled with books and pictures. "I am a suffragist," she wrote with a characteristic mix of pride and humility, "[and] I still lose my umbrella." She married fifteen years later.

But for the most part Wellesley's unmarried graduates toed the social line. They knew that single women who left home were often haunted by rumors of sexual license and constrained by low-wage jobs. It's not surprising that most stayed home. And it's not surprising that those same restraining influences persisted in small towns and ethnic urban neighborhoods across the U.S. until well into the 1960s.

"It was almost unthinkable for a person to come back to her own home town to teach and not live with her family," explains Kate O'Connor, whose home town lies eight miles from Lake Michigan. At sixty-two, she is retired and living in that same small town. Returning from college in 1952, she moved back into the house she had grown up in, back into the very room she'd slept in as a girl. Her father fixed farm machinery; her mother was a full-time homemaker; Kate landed a job in the local school system, where she taught for thirty-five years.

The house, a two-story building on the edge of town, was her mother's home, plain and simple, and Kate was an adult daughter who followed her mother's rules, schedules, mealtimes. On holidays Kate's sisters and their kids came out to the house, and her mother presided. The only space that was truly Kate's was her bedroom; the only time that was truly hers was her work time.

"Maybe that's why I decorated the classroom so much," she observes now. "I went a little crazy on that." She stayed late and worked hard. Her classroom brimmed with the kind of energy only adolescents can generate. She loved their humor; she favored the rebels. She made a place for them that encouraged their creativity. In particular, she encouraged the writers.

Just before her father died, he warned his daughters that Mrs. O'Connor must not be left to live alone. "That was an awful thing to say to somebody," Kate says now. "It was unfair." Janet had a growing family, Mary Ellen had entered the convent, Eileen had married and moved to Iowa. The responsibility fell to Kate.

And so the arrangement continued until Mrs. O'Connor was unable to handle stairs. One day, without any preparation at all, Kate went out and bought a ranch-style house. "It had a furnished basement," she says, smiling and pointing through a doorway, "and I knew that she couldn't go in there. I could live down there in the basement at least, and that would be fine." She was anticipating a territorial struggle over the house and she got one. Her mother staked out the kitchen, presided over the holidays, and attempted, as best she could, to control everything around her. Kate was fifty-two.

Today Kate lives in the house alone. It's a pretty little place, fully carpeted, with color-coordinated drapes, overstuffed chairs, and a cat named Colleen. Her mother died several years ago after a series of strokes. When the ambulance came to get her the last time, she was awake and lucid. "You have a nice place here," said the ambulance driver. "It's not my place," replied Mrs. O'Connor. "It's my daughter's."

Kate tells this story, stroking the cat. Maybe she realizes that in some way she'd made a home in her school long before she'd made a home in her house. Maybe not. But you can tell from the look in her soft brown eyes that she treasures the moment when her mother understood that ultimately Kate had made a home for both of them. You can tell that she wanted both that home and that recognition.

Why is it that establishing a home outside marriage is such a delicate emotional operation? It's not just a matter of shedding the sentimental residue from years of viewing *Leave It to Beaver* or *The Brady Bunch*; that complaint—daily registered by the angry twenty-somethings that I teach—doesn't wash. It was difficult for a woman to make an emotionally satisfying place for herself long before young people decided that Mrs. Cleaver was a real person who had special insight into emerging social structures.

No, I think it's difficult because in the traditional movie women generally make homes for *other* people; making a home for others makes her useful. Establishing her *own* home is difficult because even when she has the financial means, sexual license, and parental permission, she faces a task that forces her emotional hand. She must focus on herself in a way that Jean Baker Miller and Dana Crowley Jack tell us she was not raised (or, in Sigmund Freud's opinion, *designed*) to do. She must declare herself a whole and separate adult without the guidepost of marriage; she must declare herself capable of choosing a neighborhood, deserving of a set of dishes, and worthy of a stereo that doesn't make the philharmonic sound like a junior high school band. Making a home is making a bold statement of identity, a singular identity. In fact, it may well be the boldest.

Of course, there *is* help out there. It is much subtler than the stuff of Wendell Wilkes and *Vogue*, but it belongs to the same conduct tradition, the tradition that tells women to wait, to work on their self-presentation, to see themselves as half-adults, unable to choose what's really good for them.

Probably the most famous book in this genre was published just about the time that Kate O'Connor accepted responsibility for her mother's well-being. In 1962 the indomitable Helen Gurley Brown published *Sex and the Single Girl,* devoting an entire chapter to the art and artifice of the single "girl's" apartment. In Brown's world the first thing a single girl does is ship her parents off; a life shackled to family just isn't worth living. As for the single "girl's" apartment, it is an interior-decorated mantrap, well stocked with the right kinds of alcohol, a decent stereo system, well-chosen chintz, and a wall full of pictures ("men are usually much taken by them"). This was radical stuff in the early sixties; it was the stuff of individual gratification and women who said "yes." But it was not a step forward; it was interior decorating as a form of public defense. "A chic apartment can tell the world that you, for one, are not one of those miserable, pitiful single people," explained Brown, who didn't much care whether a woman's real tastes ran toward the un-chic. Brown's was a recipe designed to facilitate a man's sexual arousal, not confirm a single woman's sense of identity, home, or comfort. It was the housing corollary to high heels. It was an exercise in the false self.

The descendants of *Sex* are not much more help. Published twenty-four years later, Janice Harayda's book *The Joy of Being Single* is typical; it seems to address the issue of the real purpose of a home and then backs off. "I often believe, in a single woman's apartment, that the whole thing should be stamped: Perishable," she writes. "Live with your place," she tells us, but within a few pages she begins to pick apart the places we live in. She inveighs against anemic spider plants and wobbly rattan furniture, and wags her finger at posters that might be perceived as negative by potential mates (for example, the one that says, "In order to meet your prince, you have to kiss a lot of toads"). Single people just aren't experienced enough, we just don't have the taste, to fix up a place correctly the first time, she explains (equating, rather miraculously, our interior-decorating IQs with our dating histories). The solution? Buy the most expensive oriental rug you can afford and recognize that "beautifully finished hardwood floors are every tenant's dream."

This is a recipe not for developing a home but for decorating a showplace (while simultaneously shelving any self-esteem you may have inadvertently accumulated while sitting in your rattan chair). It's an exercise in self-doubt.

Another more recent entry into the genre, *The Art of Single Living*, counsels against Harayda's showplace recipe. But even here the reasoning soon falls apart. Beware of chintz and state-of-the-art video equipment, says the author, because "If you make your nest too comfortable, you may be tempted not to leave it" (a worry I've never seen applied to couples; for instance— "Don't make your kitchen too comfortable or your husband may be tempted not to catch the 7:22 downtown . . ." Why doesn't anyone worry that her readers *might not want to go home* to a place decorated for someone else?). Make a home, say the books, but don't make a good one, a home that you might like to stay in. Make a home, say the books, but make one that expresses the temporariness of your situation, the incompleteness of your life. Make a home, but don't live in it.

And that is a recipe for emptiness.

⁊ᴇ

The concept of looking something like this up in a book positively confounds Ellen Adams. When I ask her how she knew how to make her own home, she is confused. "It's never been an issue," she says. "It's there; it's where I am."

"You mean anywhere you go, anywhere you live—"

She nods. She's in jeans, a T-shirt, and a pair of decomposing running shoes, and I suspect she has never owned a Crock-Pot. "Even a campsite."

She grew up in a suburban house with an oversized playhouse out back. Her widowed mother raised six children there, waking up in the early hours to switch the clothes from the washer to the dryer or type someone's history paper. There were milk dishes and meat dishes; there was a garage full of bicycles. Since then, Ellen has lived in a geodesic dome in California, a cabin with a separate shower house in Paraguay, and an apartment on the coast of Oregon. This house on Puget Sound, the first she's owned, is filled with underwater photographs and stained glass; ecology magazines clutter the end table, and the smell of fresh-ground coffee hangs in the air. The place is lived in and welcoming, but also idiosyncratic and private.

She's really trying to help me with this concept. "The dog helps," she says, indicating Hershey. But the dog isn't it, she admits. She had a home before she had a dog. She shakes her head. "Your home is where you are," she says simply.

This is so simple it takes a couple of days to sink in. Home is where you are—where you are emotionally. If you're living in suspended animation, waiting for a life script to appear, your home is a kind of biostatic hotel room, barely comfortable enough to feel at home in. If you're preparing yourself for a cinematic romance that will take you away from all this, your home is a staging area, a *Cosmopolitan*-style set piece that might become useful during the transaction. If you're living a full and active life, a life that feeds you and keeps you growing, your home is a comfortable place that mirrors and supports that life. Home is a reflection of who you are—your emotional state, your values, your expectations, your circumstances—at any given time. It reflects your state of mind and, in some ineffable way that psychologists should study, it seems to perpetuate it.

It seems to act as an emotional mirror. And for many women, especially when they're in their twenties and thirties and the floor seems to be falling out from under them, the image in that mirror is not pleasant. In the naturalist Sally Carrighar's autobiography, the low-rent furnished rooms where she wrote articles and struggled with suicidal thoughts are oppressive just to read about. For the writer-philosopher Alice Koller, the string of featureless shared apartments became a blur. "I don't live anywhere," she wrote in 1963, at the age of thirty-seven. "I perch." One woman I met, who feels herself dangling indefinitely between the life she has and the life she wants, describes her studio apartment as dark and small. For a long time, I walked into a half-furnished apartment that reflected the break-up of a live-in relationship: I'd gotten the kitchen table but not the bureau; I'd gotten the spatula but not the ladle. I just couldn't fill the place up. I bought a couch, a bed frame, a VCR. Someone gave me a rug. But even with its Salvation Army chairs and apple-crate bookshelves, the place had the cool edge that hotel rooms have, and there were times when I thought I'd be better off in a hotel room. At least the towels would match.

Four or five years ago, Susan Ryerson, the L.A. fire fighter, faced a similar passage in her life. But she handled it differently. A woman who sets goals and achieves them, Susan has a quiet, forthright, nearly methodical way of reviewing and pursuing her life choices.

Having left home at eighteen, she'd lived with a series of roommates with varying rates of success; as a social worker, she'd spent her nights supervising a group home for adolescents. Sometime in her mid-twenties, she'd lived with a man but decided that he was using her. "George was using my apartment; he wasn't paying the rent," she recalls. "But you know, I was so picky; it was like, 'You used the last of the toilet paper, go buy some more.'" Eventually she hit a real snag: she discovered he'd lost his job and hadn't told her. So she kicked him out. After all, her widowed mother had raised her family alone. "You know, I wasn't used to seeing a woman kowtow to men. So for him to expect me to—" she sputters a bit. "So I told him that he had to leave. He had two months."

Then Susan fell in love with a man that she would stay with for nine years. They kept separate apartments in the city but saw each other almost every night. "That's why I think our relationship lasted so long," she observes now. "We always had our little homes to run to. And even if it's just for a change of clothes or to pack a bag or whatever, it's space that's yours, and you're there for an hour and you know this is my space. And you have this sense of identity by being surrounded by things that are just yours."

But the relationship began to wane. Susan veered between pressuring Jim to marry her and working intensely on her next career step—passing the exam to become a fire marshal. "I did that for a solid year—went to classes, did my studying, took notes to the store, and stood in line reading notes," she recalls. She also began to look for a house, using the same unwavering methods that got her through the exam. By the time she moved into her two-bedroom house, the relationship was over. Jim married someone else nine months later.

The house brought her comfort. "I think it was responsible for my sanity when I broke up with Jim—in times of low self-esteem, it was something I had. And I knew it at the time . . . I remember looking out the window and thinking, 'God, am I glad I have this house.' The thing is, you *do* think what your friends think, especially in my case, that he dumped me." Now she is not sure about that interpretation. Maybe buying the house was a silent declaration of independence, a way of packing her emotional bags and announcing that it was time to move on.

In any case she settled in, gathering cherished things from her past, buying furniture, attracting a herd of stray cats that congregates each morning on her back step. Even at the time she understood it was a turning point and she thought about it carefully: "My turning point was my break-up with Jim. And one of the things I did to cope with that was I looked at my life before him.

And except for that few months with George, I had been alone, and I was having a ball. I loved my life. So the thread in that was I was alone, I liked it, so it can happen again."

And it has happened—largely because of her home, she says. She walks in and what she sees confirms her: "It is who I am. I have surrounded myself with things that bring me joy, bring me comfort, that remind me of stages in my life." Dozens of books line the living-room wall and spill over onto chairs and tables; pictures of friends dot the refrigerator door. On the side of the refrigerator, a cartoon shows a haggard woman saying, "All those women who are moaning about finding a husband have obviously never had one." This is just the kind of place Janice Harayda would hate. But it is a reflection of Susan: her past, her values, her state of mind. That may be why she once brought a man she was dating over and showed him the second bedroom, which is stacked with books and papers, photos and clothes, and furniture waiting for a final assignment. "I've been working on this room for two years," she warned him with a laugh, "and *this* is what it looks like." He took the news well, she says. And I can see why. As I sit in her neat yellow kitchen, drinking Earl Grey tea and listening to music, I can feel the vibrancy of the place. There's a life being lived here, lived comfortably, lived fully.

❦

Like Kate O'Connor and Susan Ryerson, most of the women I met have struggled—or at least paused—before achieving a sense of home. "I always thought that I'd be married," goes the refrain, followed by a few acute observations: "I'm considering buying china. . . ." "I thought, if I do this, am I just giving up?" Warned by self-help books and well-meaning friends, buffeted by images of old ladies talking to invisible audiences as they make chamomile tea, they hesitated. It was not always conscious: it was buried in that sense of waiting instead of being, that sense of waiting for the movie to start rather than starting their own. But at some point, usually sometime after those first glimmers of self-acceptance that marked their singularity, they accepted their homes as *real* homes; and singular women count this acceptance as one of the most positive experiences of their lives.

Years after her crisis at the bottom of the Grand Canyon and a few months after buying her house in a woodsy suburb of New York, Christi Wagner spent a New Year's Eve eating her mother's homemade sausage, drinking wine, and reading *The Sun Also Rises*. "And I thought, 'Yeah, this is what is so important, this is what is really important to my life,'" she recalls now. "'This is *it!*'" It wasn't the ownership so much as the atmosphere, she says; it wasn't the house (which she later sold so she could travel), as much as it was the liberating feeling of being herself in her own space.

"I love it," Mary says of the little house she bought after months of anxiety. She is sitting in the screened-in back porch, overlooking a huge yard where a neighbor is playing with her dog. "It's my haven in the storm, I guess."

"That was as good as getting married to me, getting that house," says Linda Schindler. "That really helped me a lot, to know that I would have a place to live." She pauses. The extra financial security was important, she says, but there was more to it. "I know that the peacefulness came over me when I moved into that house."

"I admit to putting my arms around trees and hugging them and saying 'mine,'" jokes Lisa Nolan, who at forty-nine now owns her third home. In a more serious vein, Lisa says that her house is truly important in her life: "Just making my surroundings comfortable and me comfortable in my surroundings. When I think of what I do when I don't have any goals for the day, it's making the house [better], making it so I can see the washer." She would like to build her own house high in the Rocky Mountains. "I know exactly what I want and where I want it," she says.

Still, it's not a cure-all. Even after they allow themselves this critical piece of identity, even after they make a move, settle into a house or a niche in someone else's house that they can make their own, there are difficulties— both emotional and physical.

Of the thirty women I talked with, three lived with their families of origin, three lived with their children, one shared her house with a friend and her grandson, and twenty-three lived alone. When I asked these twenty-three what the hardest part of living alone was, one mentioned upkeep on her suburban house, a couple mentioned the fear of life-threatening illnesses; about half said "the loneliness." But when I asked about the loneliness, only one said it was severe or even frequent; few were even really sure it was loneliness. Are women who live alone lonely or aren't they? I think the confusion lies in the definition.

According to psychologist Robert Weiss, there are two kinds of loneliness. One, emotional loneliness, is a painful awareness of the absence of intimacy, a neediness that can be answered only by close emotional contact. The other, social loneliness, is characterized by restlessness and anxiety; it's that antsy feeling of being disconnected and bored that sends us to coffeehouses in the evenings or to a party where we don't really know people. The stimulation, the conversation, and the experience of just of being around people often take the edge off social loneliness. But if you're emotionally lonely and you go to a coffeehouse or a birthday party (or a wedding), you'll feel worse: the emptiness inside is exacerbated by the emotionally distant contacts. You start counting couples and feeling overtly extraneous; you feel an overpowering sense of loss, an emotional hole that grows bigger by the minute.

When you ask ever-single and divorced women what their fears are when they think about not marrying, they often say "loneliness," meaning emotional loneliness. When you ask ever-single women about the downside to living alone, they sometimes say "loneliness" and they apparently mean social loneliness—and then they discount it, much as women answering a 1993 survey apparently did when they said, overwhelmingly, that people who live alone are *not* lonely. Apparently single women experience social loneliness and call it something else: restlessness, boredom, isolation.

In their description, it's an amorphous and uncomfortable feeling. Christi recalls moments—on a vacation in Greece, during scattered evenings in her condo in New York—when she has felt nervous and directionless. "Maybe it *is* loneliness, and I'm not saying it is," she muses, and then rejects that idea. "Not lonely," she says more firmly, "but sometimes bad, sometimes anxious, worried. No, I cannot really say that I'm lonely."

Ellen is cautious in her description too. A vague feeling creeps up on her when she feels overwhelmed by all the work there is to do in the world; the feeling lies somewhere between sadness and anxiety. "I'm lonely during those times when things just get to me," she explains. "Just those times when I want someone to share the world's burdens with me." Then she smiles. "Oh yeah, and those times when I really want someone to rub my back."

"I just get restless in the wintertime," says Rachel Jacobs, the biochemist who left a tight circle of friends to move to the Midwest four years ago. But is it loneliness? If so, it's a garden variety: "I think everyone pretty much goes through this."

When she feels this way, Susan calls a friend. "I have a couple of people I can say to, 'I feel lonely. I just want to talk.'" Rachel is considering joining one of the computer on-line services. Other ever-single women go to church, to films, to cafés; a lot of them read.

It's not that they don't experience that harsh, piercing, hole-in-the-heart feeling of emotional loneliness, but they associate that feeling with *being* alone—being without a relationship—not *living* alone; and they point out that you can have that hole-in-the-heart feeling in a marriage too. "Sometimes I don't think that single women know that, that you can be lonely in a relationship," observes Linda Schindler, who works as a psychotherapist. "That I think is an awful kind of loneliness," observes Kate O'Connor. "To know that you've chosen something that doesn't fill that loneliness at all. I would think that would be almost worse."

Like social loneliness, the exasperations of living alone—roofs that leak and furniture that requires two people to move—can be handled, most women say. Marguerite Ramanis used to have roommates and she wields a mean wrench. Ellen hires help. Mary keeps a running list for her brother's annual visit. "I have a list of, you know, could-you-look-at-this, could-you-look-at-that," she says. "It'll probably take two minutes, but either I don't know what to do or I'm not strong enough to do it."

More critical is the issue of illness. Linda recalls a mind-numbing, body-stopping flu that had her flat on her back for days. "I crawled to the phone and I talked to this friend of mine, and I really had to almost beg her to come over and bring me some soup. She said, 'Okay, but I'm really on a tight schedule.' She brought me the soup, and I felt better—I had to." Linda felt vulnerable: "That stuff scares me." I know what she means. There was a moment a few years ago when I realized that I had only one phone call left in me; in a half-haze, I called my friend Betsy, who didn't have her car at work but found another friend who did. Between them, they picked me up (literally), took me to a clinic, filled the prescriptions that would get my kidneys working again, and arranged a schedule of friends to come in and take care of me. That evening, Betsy held me up in the shower and dried me as if I were a child. It was probably the scariest moment I've had living alone, but even now I don't know what I could do to make the next emergency any easier. The truth is I *am* vulnerable; it's an issue that accompanies ever-single women throughout life and becomes increasingly important as retirement approaches.

It's easy to get morbid about it. I do. Susan does. "The worst part of living alone?" she asks. "It's being found dead on the floor three days later." She pauses, then adds wryly: "But it's not the death—why would I care? I'm dead. It's the statement that it makes."

It's hard to escape the sense that someone is watching the unmarried woman, categorizing her, and commenting.

Mostly the comments suggest that ever-single women are just a little stir-crazy living alone with their cats. There may be some truth in this: their homes, when they really are their homes and not someone else's image of a home, often have the stamp of individuality. In the absence of a regular audience, there is a natural tendency to let idiosyncracies run unchecked. For years Ellen Adams stored her plastic bags in her dishwasher; Pat McDonald has a lawn chair in her bedroom; there are pigeon cages (sans pigeons) in Susan Ryerson's living room. Christi Wagner sometimes eats standing up, indulging in each dish as it comes off the stove: zucchini first, potato second, chicken last.

Pat, who spent her first months as a young adult in a convent, thinks there's something delightful in this; it's the chance to be oneself unedited, a chance that is rare in the lives of women. With each year, some new aspect of character, some unseen value, finds its way into her home and takes its place there in a way that would not be possible if she were a married woman managing the environment for other people. "I like that lawn chair in my bedroom," she says; then she smiles a smile that asks, gotta problem with that?

For many years, researchers did have a problem with it; they believed that living alone was a primary source of the health problems that ever-single women seem to suffer more frequently than the rest of the female population.

While these health problems have been discounted by some researchers, they're still often quoted in the media. According to these reports, ever-single women have slightly higher rates of suicide than married women, they are less physically healthy than married women, and they have higher morbidity than married women. (But they do better than men on all these indicators.) David R. Williams, a researcher at Yale, has questioned some of these conclusions, and he and his team point out that the definitions of mental health vary widely from study to study. Nonetheless, for many years psychologists have suggested that marriage protects the health of both men and women in some way—maybe by providing a living partner who shares social experiences, commitments, and obligations. If that's the case, maybe it's the living arrangement, not the marriage itself, that protects people; maybe living alone is just not good for you.

The studies on living alone are inconclusive, but they seem to suggest that health problems aren't caused strictly by the living arrangements. One study conducted in 1981 found no consistent differences on a long list of psychological measures between those who live alone and those who don't. Eight years later, another study compared women who lived with another adult with women who lived alone. Those who lived with another adult did report fewer acute conditions and restrictions due to their health, but no real difference in actual health status or morbidity. In effect, women who lived with another adult were less likely to express what the researcher called "illness behaviors," but were just as likely to be sick.

Then, in 1993, British researcher Duncan Cramer, working with a survey of nine thousand people, studied the issue from several different angles. Tracking both marital status and living arrangements, he found few differences between the health of nonmarried (separated, divorced, widowed, and ever-single) and married people. He did find that nonmarried women who lived alone consumed more alcohol than women who lived with a child of four or under, and that ever-single women were the most likely to consume alcohol. He also found that ever-single women had slightly higher psychological distress than married women but *lower* psychological distress than separated, widowed, and divorced women—irrespective of their living arrangements. He concluded in the *Journal of Community and Applied Social Psychology* that living alone was probably not the culprit in the poorer health status of nonmarried people, including ever-single women. Instead, he said, issues such as social integration and emotional support may be at work—the same results found in the friendship studies.

꘎

No one I talked to was able to say definitively, *do this* or *don't do that.* Contrary to the wisdom of Helen Gurley Brown, there is no recipe for making a home. That nebulous thing called support comes in so many forms it's tough to track. Kate clearly depends on her family. Susan looks to friends for what is mostly emotional support; the plumber she can call separately. In contrast, Rachel Jacobs and Allie Ackerman both make a point of getting to know their neighbors; in fact, Allie consciously builds a community wherever she lives, publishing neighborhood directories, revitalizing the condo association, meeting and organizing the people around her. "It's some yearning I have," she observes, "for family or community." Among her best experiences was a trailer park, which she chose after driving around for days, looking for a neighborhood where people were outside, talking to each other. "They were poor people," she recalls, "but God, what a sense of community. What a sense of helping each other!" Today she and her children live in a small housing complex where the townhouses face each other across narrow, winding roads and teens hang out admiring each other's cars. "A house for me is an island," she says. "It's a single family living with land around it, separating them from all these people."

Of course, there are a few commonalities in the way singular women live in their homes. Most have found a way to revel in the positive aspects of living alone: the control over the space and the time they spend in it, the quiet. Nearly everyone mentions the freedom. "The best part is that you don't have to tell people when you're coming home," notes Teresa Sanchez, who lived with her immigrant family for many years before going to graduate school. "You can plan things, like, out of the blue. This weekend I might feel like I want to go and spend a weekend somewhere. And I don't have to ask anyone."

Most have quietly picked over the conventions of what a home is supposed to look like and adapted them. To cook or not to cook, to entertain or not to entertain, to decorate for the holidays or to let it be: these are individual decisions that women eventually learn to make individually. Similarly, those who feel most at home, who feel comfortable with where and how they live, tend to have places that reflect their interests: Rachel's place is packed with cookbooks, computer art, and a piano; Christi's place has so many books you wonder if they procreate at night. In Caitlin McKuen's miniature living room there is art on the walls; in the kitchen, which is half the size of a VW, there are rows of oils and spices and cans of coconut milk, ingredients for Indian meals that she shares with a half-dozen friends who get together to cook in this tiny community in the deep of winter. These are places full of texture and life—far from the white-walled tomb that Alex Forrest inhabits in *Fatal Attraction*.

Why? What makes these places so full of life when only one person lives there? One answer seems to be activity. These are places where women dig in and really live, not places to visit for a change of clothes or wait for a radical change in their lives. Rachel composes fugues on her computer and plays them on her piano; she perfects bread recipes and takes her winners down to the state fair. Ellen cans salmon that she catches in the Pacific. Christi writes poetry.

It goes beyond that. The line between home and work is nearly imperceptible in many of these lives. Just as Kate made a home in her workplace, many singular women bring work into their homes. Teresa is just as likely to spend a Saturday night at home working on an academic paper as going out dancing with friends. "I always have something, some project going on," she says. "I work like crazy." Roxanne Walters takes calls at home for the association of black filmmakers that she founded. "I could not live in my place without my computer, which holds most of my correspondence, all of my accounting, two years' worth of professional scripts and projects, and a half-dozen bad short stories. I would be lonely without it."

That might sound strange to those whose time at home is structured in part by the people around them; it will sound desperate to those who see work as a necessary evil; it seems to reinforce the notion that singular women are just a little too narrow, just a little obsessive. But in these singular lives work is more than a matter of making money, of being distracted, of filling up time and space. Work is a frequent companion and a good friend; for Ellen, who works full-time at home, it's a good tenant. For many singular women, work is a primary source of identity, so it's no wonder that it makes its way home and lives there, a silent and flexible roommate.

※

Inevitably, there's someone who figured most of this out before any of us were ever born. In her short stories, Mary E. Wilkins Freeman profiled a lot of ever-single women, tough New England types who grow their own cabbage, write their own poetry, and valiantly make their ways in the world. In one story, Hetty Fifield, an ever-single woman who has worked as a live-in companion all her life, finds herself homeless when her employer dies and so moves into the town church without permission. She plants her makeshift tent near the wood stove and lives and sleeps and cooks in the church, so that the smell of her dinners lingers in the air and douses the Sunday morning worshipers.

The town fathers are not happy, but when they stage a siege outside the church, demanding that she take another job as a live-in companion, Hetty boldly objects. She wants a home of her own, she says: "I've had to fight to keep a footin' on the earth, an' now I'm gittin too old for't." After all, she *is* working in the church, taking care of the property, in essence serving as the town's first female sexton. In the absence of marriage and family, she is staking a claim to a real adult life, a whole identity, and she does it by staking out a home—and work.

At the critical moment, the married women of the town step into the scene and let Hetty Fifield stay.

CHAPTER SEVEN

Working

In winter Caitlin McKuen climbs a quarter-way up a snow-covered hill to her freestanding studio in mid-morning, and she stays there, painting, until late afternoon. There is no time, she says, when she's painting. There's no war on drugs or poverty, no rent check due, no flat tire on her used car. "I get in the studio and I'm in a little world, a cave, a kind of bubble or something."

The bubble is bigger than a fire escape, smaller than a one-car garage. A half-dozen canvases cover the walls, and a table holds ten or twelve jars of paint. Now that it's spring, and Caitlin has started her five-month waitressing stint, the space heater hovers unused in a corner along with a pair of winter boots, a couple of frames, and some completed paintings. There are no easels. More disconcerting to the visitor, there are no chairs. This is a private place. "When the paintings are finished, I don't mind showing them to people," she says. "It's harder for me to show the work when I'm working on it, when it's in progress, because then I think it's more open. I feel more vulnerable about the work."

In one painting a luminescent angel flies wingless above an unseen landscape. One painting depicts a stoic prom queen, and one duplicates a Renaissance religious painting—but the hands only, the hands poised to receive the Christ child, the hands raised in awe of him, the hands of the child himself praising God.

It has been a long journey—through work as a bartender and flight attendant, through study in Rhode Island and India—to get to this work, but *here it is, embracing her and confirming her. "It feels very intimate when I'm working," Caitlin says. "I'm up here physically working on some piece, and it's kind of like a relationship. My relationship is with my work, I think." She stops, and then she adds, "My most serious relationship."*

~

"A woman's work is never done," they say. Of course, they're not talking about Hetty Fifield cleaning up the church pews. But they're not talking about Caitlin McKuen painting in her studio or Marguerite Ramanis buying her own commercial horse barn, either. They're not talking about Emily Brontë writing a novel. Or Emily Dickinson writing a poem.

They're talking about women's *real* work, the endless, ongoing work of maintaining the domestic machine, of cleaning it, oiling it, and overhauling it; the work of raising children and nurturing relationships, of creating family over and over again, like Penelope at her loom. This is the much praised and yet economically undervalued work of women who marry; and it is the invisible stamp of a woman's public worth. As for women who don't marry—well, they do other work.

But the work ever-single women do is in fact extraordinarily important to who they are and how they feel. Indeed, the breadth and depth and power of the opportunity to work are inestimable. Studies tell us that outside work is an indicator of mental health and happiness for women—married and unmarried. And for the ever-single, it is probably even more crucial, if only because work goes a long way in neutralizing that nasty reflection in the cultural mirror. When a single woman is working, the judgment that she is ugly is usually irrelevant; and when she is working, the judgment that she is useless is proven untrue.

So work becomes a driving force, a pivotal element in the lives of singular women. It is the source of Pat McDonald's self-esteem, the focal point of Maureen Cabot's social contacts, the fountainhead of Caitlin's joy. It can fill in where family and friends leave off. It is a safe haven, a powerful ally, a source of identity.

~

Not long ago a new Japanese dating service saw the first signs of business failure when fewer than two dozen women signed up for its services. The business strategy behind the dating service had *looked* good: in the midst of recession, Japanese women were having difficulty finding jobs, so they would certainly turn toward marriage, popularly dubbed *eikyu shuskoku* or "permanent employment." So Takahiro Izumi, the founder of Gotanda Bridal Salon, put his dating service right in the shadow of Tokyo University, the Harvard of Japan, which turns out Japan's best catches—lawyers, policy makers, and businessmen headed for top positions. But *eikyu shuskoku*, a traditional female euphemism for marriage (as "getting hitched" is a traditional male euphemism in the U.S.), turns out not to be as attractive as it once was. Despite the recession and an acknowledged lack of equal opportunity, young women in Japan have delayed marriage in unprecedented numbers, confounding organizers of dating banquets and bridal salons, as well as their potential mates, who can't quite figure the whole thing out.

The euphemism *eikyu shuskoku* holds a key to women's experiences in the U.S. too. Although the term has the stale smell of that old Americanism "the M.R.S. degree" (or "Mrs."), which referred to a woman's college degree, it is not truly out of place in the U.S. Even if an American woman works outside the home, marriage typically defines the nature and scope of her work. In reality marriage *is* her work.

Columnist Anna Quindlen points this out in a 1994 essay called "The Out-of-Work Wife." In the essay, Quindlen, who is married, describes Lady Diana Spencer's ill-fated decision to marry the Prince of Wales this way: "Like so many other women, the 19-year-old Diana, unsure of who she was and what she cared for, decided to make her career that of a wife." Quindlen goes on to say that marriage is not a good career choice because it isn't permanent: layoffs are common, often because husbands decide that they no longer want what they wanted way back when they first made those job offers. We should take Princess Di and the thousands of divorced women who find themselves dusting off teaching credentials as a warning, says Quindlen, "of how horrible things sometimes turn out when a woman hitches all her hopes to one man's star, an object lesson in the need for self-reliance and a life of one's own."

To see these stories in current newspapers is to glimpse the primacy of women's real work (marriage). Historically this primacy was enforced by laws and economic realities; later it was enforced by medical and psychological theories (Freud, for instance, believed women incapable of invention); today it's enforced—with some confusing and painful consequences—by media, politics, even a career seminar given at one of the nation's top universities as late as April 1995.

Former Texas governor Ann Richards discovered the depth of feeling about that primacy when she gave a speech warning female high school leaders that they should not count on Prince Charming to give shape to their lives. The June 1994 speech, made a few months before she lost her bid for reelection, was characteristically blunt and it was met with outrage, especially from political conservatives, who claimed that the governor was being anti-family. In other words, conservatives claimed that by suggesting that women should develop self-reliance and professional competence as a hedge against dependency in marriage and poverty in divorce, Richards, who herself is divorced, was suggesting that women forgo family altogether. Conservatives could not imagine a world in which a woman was self-reliant and part of a family: the two goals, the two jobs, were in direct opposition.

Today in the U.S. the message to educated women about this "natural" opposition between work and marriage is both subtle and baffling: their college educations teach components of job preparedness such as autonomy, assertiveness, intellectual independence, competitiveness, and analysis, while their culture portrays femininity (or readiness for the wife job) as steeped in passive acceptance, a yielding personality, relational decision making, flirtatiousness, and unrelenting service. Apparently you have to choose one: it's nearly impossible to be both. As a result, some Northwestern University undergraduates were understandably confused when a recent women's "career" program proposed teaching the two irreconcilable sets of behaviors side by side—how to succeed in your professional "career" by being productive and how to succeed in your dating "career" by flirtatiously running your hands through your hair. Dismayed, the students protested.

Back in the nineteenth century, educated women responded to the opposition between their educations and the passivity required for the traditional wife job and the spinster-aunt job in a different way: they got sick. Unable to hold outside jobs for various reasons, British and American middle- and upper-class women were plagued by a great epidemic of something called neurasthenia, a vague set of nervous symptoms that included fainting spells, headaches, menstrual irregularities, insomnia, lack of appetite, a sense of hopelessness, and convulsions. Although men suffered from it too, in men it was often called hypochondria.

Neurasthenia played right into a well-established cult of female delicacy, of fainting pallor, corseted breathlessness, and thin-skinned beauty that had long plagued the novels, magazines, and lives of nineteenth-century women. Alice James, the ever-single sister of novelist Henry James, led a trifling upper-class life and suffered severely from it; apparently Jane Addams, who would later win the Nobel Peace Prize, did too. Returning home from her African travels, Mary Kingsley fell victim to undiagnosed nervous ills; suddenly the woman who had canoed through the Canaries and spent a night under a rock on the isle of Gomera was plagued by migraines and heart palpitations as she sat, nearly idle, in her London apartment.

Of those who escaped full-fledged illness, many nonetheless suffered despair. The letters from Wellesley's class of 1897 tell this story. Ten years after receiving her degree, one graduate wrote: "Thus far I have done nothing worth the ink to print it. . . ." Another wrote: "I have not done any of the wonderful things expected of me when I was a freshman at Wellesley. . . . I pulled Mother through a long illness, then I straightaway had the ills myself. . . . You can put me down as alive though." And others: "There is nothing significant about my 'career.'" "I have done nothing wonderful . . . two children." "I was married to a lawyer in New York City, since which time I have made New York my home, and have done nothing of importance."

Today it seems clear that at least some of this illness and despair was due in part to failed expectations. The Wellesley graduates in particular seemed to steep in a situational sadness, a sense that they weren't doing something of value, that they weren't free to express themselves, to fulfill the promise of their educations. Married and unmarried, they seemed to suffer the same malaise that Betty Friedan described in 1963: they looked out from their fathers' and their husbands' homes—just as Friedan's women looked out from their suburban homes—and asked, *Is this all there is?*

The answer was—well, yes. In the late nineteenth and early twentieth centuries, women who wanted to work faced barriers that some just couldn't overcome. The low pay, the repetitive tasks, the paychecks that plateaued quickly, the barriers to highly respected careers—it was more than many women who had other choices could handle. As a result it was largely single women who paved the way into the paid labor force.

This was a lonely and difficult path to pave in 1880 and 1920 and 1940, even in industries that appeared to welcome women. In education, for instance (just as Catharine Beecher had recommended), women teachers were paid less than their male colleagues, a practice that was legal until federal equal-pay legislation passed in the 1960s. Then, having worked for years as teachers and professors, women often had to quit when they married. In 1930, 61 percent of American schools required women to quit their jobs if they married; in 1941, only 13 percent of America's schools would hire married women. So *that's* where the punishing spinster-teacher stereotype—the featureless woman with the bun, the pointer, and the sensible shoes—comes from. To teach—to work in many American industries, including insurance companies, banks, and public utilities—for a good part of the twentieth century, a woman *had* to be single. To be a flight attendant at United Airlines, she had to be single right up until 1968.

These rules codified what a "Mrs. A." told *Mademoiselle* magazine in 1956: "I could shoot the first woman who went to work in a man's job. My ambition is to please my husband in every womanly way." Outside work is men's work. Inside work is women's work. And a woman who is doing lots of outside work and little inside work is somehow suspect, somehow not quite feminine, not quite legitimate.

Although these restrictions are now illegal, and these prejudices have eased, in reality women still face an implicit conflict between work and marriage at critical moments in their lives. Quoting a 1986 survey published in the *Wall Street Journal*, economist Victor Fuchs points out that 20 percent of women executives were ever-single and another 20 percent were separated or divorced (less than 1 percent of male executives were ever-single, and only 4 percent were separated or divorced). A smaller 1992 study shows less dramatic statistics, but the pattern is the same: women executives had half the children and three times the divorces, and they were three times more likely to be ever-single than male executives were. In Canadian politics the pattern is repeated: in 1993 one columnist noted that nearly every woman who had risen to any height was widowed, divorced, or ever-single.

Marital status also affects how much women earn. Single women (divorced and ever-single) earn more: in a comparison of the wages of married and unmarried women in 1960 and 1986, Fuchs found that married women typically start out ahead but soon fall behind—by as much as 20 percent in 1960 and as much as 15 percent in 1986. Fuchs believes that this may be the result of the same discontinuity that married women incur in their emotional lives. In the course of their marriages women tend to interrupt their paid careers, cut back to part-time, or transfer from the demanding profession they anticipated to a less demanding one, while unmarried women plug on continuously. And plugging on seems to pay off: ever-single women who work full-time actually out-earn ever-single men on average—apparently because of their higher credentials and better health.

An ever-single woman, then, has a different hold on work than her married sister does—and work has a different hold on her. Still steeped in the implicit contradiction between marriage and work, the culture around us—especially the people who make media—don't understand the nature of that hold and they draw caricatures of narrow, obsessed single women, subliminally unfulfilled. But singular women do understand the rich and complex role of work in their lives. They understand it well.

🌿

Contrary to the image in the cultural mirror, no one I met recalls choosing work over marriage.

Susan Ryerson didn't sit down one day and say, "If I marry, I'll never be a fire marshal." Teresa Sanchez didn't arrive at graduate school and suddenly choose an academic career over a domestic one. And when Rachel Jacobs left her boyfriend to move to Albuquerque for a job, she wasn't choosing the abstract concept of "her work" over the abstract concept of "all marriage." But Rachel has had a hard time explaining this to outsiders. "My sister gave me a real hard time about this," she recalls. "She said, 'How can you do this? Where are your priorities?'

"I don't remember exactly what I said," Rachel continues. She's sitting at the kitchen table, chopping tomatoes as she talks. She has the quiet, unflappable voice of a well-schooled scientist, an observer who is never surprised, never angry, never exuberant—but it's an illusion. Rachel is a risk-taker. Last year she learned to jump out of airplanes, and every week she drives into one of Chicago's poorest and most dangerous neighborhoods to pick up the young girl she tutors as a volunteer. "You just had a gut feeling of what the right thing to do is, and I just felt that the right thing to do was follow up on my education. And I really learned something from that because things worked out in Albuquerque; the job there led to another job up here . . . and I kind of felt like I did the right thing, looking back."

"Do you still?"

She doesn't hesitate. "Yes," she says. "Especially looking at him and seeing that he's still in that same apartment, hanging around with the same people. I mean, I've just seen so much and met so many people since then." Among them, she says, is a boyfriend of three years.

No one says that she chose work over marriage, but nearly all remember finding reinforcement in work, finding meaning and purpose. Often this happened early, in the twenties. It was then that Karen King and Christi Wagner became dedicated teachers; it was then that Ellen Adams found her work as an environmentalist. When I ask retired executive Diane Faverty, seventy-four, what the best part of her life has been, she talks about work—filming the first black-and-white TV commercials, traveling around the country, formulating a product strategy aimed at women consumers. When Jillian Goodman talks about her first glimpse of an American hospital, you can almost feel her twenty-eight-year-old self quivering. "Here I was in this big hospital and learning how to start IVs and EKGs and things that British nurses didn't do," she recalls. "It was beautiful—I remember my first week here, I took a photograph of the supply room. It was wonderful. All those supplies, you know. I mean, coming from socialized medicine, that was something special."

"I really feel like I fell into the right profession," says Janice Patinkin, who has been a dental hygienist for sixteen years and is often requested by patients. "How many people can say that about their profession—that they constantly get a pat on the back?"

It may be a kind of falling in love—a kind of falling into purpose. In work the ever-single woman is reinforced and valued; in work she produces, she makes changes, she creates. On the outside—at twenty-eight and thirty-two and thirty-five—she may feel out of step with peers who are marrying and having children and struggling to find good day care; but at work she is in step with her peers. She's accepted largely on the basis of what she does and, in some senses, for who she is—her real self, her real capabilities, her real concerns. At that critical, difficult time, when friends seem to withdraw into marriages, when the family shifts, when the script disappears—there is work, and it feels good.

Although work was initially a waiting station for Maureen Cabot, the stenographer who once told her boss that she wouldn't be around long enough to get a ten-year pin, it soon changed. Maureen fell into its rhythms and its reinforcement, and work soon became the center of her social life. It was the place where she met women who were leading similar lives; it was the place where she met the men and women she would travel with; it was a place where she could let her talents and her humor shine—and be appreciated for it, quite naturally. In fact, that's how Maureen got promoted.

One day during World War II, a manager spotted some cartoons she'd drawn for a colleague's son who was serving overseas. He told her, "You can write. Why don't you go into public relations?" For years Maureen hesitated, moving through the secretarial ranks in the expected way, flexing her humor and her talents spontaneously, while the manager continued to encourage her—until she finally leapt up into the new, more challenging job. By then, though, it wasn't the content of the job so much as the fact of work that she'd come to appreciate; she had come to see herself as a "working girl." Along the way, she'd come to value the nature of her professional skills and what they bought her: the freedom and the means to travel; the circle of friends; the autonomy that she didn't see in her married friends. "I'd see certain friends who are involved with children and certainly I don't mean that they were miserable, but they look back and say, 'Oh! look where you've been!'" she says. Then she adds, "There are good things about both. You're not going to have it perfect."

The trick is to find work that satisfies, that talks back happily, that soothes and provides a sense of worth. It's not always easy—in fact it's not always possible. Victoria Mason remembers working a twelve-hour day at a neighborhood liquor store for seventeen dollars, a wage that was well under the legal minimum and can still pique her anger. "But I did my stint on welfare," she recalls, "and I was like 'No, no, *no*.'" Finally she quit, found a better job at Marquette University, moved from there to the County, and from the County to the Board of Education. Her work served her other purpose, the purpose of raising and protecting her children, but it never satisfied: "I don't think God meant me to be a secretary," she says. "I'm good at it, but I don't think that's all, that's it." Facing another five years of college tuition, she works her secretarial job at an elementary school, where giggling children race down the hallway to hug her, and another job at a currency exchange, where she cashes poor people's checks. But mostly she looks ahead toward new work that will fulfill her—college, maybe filmmaking.

Some of Susan Ryerson's early jobs were similar. Right out of high school, she took a job at an L.A. department store. "It was a bus ride away from home," she recalls. "And I think here's what convinced me: you see these middle-aged women and you see what they're doing." They were doing boring jobs and they weren't making much money; it was clear she was going nowhere. She remembers selling a pair of men's socks and thinking, "Gee, I don't want to be here *forever*." After six months, a stranger on a city bus saw her reading a book and urged her to join a minority college prep program—the same program her mother had been recommending for months—and she pursued it. But there were still boring, low-paying jobs ahead, sometimes two of them at a time (one of them in the back room of yet another department store), as Susan looked for a way to live and work happily.

Unfortunately, this avenue to singularity—finding work that confers and confirms worth—may present new problems. There's a danger in finding and focusing on good work, ever-single women say, and the danger is that work becomes everything. In the absence of the traditional structures that give form to a life, a woman can get lost in her work, lost and a little limited.

Teachers are the first to point this out. There are always extra committees, extra projects, and problem students needing attention. The schools need dedicated teachers, and that's important—and maybe just a little seductive. As an active teacher, Karen King rarely misses a day of work and used to sit on every committee she was asked to join. "It was my total life, so to speak, before I decided to adopt either of the girls," she recalls. "I mean, I worked on this committee and that committee; I was running at night going to this meeting and that meeting, and it was very much part of my life. I liked the people I worked with and I like to be involved in decisions and all that." But raising a family changed things: "I had to begin to realize that now teaching couldn't take up as much time, you know, and so I started backing off." Now she does take days off—mostly to chaperon Faith's field trips.

But many ever-single women don't have the kind of outside stimulus that forces them to adjust the way Karen did. For many the concern and the adjustment must come from within. In Pat McDonald's case the adjustment came as part of her journey toward greater self-realization. "I'm wondering at times if I sometimes use my work, you know," she says, "because of the struggles with self-esteem. Maybe that's why I haven't gotten out socially more." Never a clock-watcher, she has traditionally served on school committees and gladly attended extra meetings, but in an unprecedented move, she complained recently when a new program got out of hand. "I was able to go to the principal and say, 'Hey, this is tough!' . . . At first he just kind of gave me a pep talk, but then I went back to him again, and meanwhile he began to hear it from other people." Pat's effort to change her lopsided life actually changed her lopsided work environment, too. "It took someone to break the barrier," she says with her quiet brand of pride, "and he's made some changes."

Doing this isn't easy. In the absence of a key relationship that draws her away, the ever-single woman who feels herself being absorbed into work has to reach out, all on her own, to something else that will feed her. Susan Ryerson calls that something else an avocation, and she claims that work doesn't drive her life—her avocation does. Early in her twenties Susan learned to play tennis; by twenty-seven she was good enough to play in the World Cup. She chose a night job, a position working in a children's shelter, so she could practice during the day. Tennis and books (and books about tennis) animate her life. "This is a profound thing coming from a black person," she says, "but tennis for me was like being able to dance. I was a lousy dancer as a kid, so, you know, here's this black girl who can't dance. But tennis I took to—physically it was wonderful. It was my way of dancing . . . and I found that the harder I worked at it, the better I got."

I watch Susan "dance" one Sunday night on an indoor court. Her worthy opponent is a buddy, a forty-year-old father of two whose forehand speeds over the net like a .45-caliber bullet. He and Susan are part of a loose-knit group of black tennis players who travel to tournaments together and hang out at the nearby public courts. "It's a loose circle. They don't demand anything of you," she says. "You just have to contribute a six-pack now and then." Tonight she loses the first set, but she wins the next two, game after game, pummeling the ball and placing it devilishly along the alley. She's disappointed in her net game, she tells me later, and she was mortified to lose that first set. "I should have beat him," she says, and I recall stories I've heard of Susan's buddies coaxing unsuspecting players in the park—*Hey, why don't you play with her? She's good for a woman, but you can beat her*—a practice she now discourages. It's clear that tennis has brought her confidence and friendship. Tennis has brought her an unexpected dimension. "I can't imagine my life without it," she says.

Indeed, most of the singular women I met—the women who are most comfortable with their lives—have found an extra dimension in nonwork activities that spark their interest or use their skills. Mary Stendahl runs—a lot—and she's recently joined a group that runs team marathons. When she's not taking risks, Rachel has taken courses in painting and lessons on the piano—and she's good enough to mount a formal recital on her own. A few years after moving to Seattle, Janice joined an organization that sponsors group activities like bike hikes, orienteering, and camping trips—a group that she credits with turning her attitude toward Seattle around completely. These singular women choose avocations that give them something back, that confirm their abilities, that put them in touch with other people, that enable them to be more of who they are.

Still, for most singular women the source of pride, pleasure, and achievement lies mostly in the work. "It's ironic that we're facing layoffs," says Rachel, who works in the research division of a health-care company that is running scared over health-care reform. In her nearly unmodulated voice, she expresses her sense of achievement and her sadness: "This is some of the best work I've ever done." Even Susan Ryerson's emphatic claim that leisure drives her life is only partially true. Susan has spent many off-hours trying to recruit minority men and women to the fire department, and twice she has spent long months coaching women to pass the difficult physical test for the department (they do things like wear fifty-pound sacks while climbing a stair machine for five minutes). As much as she has found herself in tennis—her avocation—she has also found a part of herself in work. She is, even if she seems to deny it, dedicated.

꽃

"Why is this news?" a singular woman asks me. "Isn't it obvious that women get something out of work?"

Apparently not, although it *is* true that some thinkers have come up with the notion before. Back in the 1800s, Susan B. Anthony believed that the

whole image of the spinster—gnarled and shrunken and narrow—was the result of enforced uselessness. In 1918 H. L. Mencken, a popular columnist on
the order of Andy Rooney, noted that work provided the single woman with
enough psychological feedback and enough income to make marriage
optional, and he argued that women were more diligent than men. "If the
work of the average man required half the mental agility and readiness of re-
source of the work of the average prostitute," he wrote in *In Defense of
Women*, "the average man would be constantly on the verge of starvation."
Less offensively, and maybe more surprisingly, in the 1930s the Jungian psychologist M. Esther Harding speculated that work—not marriage—was the
quickest avenue to the development of an adult female consciousness capable
of equal relationships. And in the late forties the French feminist Simone de
Beauvoir described the challenges and rewards of outside work. At various
times various thinkers—mostly female and often singular—have thought this
one through, but the popular culture, the world we inhabit and the mirror we
look into, systematically resists it. And that resistance—masked though it
sometimes is—often intrudes into the lives of singular women.

It intruded into mine one day in the late 1980s when a client, the president of a plastic fencing firm, brought his beliefs about women's *real* work to
the conference table. In the middle of a meeting on engineering for new mar-
kets (they'd made too many plastic fences and wondered what to do with
them), he turned to me and demanded, "What's with you, anyway? Didn't
you *try* to get dates in high school?" At first I looked for the connection between plastic fences and dating; then I looked for an appropriate response;
then, caught as I was in that awful *what's-wrong-with-me?* stage, I obsessed for
weeks, believing that if I were just a little more feminine, a little better
schooled in the ways of women's magazines, I'd never have inspired such a remark. But in fact, the problem lay in the cultural contradiction between the
nature of outside work and the prevailing picture of femininity; more to the
point, the problem lay in his belief that as an unmarried woman, I'd failed to
do women's *real* work and that as I sat relaying market research on product-
conversion opportunities, I was engaging in some kind of bizarre and unnatural substitution.

A much bolder example of this belief occurred back in the 1830s, when
the *Boston Post* took on Sarah Moore Grimké, an ever-single Quaker woman
who dared to campaign against slavery in front of mixed (male and female)

crowds. "Why are all the old hens abolitionists?" the *Post* asked in frustration. Of course the paper had a theory: "Because not being able to obtain husbands, they think they may stand some chance for a Negro, if they can only make amalgamation [integration] possible." But the *Post* was wrong about Grimké: as a young adult, she'd had two (count 'em) marriage proposals. Her work emanated from her moral convictions—not from the hope that she might marry a freed slave.

Today the message is a little more subtle and yet it's similar. Throughout the twentieth century the single woman who focuses on work has been the focus of misunderstanding—especially in the movies; there, it's clear that the working single woman is engaged in a bad substitution, a poor replacement for the real work she would have done if she'd had the chance—if Prince Charming or Prince Charles or Prince had come along.

In the movies this unnatural substitution taints her work and warps her character. The aging actress Margo Channing in *All About Eve* (1950) is stuck in an artistic rut—and she's narcissistic. The spinster-teacher Jean Brodie in *The Prime of Miss Jean Brodie* (1969) is a bad teacher—and morally corrupt. The beautiful aging dancer Emma in *The Turning Point* (1977) has outlived her excellence as a performer; she has given up way too much for her career ("She travels with three little dogs," her married nemesis observes ruefully)—and she's morally corrupt. The high-powered power broker Katharine Parker in *Working Girl* (1988) flubs an important business opportunity—and she's morally corrupt. The wildly successful journalist Seleena St. George in *Dolores Claiborne* (1995) is an addict—and she lies to get assignments. Something's wrong with the single woman who focuses on work, and something is wrong with her work.

Bravely, the pro-college, pro-career *Mademoiselle* tried to debunk this image in the 1950s with an article entitled "What's Wrong with Ambition?" Although *Mademoiselle's* survey of working women showed that they treasured their freedom, enjoyed their work, and had no regrets, the writer got lost in a thicket of prejudice and fears. In the end she reconciled ambition and femininity by declaring all women, particularly mothers, ambitious: "Marriage and children are part of a very ambitious woman's ambitions," she wrote. "Children give their owners more status than diamonds do in practically every community today. Mothers are known for their little brand-name products as surely as Elizabeth Arden is for hers." In other words, ambition is okay because women who do *real* women's work (get married and raise children) have ambition too.

These powerful images serve as a warning to women; they feed their premarital panic and they undermine the true reciprocity some ever-single women have with their work. At worst they warn the single woman that in substituting other work for women's "real" work, she boards a train that takes her far from her natural destination, and it's terribly hard—nearly impossible—for her to get back on the right track. Success will make her inaccessible to a marriage partner who must be older, richer, and more accomplished than she is—a problem *Newsweek*, George Gilder, and others have noted. And if that's not bad enough, work will squeeze something essential out of her, something pliable and soft, something marriageable.

The problem with these warnings is that there are some quarter-truths lurking somewhere in the shadows there, tapping the ever-single woman on the shoulder, making her wonder if she has made a terrible error by working hard and true.

One quarter-truth is that the marriage gradient traditionally places older, educated, successful women out of reach and out of favor with traditionally minded men. That's why not long ago Teresa Sanchez tried a couple of end runs around the issue of her professional status—but she found that it didn't work. At a singles' dance she introduced herself as a teacher. "So they start saying, 'What school do you teach at?' and I say, 'I'm a university professor,' and boy, that freaks them," she says unhappily. "It changes [everything]."

But if it's true that being a professor of comparative literature places Teresa outside traditional patterns, it's also true that any woman who reaches thirty-five and forty-five and fifty-five without marrying is not probably not traditionally minded and would not be happy with a traditionally minded man anyway. Only two women I met feel that they stumbled into their success and say that they might have traded it for a marriage. Gretchen Wentworth, who spent twenty years in the fashion industry, is one. "If I'd married I'd have quit my job," she says. "I'm old-fashioned that way." But for most the work that they have done is so much a part of who they are that they can't imagine such a trade; most look for marriages that could allow them the full identity—and at least some of the autonomy—that they've achieved.

The other quarter-truth is that achieving professional competence and economic independence will change the way a woman looks at traditional marriage. Maureen Cabot says it best: "Part of it is that when you consider marriage, you want to improve, you want life to be better," she notes. "But when you start earning good money and you have friends and you're able to travel, it would take something more to make you choose it. You're not going to get married unless you think it's a step up," she says and immediately adds: "And I don't mean necessarily financially. I mean that you're going to find something that you don't already have."

But I think the last antiwork warning is the scariest of all. It tells the single woman that even if she finds someone to accept her success, even if she adjusts to being a little less independent, she still won't be a true and attractive woman anyway. Work may well have wreaked some irreparable damage. *All About Eve*, which was made into a popular Broadway musical in the 1970s, is particularly explicit on this point. Toward the end of the film, Margo Channing looks back on a successful acting career but worries that she is no longer capable of marriage: "Funny business, a woman's career," she muses. "The things you drop on the way up the ladder so you can move faster! You forget you'll need them again when you get back to being a woman."

Being a woman is a career in itself, says Channing (predating Anna Quindlen and Ann Richards by forty-four years); it's the job that buys a woman love, which in turn buys her an identity. "Sooner or later we've got to work at it, no matter how many other careers we've had or wanted," she says. "And in the last analysis, nothing's any good unless you can look up just before dinner or turn around in bed and there he is: without that, you're not a woman. You're something with a French provincial office or a book full of clippings, but you're not a woman." Some forty years later, *Working Girl*, *Newsweek*, *Slow Dancing*, and Northwestern's career seminar all said nearly the same thing—if a little less articulately.

What does a singular woman do with these kinds of judgments? When a woman is happy in her work, when she is fed by it and engaged in it, she ignores them. Like Teresa Sanchez, like Maureen Cabot, she draws on her resources—her family, friends, and yes, her work—to discount the image in the media mirror. When a colleague recently explained to Roxanne Walters that although there were a lot of guys in the filmmakers association who were interested in her, none of them was likely to ask "the boss" out, she shrugged—and kept her position as president and founder. To abandon a role that she had worked hard to create would be to abandon some part of herself—which is a false way to start any relationship.

Still, the imagery is potent. It's no wonder that the adolescent crucible—which rewards the social skills and self-packaging that are preparatory for marriage over the more concrete skills that are preparatory for work—remains so fiery. And it's no wonder that the singular woman, supported by her family, accompanied by friends and neighbors, involved in her work, and flanked by interests that feed her, goes nearly unnoticed. Hers is not a warped life; it's not a working life corrupted by amoral ambition; it's not the stuff of pop culture, of Jean Brodie or Katharine Parker. It's a quiet life charged with energy and focus, the life of Susan Ryerson, the life of Rachel Jacobs. These are current, low-profile movies made of real women making real connections and doing good work that goes (contrary to the myth) unpunished.

🐦

"I think these paintings are about a single woman, the ones I'm doing now," Caitlin McKuen tells me. "Because one of the things I was thinking about during the six years that I was celibate and out of relationships was what does it mean to be a woman? What makes me a woman?"

We're sitting across from each other after the tour of her studio, and she's looking at me so directly that it's almost uncomfortable. Goodness! I think, fresh from a screening of *All About Eve*, I hope I'm not supposed to come up with an answer!

"My decision to have my tubes tied completely redefines me now," Caitlin continues. "Because before, even though I was independent and kind of strong-minded and strong-willed and self-sufficient, I could still be what women should be—a wife and mother. And now, although there's a possibility that I could be a wife, I won't be a mother."

So Caitlin is left without a definition, and her paintings seek the definition for her. "They're very personal. They're real deep, maybe from things that I don't even understand," she says. "So I guess the work would just automatically have to be about my life as a single person living alone."

Simone de Beauvoir said it was rare, and perhaps it is, but in Caitlin McKuen and a few other singular women, I see an experience of work that reaches beyond social structure and economic independence, beyond the simple act of finding purpose. In Caitlin, in Ellen Adams, there's a profound sense of having come home to work. They live in their work; it is one with their characters, their concerns, their spiritedness. De Beauvoir said few women attain true involvement and true artistry, but I think both of them have.

Caitlin likens her dedication to her art to an intimate relationship. Ellen says that her environmentalism drives her life: where she lives, what she buys, how she works, what she does in her spare time. Each worries that when a relationship with a man appears, it threatens to drain time away, to distract and cloud her purpose. Ellen says that she changes when she's in a relationship. She says she shifts focus and steals time from her work. "Who would have the time to do what I'm doing if they have a primary relationship? Or if they were fair to a primary relationship?" she asks intently. "If I get involved in a relationship, I know I'll have to cut back 'cause there's no extra time or energy to give." Being in a relationship is different for men, she thinks; they're less likely to lose focus or compromise their work. "Men feed from a relationship," she observes. "They take as much time as they want away [from it] and [then] come back and get taken care of. For women, that's not the case."

There are no signs of the narrowing, confining effects of overwork that Pat McDonald experienced in her work as a teacher; there's none of the exhaustion I remember during my four or five years as a workaholic, working twenty-eight days straight, taking one day off, and working another forty-two days without a break. In these lives all the stereotypes of the limited, warped, frustrated woman who loses herself in her meaningless job are banished: you see the work and the woman, and they're intimately connected. It is like a marriage, a marriage of identity and purpose, character and work, work and—the best I can come up with is . . . devotion.

In my journey toward singularity, I note these two wonderful, purposeful creatures along the way and wish I could be like them. But I realize that this kind of bond with work, like a truly good, lifelong marriage, is rare. So instead I look for tips, for lessons.

In Ellen I see an ability to accept—and maybe use—the persona that her work has lent to her. She accepts her stage role—but she does not internalize it. It's something she may have learned while working among the indigenous peoples in Paraguay. "They call me 'that little hippie lady with the dog,'" she says of the townspeople who see her walking to the post office out there on the Olympic Peninsula every day.

"How do you know that?" I ask, a little stunned. Who would relay such a thing?

"Oh, Gary Peterson—he's on the planning council with me—told me," she says and shrugs. "I'm like the little old lady in tennis shoes working to see that the boats don't get too close to the whales. I'm sure they say that." She smiles and shrugs again. "But it's like—I'm *glad* there's a little old woman in tennis shoes out there!"

In Caitlin I see a willingness to grasp her challenges and examine them so thoroughly that they become odd and curious in their own right—the way an object like a bolt or a phone taken out of context and stared at will take on a purity, an inexplicable objectness all its own. In Caitlin's house is a window taken from her grandfather's dairy barn. On the glass she has made the counting marks that waitresses make on their order pads, four vertical lines and a diagonal, four vertical lines and a diagonal, over and over again. In her living room the window hangs flush against the white wall, marking, it seems, a whitened landscape. It is called *Counting the Days of Winter*, and suddenly all the frozen, white-out Midwestern days of eighty below, all those empty winter days that I have dreaded and hated, are changed for me. Caitlin has taken a part of her singular, solitary life, a piece of the life challenge she faces in her isolated studio in a snowy land, and made it something nameable, special, and pure enough to speak to someone else. Her work and her life are integrated indescribably.

And that is an extraordinary accomplishment.

CHAPTER EIGHT

Finding Intimacy

The bartender is in her mid-twenties, pretty and blonde, an undergraduate studying communications and women's studies at a local college. "Are you here for the party?" she asks, pouring a beer. "You're early."

The party is the brainstorm of "Emily" (a code name). Months before, Emily and three friends had posted a series of billboards in Chicago advertising for husbands: "4 Professional Middle-Class Women, Ages 29–31, Seek Husbands. P.O. Box 175B, Chicago IL 60614." Some 250 men had responded to the billboards, and Emily and her friends had jointly screened the promising candidates. Then, explains the bartender, Emily had conducted some of her solo dates here, one after another, sometimes several dates a night.

So this party is for the men who didn't make the cut as well as 100 eligible women that Emily has recruited through a radio talk show. She called me personally because I'd written her when I first saw the billboards. "How old are you?" she asked.

"Nearly forty," I said.

"Oh, you're too old."

"Can I come anyway?"

The party is slow to start. Pretty, likable, predominantly suburban women cluster at the tables, laughing, talking, planning vacations. They're too well trained, it seems, to approach a strange man. Meanwhile, likable, approachable men watch sports on big-screen TVs; they're too shy, they tell me, to approach a whole group of women. Nearly two *hours pass before the crowd begins to socialize. Rumors run through the women about this good-looking guy or that one; people post notes on a special bulletin board for one another; they meet, talk, and drift away, disappointed. A few come away with dates.*

As I leave I see the bartender standing at the end of the bar, watching. "This isn't the way to do it," she says.

"What?"

"This isn't the way to find an intimate relationship."

I think she's right. But I wonder how at twenty-six she can be so certain, and so comfortable with her certainty.

🍂

What is intimacy? I think, driving to pick up my date for the evening, who has been baby-sitting my dog. Are we intimate? He knows that I don't own a potholder, that I can't stand cantaloupe. I know he loves flying airplanes and doesn't like the way I let my computer files just pile up, like dirty dishes after a banquet. What is that? That's familiarity, I decide. That's knowing somebody. What is intimacy?

According to some psychologists, an intimate relationship has three characteristics: involvement or closeness, commitment, and symmetry or equal levels of investment. For true intimacy to exist, the two selves must be whole, intact, and engaged. The resulting relationship is something living and unique: it can never be duplicated in every aspect, which explains the gnawing emptiness of that famous scene in the movie *Annie Hall* (1977) when the main character, played by Woody Allen, invites a new girlfriend over and tries to duplicate an intimate, exuberant lobster dinner he once had with Annie. The sad, bitter message is clear: you can't replicate an intimate relationship that you've lost.

What's most interesting about this definition of intimacy is what it doesn't say. It doesn't say that intimacy involves sex. It doesn't say that intimacy resides in marriage. It doesn't say that intimacy exists only between a man and a woman. It doesn't mention dating, economic support, longevity, or even proximity.

When I ask ever-single women if they have intimacy in their lives, most of the singular ones, the ones who feel most comfortable with their lives, say yes. Christi Wagner, the New York teacher, has it in her relationship with her sister. Lillian Salinger, the Illinois farmer, has it in her relationship with her brother; filmmaker Roxanne Walters in her relationship with her mother. Kate O'Connor finds it in her lifelong friendship with Clarissa.

But others sigh, fidget, and tell me no—they're not in a *relationship* with a capital R. And I realize that there are two issues here. One is the issue of intimacy, of closeness and connectedness. The other is being in a primary relationship, the feeling and the fact of being the primary character in someone else's life—which most people achieve through marriage. Clearly there are intimate relationships that aren't primary, and there are primary relationships—marriages—that aren't intimate. In the rush and hustle and fear and frenzy of those days when women court and hope to be courted, when the marriage choice looms large and identity is still in formation, when sexual desires run high, it's easy to get those things mixed up. It's easy to search for one thing—primacy—and call it another—intimacy. And it's easy to search for intimacy and choose, unconsciously or maybe consciously, primacy.

If ever there was a delicate and nagging issue for an ever-single woman, this is it. It weaves through her life like a sentimental song, haunting her, sometimes ambushing her. But if ever there was an important discovery to make, this is it: intimacy and primacy are not the same thing, and marriage is really a vehicle that *may* or *may not* provide both. This discovery may not silence the song always, but it opens up a world of understanding about choices, about dating, about sex, about being singular.

❦

Surprisingly, some anthropologists claim that marriage was never meant to be the repository of intimacy. Historically, marriage was an economic and sexual partnership—until sometime in the eleventh century, when Western Europe began to embrace the idea of romantic love. With romantic love, the notion of involvement or closeness entered the picture, adding a new expectation to the marriage tie. Similarly, during the period just before the American Revolution, the notion of individual rights, especially the right to pursue individual happiness, began to seep through the culture; the notion would eventually reach women about the time that equal-pay legislation did. This added yet another expectation to the marriage tie.

Meanwhile, in the nineteenth and twentieth centuries, the economic balance shifted and women were no longer completely dependent on marriage for survival. Then contraceptive technology improved, and men and women were no longer dependent on marriage for sex. Even after the sexual revolution of the 1960s, sexual activity among single women continued to increase: in just the five years between 1982 and 1987, sexual activity among ever-single women between fifteen and forty-four increased 5 percent, making more than three-quarters of ever-single women sexually active. Similarly, the number of cohabiting couples skyrocketed between 1960 and 1985, from 450,000 to two million. Armed with this increased economic independence and the license to be sexual, single women stared down the stigma of having children out of wedlock; in 1981 they actually formed a national support group, Single Mothers By Choice, for single women who choose to have babies on their own.

Rather suddenly, the western marriage was no longer primarily economic or primarily sexual. There was nothing in it that you couldn't get elsewhere; there was nothing inherently binding. Yet marriage was supposed to fulfill our needs for ephemeral, elusive things like romance, intimacy, and individual happiness. In effect, the marriage tie was weaker than it had ever been, yet it was burdened by greater expectations. The results: a disconcerting divorce rate and a mounting confusion over the nature of marriage, the purpose of it, the advantages to it.

Karen King ran into these issues head on early in life. Years ago she dated a man, a public prosecutor, and they were close. But when Karen told him that she wanted to adopt a child and that she had started to buy a house, the prosecutor balked. "This is something I wanted to give you," he told her. "And now you've got it."

Karen understood that they'd reached a critical moment, a discussion about what marriage really was about. "I don't need you to give me a baby," she told him. "I can get ten babies if I want them without you . . . [and] I don't need you to buy me a house. I have a job, I'm not rich, but I can afford the house I've bought, and so, if you're intimidated by that, this relationship won't work."

What *did* she want out of a marriage, then? Intimacy, she told him: "I need companionship and love and caring and doing things together and talking."

Looking back, she adds, "They want to put you in a house and give you the kids and do all this for you." But while that's nice, she concedes, it's not the sum of what she's looking for. "I can live without someone doing those things for me."

That's a kind of clarity few people have. Most of us spend our twenties and thirties in a kind of dating fog, confused by media images and our emotional needs, by the desire to be central in someone's else's book and by the accessibility and power of sex. In that kind of atmosphere, it's no wonder that many women look for intimacy in all the wrong places. Billboards, for instance, or crowded bars on a weekday night.

Of all the women I met, Linda Schindler has struggled with the search for intimacy the most openly. As a therapist she deals with the issue daily. Her clients—married, divorced, widowed, separated, and ever-single, men and women both—look to her for wisdom and she does what she can to comply. "As a matter of fact, I did talk about intimacy just last night," she tells me one early fall afternoon. "I did, with a man who's getting divorced . . . and I think that intimacy is when you are first of all very comfortable. Number one, you have to be yourself. It's to share all of your feelings, which I think is very hard for both men and women."

At forty-seven, Linda knows that she has intimacy in her life—she has extraordinary friendships—but she wants a relationship that offers both emotional and sexual intimacy, one that fully engages who she is. She's clear about that—most of the time. Other times, especially when she tries to do something about it, she gets dangerously close to getting mixed up.

Sometime after she passed forty, Linda decided that she wanted an intimate marriage. Funny, energetic, self-aware, and self-assured, she took it on as a project along with three other close women friends. She answered the personals. She cased out all the singles dances in the area. At one point she joined an expensive video dating service.

With that, Linda entered a growing, rough-and-tumble world of well-marketed businesses and classes on flirtation, of syndicated advice columnists and singles events. The number of social introduction services in her home town, Chicago, tripled in the fifteen years between 1978 and 1993, and the number of personal ads in the free newspaper tripled between 1990 and 1993. One very exclusive matchmaking service was charging $7,000 for a two-year contract in 1993. It's a pressurized world built on traditional ideas (Linda was told by one service that she was demographically undesirable), hit-and-miss results (between 5 and 20 percent of dating-service clients achieve marriage through the service), and methods that have a lot to do with primacy and very little to do with intimacy.

Two years after Linda and her friends launched their marriage campaigns, two of the women were married and two weren't. Linda isn't sure why. "The two that have succeeded at this point have done nothing more than what the other two of us have done," she says. In search of an answer, she sat down with the management of the video dating service, looking for something to change in her personal videotape. Hearing this I cringe, thinking of all the women I have known—friends and teenagers and students—who have reviewed themselves in the mirror, unhappily looking for something to improve. It's the first step backward into a false self, I think, the first step into that awful, unproductive state of constant self-revision. But Linda is stronger than most women I know; she hasn't fallen into the trap of thinking that if something needs fixing, it must be her.

"What do *you* think the problem is?" she asks me point-blank.

"I think it's the process," I tell her.

I'm actually quoting Robert Weiss, the researcher who gave us the notion of two kinds of loneliness. Although Weiss had long contemplated the pain of loneliness, he wrote that launching "a campaign of search for an attachment figure" was a questionable approach to resolving loneliness. Singles groups, personal ads, and other efforts to "meet someone" will lead to meetings and dates, but the "relationships are thinly based and fragile," and the searcher is likely to experience a sense of repetitive loss. The campaign is probably going to be unsuccessful, Weiss concluded, and it may well be damaging to the self-esteem.

The underlying reason for the failure seems to be the vast gap between the nature of the *goal* and the nature of the *process*. The goal—intimacy—is about the whole person: her context, her work, her friends, her family, the life she has constructed, her interests, the way she listens, the way she shares, how much she has to offer, and how much she wants to take. The process—services such as video dating and personal ads—removes her from her context and draws attention only to what she has to show—her face, her figure, her ability to say something pithy in two minutes on tape or forty-five minutes over coffee. The goal is mostly about invisible things such as values and character; the process is about surface things such as sex appeal and verbal skill, visible things that form, as Weiss said, a fragile basis for a relationship. To put it more concretely, you couldn't intentionally make a goal and a process much farther apart, unless you trained someone to be a pastry chef by teaching her to drive trucks.

It's not fair to say that the process is inherently painful. But if the stories that Felicia Collinet and Teresa Sanchez tell are any indication, believing that the process will lead to an intimate connection—a connection marked by closeness, commitment, and symmetry—is certainly a setup for frequent disappointments and rejections that have nothing to do with who the whole woman is. "It was the worst date of my life," says Felicia of an evening spent with a man she met through the personals. "It's just that the men, they don't want a relationship, a friendship or whatever, but they immediately want someone to sleep with. I don't tolerate that."

For some women it is possible to accept the process for what it is—an arbitrary, inefficient process that depends on surface things, a process that can lead to meetings, maybe to dating, maybe to a romantic relationship, but rarely to intimate marriage. Marguerite Ramanis, the woman who once took herself to her own prom, takes that approach: when she still worked in the electronics industry, she kept her pitch letter on her office computer and sent it whenever she saw an interesting personal ad. She met the respondents at lunch, and she took the whole thing with a large grain of salt. "Some—well, I met one weirdo who was truly a nerd in the true sense of the word," she remembers. "But otherwise they were just nice people who saw this as a vehicle to meet other nice people, and you could tell on one date whether things were going to click or not," she says, apparently without despair.

At thirty-seven she is even more relaxed than ever. "I think the term *searching* is what I object to. I am not searching right now," she says. "I have at times thought to myself, 'Gee, I should spend more time and effort looking for a mate,' only because as good little M.B.A.s, you have a plan and you work a plan and then you get to your ultimate goal, whatever it is." At this moment, Marguerite and I are sitting on a bench in her commercial horse barn, the place where her goal-oriented M.B.A. training has led her. She has invested her savings, changed her lifestyle, put her house up for sale, and planned her cash flow, carefully, precisely, within specific parameters. "You tend to be very goal oriented and project oriented," she continues. "But I don't think human relationships lend themselves to such structure."

Maureen Cabot agrees wholeheartedly—and applies her usual brand of wit to the issue. She recalls standing at singles dances forty years ago watching the young men watch her. That's when her best friend leaned over and noted that the whole scene was remarkably like a slave market. And she was right, Maureen explains: "They did everything but look at your teeth."

The fact is, few people really like the process. At the billboard party, even the pleasant-looking fiftyish woman who finally admits that she is Emily's mother doesn't like it. "I was embarrassed when I found out," she says as we sit in the dark bar, watching people literally bump into each other. "I thought they must be terribly desperate to do such a thing [put up billboards]. But then I realized things have changed. They're not like when I got married," she says.

She is more right than she knows. These women hunting for husbands in this darkened bar have far more on their plates than Emily's mother probably had: they are looking for more (more intimacy) and for less (less economic support) than she probably looked for—and they are hampered by the added confusion of accessible sex.

❦

"You're gonna talk about sex, aren'tcha?" the cab driver asks. He's in his sixties, a hard-working man whose marriage of thirty years ended some time ago. He had affairs, and his wife objected, but they're still friends. As an astute observer of human behavior, he announces as I get into the cab that it's clear that I've never been married ("I knew it," he says, slapping the dashboard in victory when his theory is confirmed; "I knew it because you look so *happy*"). Then he tells me that sex is what sells books and movies. "No one's gonna read a book that doesn't have sex in it," he warns.

"Many of these women have never had sex," I point out.

As a man of the world, he can't believe this and tells me I must be wrong.

"Of course, many of them have," I add.

"See there? You put that in there," he advises me.

To "put that in there" isn't that easy to do. Because the thirty women in this book came of age at various times between 1937 and 1983, their experience of sex, sexual mores, and the search for intimacy varies widely. Yet many have at some time or other questioned whether sex and intimacy are the same thing; and most have wondered how their search for emotional intimacy has affected or been affected by their sexual lives. If there is a theme that periodically resurfaces throughout the age groups, it's that sex is confusing—and far less important than the culture makes it out to be.

Their experience of sex truly reflects their ages. When women who now are in their sixties and seventies came of age in the 1940s and 1950s, the notion of marriage as the place for sex and economic security still governed; sex and intimacy were regarded as inextricable, and both belonged to marriage. These are women who grew up when my mother did, my mother who once explained why it was inappropriate for a married woman to have lunch with a non-related man. Such a meeting was too intimate, she said; and I realized later that in our small town in 1963 such a meeting was tantamount to public foreplay. In such a setting, at such a time, an ever-single woman wouldn't have had much room for exploration or even friendship with a man.

Kate O'Connor, who returned to her own small home town in the early 1950s, has thought a lot about these issues. As a young woman, she dated a man who never married. Today she believes he was gay, and she has asked herself whether she has a sexual interest in women. But she has thrown that idea out. "I am asexual, I guess you would say. I don't think I have a strong sexual drive," she says. "I'm quite sure I don't." Without exploration, without experience, residing in a small town, living as a devout Catholic, it would be hard to know otherwise. But it's clear that she has emotional intimacy with her family and friends, and it's clear that she is not uncomfortable with the notion of sex. Kate brought the subject up—I didn't.

In contrast Janice Patinkin, the woman who once told her family to stop nagging her about marriage, grew up in the 1960s, and her experience reflects her generation, which has had many more sexual partners than any other living generation. "Sex is very natural, healthy, and you should never go without it," Janice says. "I had this guy, a summer relationship, once, and his idea of life was that you have sex, and then you do stuff, and then you have sex, and then you do stuff: life is just full of stuff and then you have sex." Petite, athletic, dressed in jeans and a sweater, she's sitting cross-legged on the carpeted floor of her apartment, laughing. "And I said, 'You're right!'"

Between these two poles of experience lies a range of attitudes, many belying confusion and others, a kind of conscious, nonplussed disengagement.

"Don't miss it," says Susan Ryerson bluntly.

"I *would* like to find out," Victoria Mason says ruefully, "what the fuss is all about." On the other hand, finding out what the fuss is all about isn't enough motivation to look for a relationship at this juncture, while she's working two jobs and supporting two children. "I don't know," she says. "I don't know whether I really do want to date."

Roxanne goes further. By the time she hit high school in the late 1970s, the sexual revolution had firmly separated intimacy from sex and sex from marriage. Pervasive pop messages such as "Love the One You're With" had winnowed their way deep into the culture. But powerful traditional messages also appeared in unchanging wedding and honeymoon rituals, in soft-rock songs and romance novels, and the result was a muddled message that seemed to suggest that sex may or may not have something to do with love, depending on your gender.

She had sex for the first time at sixteen. "I particularly would tell teens in a minute, 'Don't do it,'" she says. "Because I just find that sex complicates things, and you can't figure it out. It takes you a long time, the younger you are, to figure out the difference between sex and love." Her first sexual experience was loving, she says, but then the confusion began. "I didn't know that not all men engage in sex because they love you. They engage in sex because [of] what it is. And so I have to start trying to mature and figure out—if I'm going to engage in this type of behavior, I have to understand that not everybody does it for love. Do I do it for love?" she asks frankly, looking back over the last couple of years. "Do I fall into this thing of thinking . . . your sexuality is just part of human nature? It gets complicated."

Part of the complication, she says, is that the quality of sex becomes too important too early in the relationship. "Had I never, ever experienced that . . . I'd have no idea of good from bad," she explains. "So once I made a connection at this age, I think the sexual thing would not have been a determining factor . . . I wouldn't know an orgasm from a cloud in the sky. But I do know. So it's harder, because this guy might be wonderful, but the sex might be horrible."

These feelings about and reactions to sex are very different from the popular images of single women, images that suggest that the hot pursuit of or cold lack of sex is what differentiates them from married women. "The images move from one end of the spectrum of this swinging single chicky who's got sex going on for days to this dowdy, downtrodden individual who couldn't buy a date on a Thursday night," observes Victoria angrily. "There's no middle ground." More pointedly, popular images of single women nearly always speculate on their sexual experience, and this preoccupation with the sexual experience of single women can be limiting, even damaging.

Typical of this preoccupation is Sherwood Anderson's 1919 story "Adventure," in which aging, lonely, ever-single Alice Hindman suddenly bursts from her mother's house and runs down the streets of Winesburg, Ohio, naked; she is sensuality unbound until she runs into an old man, realizes what she has done, runs back to her room, and bars the door with furniture, as if she cannot trust herself to contain her desire. In more recent years, seedier versions of this story have occurred regularly in Hollywood movies such as *Looking for Mr. Goodbar* (1977), *Single White Female* (1992), and *Basic Instinct* (1992).

For a real-life version, look to Congress, where the Republican effort to discredit Anita Hill, an ever-single lawyer who accused then–Supreme Court nominee Clarence Thomas of sexual harassment in 1991, indulged in the same preoccupation. In an attempt to undermine her testimony before the Senate Judiciary Committee, Hill's opponents proposed that she suffered from a rare psychological condition called erotomania, which caused her to fantasize that Thomas had been courting her. Alternately, they implied, she'd solicited Thomas, failed, and was now getting her revenge. Whatever the real story between Hill and Thomas, these two particular theories were clearly based on a readiness to believe that ever-single women are desperate and sex-starved; it's unlikely that the word *erotomania* would have come up if Anita Hill had been married. In the end the Republicans abandoned the erotomania theory, and the psychiatrist who served as their source admitted that there was no evidence that Hill suffered such a debilitating condition.

Another part of this sexual mythology is the notion that ever-single women regularly prey upon other people's marriages, the way Alex Forrest preys upon Dan Gallagher's marriage, the way Eve of *All About Eve* encroaches upon her producer's marriage, the way Emma of *The Turning Point* encroaches upon an admirer's marriage. Not surprisingly, sexual misconduct was one of the first issues the audience raised with a panel of ever-single women on a 1995 segment of *The Phil Donahue Show*. But in fact, only four of the women I met had ever had affairs with married men—among them Allie, who conducted one affair for thirteen years, and Gretchen, who conducted an affair for nearly twenty. Most of the women say that such affairs are counter-productive; while affairs may be sexual, these women note, they are not truly intimate. And they're probably right: affairs with attached men are not committed, and they often lack symmetry.

Christi Wagner's opinion is typical. She says that one of her most painful times occurred years ago when she realized that her dalliance with an attached man was leading toward an affair. "I didn't have an affair with him—no, because he was in another relationship and . . . with me if it's not total, I have to stop it somehow. And the thing wasn't total," she says. "But I was in agony. It was absolute pain and agony."

The final, most enduring part of the sexual myth is the dowdy, downtrodden image that Vicki so dislikes, the image of ever-single women as prudes, as passionless women whose desires are blocked, whose feelings have turned to sawdust. These are the Miss Gulches, the finger-thin, frigid types, the women unable to give sexual love or receive it.

If there is a one-woman answer to this image, she's probably Lindsay Cordell, the woman who brought her father to tears when she told him that she planned to go to college. When Lindsay finally came to terms with her background and identity, she chose to remain in the Church of Jesus Christ of Latter Day Saints and she chose to remain celibate before marriage. But Lindsay is not a rigid, sanctimonious, sexless Miss Gulch. In fact, she is energetic, sensual, attracted, and disciplined. And she has a great sense of humor about her situation.

For instance, she tells me, when she recently started planning a vacation in the Virgin Islands, one friend asked her if he should pay her alms—*was this some kind of pilgrimage for her or what?* Repeating this comment, she laughs with such delight that her blues eyes nearly tear up. Then there's the date who once announced that her virginity was a sin in itself. "This is like having a Corvette in the garage and never driving it!" he told her. "He was hilarious," she says now, "and he made it his personal quest to try and break me of this habit. And we're still friends. We just bike. His friends told me that they loved having me as his girlfriend because he rode a lot harder." She flashes a mischievous smile and adds, "I guess he had a lot more stamina."

But then she turns serious. "It *is* odd. I think it's incredibly odd," she says. "I don't think it's natural."

"You *don't?*"

"No. I think we're meant to be sexual creatures. I think this is incredibly odd. Especially for a thirty-year-old woman. I feel things now that I never felt when I was twenty, twenty-two, you know. It gets stronger and stronger, those physical passions."

She resists those physical feelings because she believes that there is much more than physical release at stake. It has something to do with securing a sense of self—and holding on to it. "I'm a sexual creature who lives an asexual life . . . in a sexually soaked culture. I think the hardest part for me is . . . as women, we're very sexual creatures. We're looked at sexually. So, to establish an identity and a self-esteem that is based separate from being a sexual identity has been very difficult."

But she has achieved it, and she believes that this achievement is actually a step toward intimacy. Not only has she found an identity all her own, but she has kept herself relatively unencumbered by fear and pain. "It's also very liberating," she says. "Because I'm intact. I've never had to piece myself together, except for my heart, and so I give that pretty freely." When she achieves the intimate relationship she wants, she'll share her sexual self. "I'll just give it to one person and hopefully they'll take care of that," she says. "Otherwise, I'll take care of it."

Such clarity, I think, listening to her as she sits in the school cafeteria with the sound of Muzak love songs in the background. At thirty, Lindsay has an understanding of herself, of marriage, of sex, of intimacy that goes well beyond anything I had at her age. The fact is, at her age I was miserable. But it wasn't really about sex. Or intimacy. It was about another thing altogether.

❦

If you had asked me what I was missing when I was thirty, I would have stumbled around verbally for a couple of minutes, fighting back the heat of tears rising behind my eyes. Then I'd have said something vague and incomprehensible about a primary relationship; if I were really on a roll I might have thrown in my birthday or the fact that there were no family pictures on my desk at work. I might have said something about vacations, home movies, aging, and those first few moments when I'd arrive home from a business trip and my dog was still in the kennel. If I were being brutally honest, I might have confessed that what I really missed, what I really wanted, was to be undeniably, irrevocably important to someone else.

I wanted to be primary, and to me, being primary was inextricably bound up in being intimate, and being intimate was inextricably bound up in being married.

Being primary is walking dead center down an aisle in a white dress and having a hundred people watch you do it, I thought; being primary is having a relationship that makes it nearly criminal to miss a birthday. Being primary is having someone ask, *How was your trip?* not four days after you get home, but the moment you arrive, the moment you need to be told, *Things weren't the same without you.* In my thirty-year-old mind, the people who had this were deeply entwined in real, intimate relationships—marriages, not friendships. In my thirty-year-old mind, I was nowhere because I was not primary.

My feelings were not unusual. Many of us hanker after stardom. Some of us dream of being primary as much as we dream of intimacy. That may be why the wedding itself is such a powerful image for women; the dress, the flowers, the music, the day—all exist separate from the marriage, isolated in a dreamlike bubble of magic that may itself live long after the marriage has dissolved. "Ask any woman about her wedding, and no matter how long ago or how ill-fated it was, she will describe it down to the last hors d'oeuvre," Mary Cantwell, who says she is ambivalent about marriage, wrote in the *Chicago Tribune.* "Ask me about my wedding, and I'll tell you how it felt to slide on my garter and zip up my beige silk taffeta and pin a wreath of white roses in my hair. I won't tell you the rest," she wrote, "but I'll tell you that, and when I do I'll glow." The wedding is an eloquent symbol of primacy; it's a public announcement of a woman's importance, her new status, her new placement.

For me the strange, painful sense of being *unimportant* surfaced most often at times when I had no witnesses and felt that I should have them: when I felt my joys and achievements going by nearly unnoticed, certainly uncelebrated. Living alone and working alone as a writer, I lived an unwitnessed life; there were no home movies, no Kodak moments; there were few visits from family and no innocent bystanders who could laugh when I made a stupid mistake or applaud when I got a promotion. Felicia Collinet has had similar feelings. "I felt lonely when a month ago I got this promotion and I called my friend Tom and said, 'Listen, I got this promotion' and he was barely even positive," she tells me in frustration. "I didn't really have anybody to share it with and I would have really liked someone to share that with me."

Yet even at thirty and thirty-five, I knew that being primary didn't mean being loved or even being taken seriously. I'd worked with mostly men during the early years of my working life and I could recall a number of cringing, crazy times when one or another had forgotten an anniversary or a wife's birthday and sarcastically, resentfully rushed around Palo Alto or Phoenix or (in the worst case) the Denver *airport* looking for something appropriate to fulfill what was obviously an obligation (as I remember it, the Denver shopper ended up with an overpriced oil painting, unwrapped and clearly unplanned). At thirty I'd seen my share of perfunctory marriages in which the partners fulfilled their responsibilities but no longer shared themselves. The partners were primary—and very nearly strangers. I knew this and I instinctively recoiled from the underlying emptiness of it, but it would still take me years to accept that primary does not mean intimate.

Primary may not mean intimate, but in most lives, it *does* mean marriage, and that's where I was getting hung up. Marriage—unlike friendship—does provide that function, that fact of structural significance. In fact it's probably this function of marriage that keeps people together in nonintimate marriages: as Weiss has observed, marriage depends less on love than it does on attachment, which is composed (in part) of shared presence and familiarity. Marriage provides each partner with a "valid place" in the world, a social home—irrespective of the extent to which the marriage is emotionally satisfying.

So how do singular women resolve this lack of structural significance?

In some lives the family of origin lends a sense of being important. For a woman who lives with a parent, for a woman who lives with a brother or sister, there's a built-in role that is recognized by everyone around her. "I can't imagine being single without a family," seventy-five-year-old Rosalie Morgan, who lives with her sister and nephew, says bluntly.

In other lives children lend the ever-single woman her primacy. Allie Ackerman is indisputably a primary figure in her children's lives: they count on her; they rebel against her; they perform for her; they expect her call when they're separated from her.

In still other lives it has never been an issue. Women like Caitlin McKuen, Maureen Cabot, and Ellen Adams seem to have internalized the natural significance their families see in them and carried it with them as they traveled the world. Yet, even though she's the kind of woman who would choose to hike the Continental Divide alone, Ellen can sense the emptiness other single women feel: "I guess they must want to feel important to some-one," she observes. "I can see that."

Victoria Mason remembers it. "There was a time in my twenties when I so desperately wanted to be married . . . I don't know why," she says. "I think it was just because I wanted the ring. You know—*get the ring.*"

But the strange, painful truth is that as much as they want to be primary, being primary just isn't enough for some women. "I don't understand women who marry without [intimacy]," says Janice Patinkin rather fiercely. She has dated actively all her life and, although she still wants to marry and have chil-dren, she has turned down several proposals. "I don't respect women that I think that has happened to. I don't understand women who choose to be married for security. . . . Some of these women can't go to a restaurant and have a conversation. What is that? That can't be a marriage. It's scary to look at a couple in a restaurant and think, they're in prison. They don't want to be with each other anymore."

Some women make nonintimate marriages, she guesses, because this is the best that has come along or because they're afraid to be alone. "Why would they do it?" she continues speculating, sure that there must be a deeper answer. "Low self-esteem; they don't think they can get along by themselves, in and of themselves." As sad as she sometimes is, she would rather be alone, Janice says, and she will be until she finds what she calls "friendship intimacy" and "sexual intimacy" in the same relationship.

Not long ago, Linda Schindler had a similar realization. When a match-maker told her that many people marry just to have company, she was baffled. "I don't know why one would do this," she says. "Just for companionship? I wouldn't. I think it would be horrible to be in a [nonintimate] relationship and feel alone. There's nothing worse. I dread that."

For some women the distinction between intimacy and primacy became clear as they cohabited. Of the thirty women, five (most of them baby boomers) have lived with a man. Some did it for convenience; others say that they were "trying on" the relationship. Most say that whatever they found in their live-in relationships, it wasn't enough—often it wasn't intimate enough—to stick with it. None of these women sees cohabitation as a form of marriage; and none sees company or convenience or those Kodak moments that I so hungered for as good reasons to have a live-in partner.

Their feelings seem to echo the findings of researcher Koray Tanfer, who defines cohabitation as a form of courtship, not a form of marriage. Cohabitation is a testing ground and not a very good one: historically couples that cohabit before marriage have high rates of divorce. These results are not surprising to those who think about intimacy the way these women do: heterosexual cohabitation is often characterized by asymmetry and a lack of commitment, basic structural weaknesses in any intimate relationship.

🦅

Sorting this out—separating the idea of being primary from the idea of being intimate—is difficult, but women do do it. In the process the wedding image seems to slip from its pedestal. Roxanne no longer dreams of weddings but of relationships: her ideal is a kind of Katharine Hepburn–Spencer Tracy relationship rooted in friendship. "That's what I miss," she says. "I think I would miss that more than just having a romantic relationship." As time passes there's no concrete image to replace the wedding, notes Linda: "As an older woman you don't know how to think about getting married. So it's sort of lost its romanticism."

Meanwhile, in the course of being single, some women seem to stumble on a notion that psychologist Rae Andre once noted—the notion that in order to deal with solitude, people must become primary in their own lives and they must generate their own feedback. Especially for a woman steeped in the lessons of adolescent femininity and female self-sacrifice, this may seem an impossibly intangible approach to life. But Mary Stendahl, the New England schoolteacher, has come to it in fairly concrete ways. "You do get feedback from yourself," she observes, "if something satisfies you. Like—I don't plant shrubs for anybody but myself," she says, looking out through her screened-in porch toward her back yard. "I don't garden for anyone but myself."

"But that's hard to count on, isn't it?" I ask her. "What happens if you're down one day?"

"I go running," she says, smiling.

While Andre seems to believe that achieving this skill is an end in itself, most of the women I met do not depend totally on their own feedback; they find roles that recognize and reward the self they have solidified. They find ways to play a unique role in others' lives, which may be the next best thing to being primary.

It's a kind of niche marketing: the ever-single woman offers a special gift that no one else can offer in quite the same way. This approach is particularly successful in accepting, adaptive families. "*Everyone* should have a maiden aunt," declares Maureen Cabot from the perspective of forty years. "I was the one who gave them their first Beatles records," she says proudly, and adds that in this case the feedback from certain quarters was not exactly appreciative. "My brother said, 'What are you going to do next, give 'em bongo drums?'" In a quieter vein Pat McDonald shows me a book of poetry that a nephew has written, a handwritten piece carefully illustrated, and I suspect that her appreciation—well schooled, well expressed, thoroughly sincere—was unlike any other he received. Teresa Sanchez draws pleasure and feedback from her position as family role model: as the first college-educated person in her Cuban-born family, she patiently advises her nieces and nephews. This year she prepped her college-bound nephew on where to sit, what kinds of questions to ask, and when to volunteer in class. "So he has a sense of—he's more sure of himself because it's not a big secret—you behave in a certain way," she says.

For intimacy singular women turn to friends and family. Most have come to define intimacy as something between any two people equally and honestly engaged, and some worry that intimate friendship is not possible with a man. "It's like your real friendships are [with] women," says Allie rather unhappily. "They're the ones that understand you and love you and can talk. I mean, who could sit with a man like this and talk for this long?" Fifteen years younger and still dating actively, Janice agrees: "I have a feeling you don't get that total friendship intimacy with a man. I have it with some men, but not total; the men I can have emotional friendship intimacy with—maybe I don't think what they say back to me all the time helps much. But I can find that with a woman."

Nonetheless, when they talk of marriage, they use the language of friendship. "I really want an intimate relationship," says Felicia. "I really want a good friend."

"I wanted somebody to have fun with," Maureen says, looking back, perhaps, to those slave-market singles dances. "I mean, I think any normal male and female can find sexual attraction. That just kind of comes naturally. But it's the other things. The longer I didn't marry, the more I saw how much the *other* things counted."

"I would just like somebody to talk to," says Victoria. "Somebody who would be willing to give me what I ask for without me having to give anything back sometimes, you know . . . somebody who will sit there and listen to me whine, 'Oh, the world is treating me so bad today.'" Then she gives me her classic deadpan expression and adds: "You know, I do this whine thing *so well!*"

Despite the concerns, despite the deadpan, many still hope for emotional intimacy, sexual intimacy, and primacy all wrapped up together into one relationship, a marriage. "There's always hope," says Victoria frankly. But this hope does not eclipse the intimacies she has already. "I would miss it," she says, imagining living her whole life without intimate marriage. "I would miss it, but not having it wouldn't diminish who I am."

In Janice's softer voice, the language is less adamant, but the feelings are clear and strong. "When I can give the love I have inside me to somebody, whether it's my nephews, who are two and four, whether it's my girlfriends . . ." she says, her hands hanging expressively in the air, "if I can get it out in some ways, then I'm not lonely." She pauses, perhaps reviewing the loving relationships she has created. "I feel like I've been real lucky in life," she says decisively, "except that I've never found a marriage relationship."

CHAPTER NINE

Feelings and Choices

Carrie Cunningham has a few things to say about the unmarried life. Also supportive families, good books, the reason she disliked Smith College, the importance of friends, the joy of having cats, and the glorious places she's traveled. Oh yeah, and there's that silly episode when she lived with "a fellow" and eventually made friends with one of his many extracurricular lovers. And did she mention that she doesn't mind being unmarried?

"I like it," she says over coffee in one of those cafés where the coffee is expensive and the chocolate is exorbitant. Approaching sixty, Carrie wants to make sure that I know she doesn't hate men. "I like them as a whole," she says. "I just got a lemon."

But Carrie doesn't dwell on the lemon. She takes off on dating services and singles dances, problem kids, the myths that go with aging— laughing as she goes, pausing only to see if I've caught her drift.

In the late October darkness she stops a moment before she leaves my car. "I'm sorry if I've thrown off your sample," she says with sincerity. "But the truth is, I'm happy."

The truth is, Carrie Cunningham didn't throw the sample off at all. She loves her friends, her home, her freedom. She enjoyed a close family and still misses the brother who died a year ago. Like most of the women I met with, she is healthy, active, and interested in the world; she is confident, and the regrets she expresses are minor (*Okay, okay,* she laughs over coffee, *maybe I should have dumped the man sooner or skipped living with him altogether*).

In fact Carrie is unusual in only a couple of things: she passed through her thirties with barely a ruffle, and she located her sense of joy and everyday confidence not in the content of her work as a travel agent but in the people she worked with. The other things—her satisfaction, her equanimity at not having children, her love of books, her connection with friends, her sense of humor, her wide-ranging travel, her feelings—all fit fairly well with the other twenty-nine women I met with.

In short, the feelings of these thirty women are not what people expect. People expect great expanses of loneliness, they expect depression; people expect regrets, self-recrimination, maybe even a little embarrassment, certainly a psychosomatic health problem here or there. These expectations certainly reflect the cultural mirror and they echo and amplify the experience of women in the throes of the scriptlessness and fear that haunt their late twenties and early thirties. More surprisingly, these expectations find their way into the presumably objective psychological community, which has had a tough time conceding that most ever-single women feel pretty good: in the 1970s one sociologist concluded, "On the whole the women interviewed *did not* appear *un*happy" (emphasis mine). You can virtually hear her digging in her intellectual heels.

It's no wonder that singular women like Carrie come to believe that they are breaking some kind of immutable law, a law that says: *if she is alone, she must be lonely;* or, *if she is unconnected in the conventional way, she must be unsupported and maybe even depressed;* or, *if she feels good in her single life, it must be because she chose to be single.* But none of these immutable laws holds much truth in the formal research or in this informal group that I have found.

In truth, those who listen without prejudice learn that once singular women have found their places among family and friends, once they have created their homes and their lives, they aren't particularly lonely; they are generally satisfied and healthy; and their happiness does not have much to do with choice, with choosing to be single.

The primary feeling women expect to have when they stare down a stretch of time without a potential partner is emotional loneliness. The specter of this hole-in-the-heart, empty-souled feeling is downright scary, especially in a society that offers little consolation and little community to its single members.

Sadly, part of what we fear is actually shame. As Robert Weiss has observed, lonely people are disparaged; loneliness is seen as a shameful state that the victims have brought upon themselves. They've done something—there must be some reason that they've been rejected.

"Ooh! Stay away; it might be catchy!" jokes thirty-five-year-old Nan Hansen in her best eight-year-old, "she's-got-cooties" voice. Nan is a tall, quiet woman who has worked intently in the last few years to get to know herself—so her mildly ironic manner can catch you by surprise. She pauses, turns serious, and offers her own theory about why people avoid talking about loneliness. "Some people don't want to be reminded of *their* loneliness," she tells me. "That's why they kind of start to back away from me when *I* start to talk about it."

So what is this thing we're all avoiding? Some cognitive psychologists such as Rae Andre say that loneliness doesn't exist. Andre believes it's a fog covering other feelings like anger and disappointment. Other researchers, however, believe that loneliness is a distinct emotional state; while it's associated with other experiences such as depression and low self-esteem, it has its own characteristics. In depression, for instance, a woman will feel listless and avoidant; her primary response to sadness is to succumb to it. But when she's lonely, she's likely to feel anxious and needy; her primary response to loneliness is to resolve it—to find a new relationship or repair a damaged one.

Probably one of the best portraits of a lonely woman appears in *Summertime* (1955). In the movie, a self-deprecating, middle-aged, ever-single secretary named Jane Hudson travels alone to Italy in search of something that she herself can't name, but we suspect it's romance or some kind of validation. Unfortunately, Jane's first night in Italy is not promising. Everyone else at her *pensione* has plans, even the hotel matron, and Jane finds herself alone on a terrace, suffering red-faced embarrassment as someone takes pity on her and invites her along. Jane turns the last-minute invitation down—apparently out of pride—and then stands alone on the veranda, talking first to a cat, then looking out over Venice.

Then she breaks out; she takes a walk and ends up at a piazza full of couples, where she suddenly appears—and feels—more extraneous and more needy than ever. Beset by self-consciousness, restlessness, and loneliness, Jane soon figures out how to reconfigure her table setting so that it looks as if she's not really alone, not really lonely, but merely waiting for her partner to meet her. The scene is enough to plunge even the most self-sufficient woman into total empathy and despair; it has all the earmarks of what we believe about loneliness and what we feel when we're lonely—and it's all shot in living color by the director who gave us those expansive, desolate desert scenes in *Lawrence of Arabia.*

As resonant as Jane Hudson's story is, it also inadvertently propagates some myths. For instance, loneliness is not something that hunts down and hounds single women in particular. In one of Weiss's early studies, the unmarried men were as lonely as unmarried women; the only difference was that the women often believed that the men had more freedom to combat their loneliness. More pointedly, loneliness affects the married as well as the unmarried: in 1973 one expert estimated that only 1 or 2 percent of the people he had studied reported that they had never been lonely. In fact, studies have long held that being alone and being lonely are not connected in quite the way those of us looking into the cultural mirror would expect. Studies of older adults conducted in the 1950s and 1960s showed that while ever-single men and women were more socially isolated than married men and women, they were not lonelier than married men and women. In other words, the state of so-called social isolation may not determine "loneliness" or even unhappiness—despite what we see in movies such as *Summertime.*

So if being alone isn't what causes loneliness, what does?

There are a number of surprising theories. For instance, in 1986 British researchers Judith Lobdell and Daniel Perlman actually tested the idea that loneliness is transmitted generationally. Studying 130 undergraduate ever-single women who lived at home with their parents, Lobdell and Perlman found that the way the daughters perceived their parents' emotional status was a reliable predictor of their own emotional status. For instance, daughters who believed that their parents were dissatisfied with their marriages tended to be lonelier than daughters who saw their parents' marriages as happy ones. Overall, the loneliness scores of parents (particularly mothers) and their daughters were well matched, which led the researchers to suggest a couple of possible reasons: perhaps something in the family culture or child-rearing

practices prevented the generational transmission of involvement and closeness. Alternately, perhaps women who suffer loneliness reconstruct their
childhoods and cast them in a negative and lonely mold.

Another key that shows up in recent research is the notion that we set
our own standards for loneliness. In an extensive study of older unmarried
adults, Pat Keith found that people who reported the most loneliness were
not necessarily the people who were the most isolated, but the people who
were dissatisfied with the level of social contact in their lives. Researcher
Susan Rice has come up with similar findings.

Although this research seems to leave us with more questions than answers, it does go some distance in explaining why what we intuitively expect
ever-single women to say about their feelings just isn't what they actually say.

Among the women I talked with, two—Carrie Cunningham and Kate
O'Connor—say that they have never been lonely.

"I can't remember ever being lonely," says Carrie.

"That's something that—I don't have the vaguest idea of what that's
about," Kate says, and since her memories of her small-town childhood, of
her friendship with Clarissa, of her feelings at her sister's wedding are so vivid,
you have to believe her. "I'm not lonely," she says, "and never have been."

The other twenty-eight women say that they have felt lonely, but few see
loneliness as a major factor in their lives. Most admit to some restlessness and
anxiety, the earmarks of social loneliness, but very few dwell on emotional
loneliness, which is caused by a lack of intimacy.

Reflective, relentlessly honest Nan Hansen may be an exception. Walking down the street, seeing couples walking hand in hand, calling friends and
getting answering machines, she has a heightened awareness of her own loneliness, especially during the holidays. "Sometimes I let my mind half-believe
that if I were married or in some deeply committed relationship . . . that there
would never be this loneliness," she says. Other times, she believes loneliness
is part of the human condition. And other times, she is confounded by its invisible nature. "Even with my single friends, I think they don't feel it the way
I do—because they haven't said anything to me. I can fall into that, unless I
check it out." The only unmarried daughter in her distant family, a bright,
emotionally courageous woman who is just coming to terms with wanting to
be married, Nan does see loneliness as a major factor in her life.

In contrast, in most of the other women the talk of loneliness, even the harder emotional form, is framed situationally, as if loneliness occurs inter-mittently—when times are tough, when emotional and social resources are momentarily scarce. Louise Long, now in her seventies, remembers the first trip she took after her sister got married some forty years ago. She walked into an empty hotel room in New York City at 9:00 P.M. and suddenly she realized just how alone she was. "I closed the door behind me, and this was not the first time I'd been alone, but I thought, 'If I die tonight, there's nobody that would know or care.'" It was a startling and painful moment.

"Maybe the times I feel lonely [are] when I've had a fight with my daugh-ter," says Karen King, whose second adopted daughter, Faith, is now eight years old. "There're some times when you think, did I handle that situation right? Who can I call upon to say to me, 'You should have done this or you shouldn't do that'?" Other times Karen feels the lack of companionship. "And then there are times when maybe there is something that I think about doing and I wish there was someone to do it with, other than a child, other than a girlfriend." She stumbles a bit and then clarifies her point: "But loneli-ness is not something that has ever set in on me or overcome me for any pe-riod of time," she says. "I have never been depressed because I am alone . . . and I think maybe part of this is I told myself very very early that you only be-come a victim if you make yourself a victim."

If researchers such as Nancy L. Peterson and Susan Rice hadn't already concluded that loneliness is not a big issue among ever-single women, I might have thought that what I was running into was shame—I might have thought that women were not reporting loneliness because they were ashamed of it. But given the expert research that others have done, I have to believe that what I was hearing is real: by the time these women had traversed and con-quered that scriptless decade, loneliness had become merely a visitor, difficult and frustrating, but mercifully occasional.

Much more commonly, women talk about liking solitude, about appreci-ating—even craving—psychological space. "I've always wanted to live alone," says Christi Wagner, whose condo overlooks a trendy neighbor-hood where she can wander among Mexican bakeries, small florists, and ex-otic delicatessens. "I wanted to have the space around me to see things clearly and I felt that—I still feel that—there are a lot of times . . . with a lot of peo-ple [when] I can't see clearly because there's so much yakking going on and blowing of smoke." This need for space has been with her since childhood:

"That's something I've known for a long time, even when I was a kid. I'd love it when my family left the house. I felt, now the air is clear; now I can think and see clearly."

Even so, when Christi feels overwhelmed at a party and wants to take off and be alone, to regain that psychological space, she sometimes worries that this need for solitude isn't quite right. She worries about it—and then she leaves the party anyway. "I cried last night," she tells me. "I was in my bed crying. What was I crying about? And I said, yes, you're crying because you left the party and you're worried about yourself. You're worried that you left something . . . other people like. But then I thought, wait a minute, why are you assuming what you did was bad? Why don't you just take good care of yourself?"

Susan Ryerson, with her library-like house and her tennis, is more settled in her feelings. "I like being by myself," she says. "I can occupy myself even when I'm doing nothing." She is unapologetic about this, but she is realistic too. "I know that loneliness at times is the price you pay for the good times of being alone. So I can accept that, and I can even welcome the lonely times, because it's a balance."

Ellen Adams, the environmentalist, resolutely seeks solitude. Being home alone in her place by Puget Sound just isn't enough sometimes. "I can imagine people saying, 'Why do you need to be alone [since] you live alone?'" she conjectures. "But it's not the same. You live in a house, the phone rings . . . you're in a neighborhood, you go to the post office, people see you, that sort of thing. It's not the same thing as being out in the woods."

So every year on her birthday, Ellen declares her solitude and takes off for a hike along one of the coastal trails or inland to an old-growth forest with her dog, Hershey, padding alongside her. It's a good time to reflect on her life, she says. Not that she always does—"But I always give myself the option," she says. She doesn't need to crowd her mind with issues and decisions. The hiking itself, the solitude itself, has value. She doesn't need to crowd her agenda—especially on her birthday, of all days.

If one feeling stands out among these women, it's a deep appreciation of personal freedom. They respect it; they revel in it. Even those who are in the midst of struggling with their feelings are cautious about giving up their freedom. "If I could meet someone that I was compatible with but would not attempt to hold me down—if there is such an animal—then I think I would be open to marriage," Juillissa Rivera says. "But I would never settle for anybody, regardless of the void."

Most singular women talk about the freedom that comes with living alone, eating odd things at odd times, watching late, late movies, coming and going without excuse. But for many, freedom is expressed in travel; travel becomes a metaphor for a life lived without the usual social constraints and obligations, for a life that goes where it wants to go, unencumbered.

The metaphor has wonderful roots in the nineteenth century, when unmarried women who felt constrained by the roles laid out for them broke out on their own; unable to be themselves in their own cultures, they became themselves on the road, temporarily transplanted among strangers. This was the experience of the biologist Mary Kingsley, the Victorian painter Marianne North, the explorer Isabella Bird, who travelled the American Rockies before her marriage at age fifty. It was also the experience of the writer and philosopher Alice Koller, who planted herself on Nantucket one winter in the early 1960s in an effort to find herself through solitude.

In part, the freedom these ever-single travelers find is the freedom of anonymity, the freedom from the judgment that the conventional world seems so bent on pressing upon the unconventional woman. "There is this great—like when I went to South America—I had this great liberated feeling that nobody here gives a damn what you're doing," observes Carrie. "They're not even looking at you. And, in fact, if the most entertaining thing they can find to do is sit and wonder about you . . . then you have to feel sorry for them!"

Embracing this freedom, she made a discovery. "I found I could go out to dinner. It's more fun to go out with somebody else, and my rule of thumb would be . . . to say to myself, are you not going out because you're too tired and you want to take a hot bath and you're not hungry? Or are you not going out because you're by yourself? And I would be very honest and say, well, I'm not really going because I don't have anybody to go with—*then I'd go.*"

Strangely, this anonymity brings an implicit self-declaration. For Juillissa, traveling in Spain alone, the declaration was entirely accidental. Wandering far off the beaten path, Juillissa went looking for the small towns in the south where the walls are whitewashed, the streets are narrower than bike paths, and the bus comes through a few times a week. She'd wanted to travel with someone. "I remember at one point, I turned to speak to someone as if I were with somebody," she recalls, "and I realized how much I wanted to travel with someone." But she pressed on alone, and in a small bus station she showed a picture to a widow and her daughter and asked in Spanish where she could find a town like the one in the photo. "Which one are you looking for?" the widow asked.

"Any one of them," Juillissa replied.

"Where are you from?"

"The United States."

"Where are your husband and children?"

"I don't have any."

"Oh!" cried the widow, "what a ridiculous thing!"

Somewhat daunted, Juillissa found a picturesque town and a private house to stay in. There, the women of the house were captivated by her solitary presence and they asked over and over what it was like to be unmarried. Juillissa told them that she worked and traveled and lived by herself. But the eighty-six-year-old grandmother, who had kept house, raised children, and carried tobacco on her back for much of her life, could not grasp the notion. "You don't clean up after anybody and you don't cook for anybody?"

"No, I cook for myself."

"I think I'd like that," the grandmother announced.

She took Juillissa to town, introducing her as her American niece, and as they left each shop, Juillissa could hear the shopkeepers speculate on who she was, where she was from, and how it could be that she didn't have a husband. It was clear that her freedom spoke to them, and through them, it quietly spoke to her.

Christi has tried to incorporate these kinds of travel experiences into her everyday life. "I was able to take . . . my solitary aloneness and live in the world and have the world open up, just crack open," she says of an extended trip to Greece. "I always suspected even when I was a kid that it was possible to live alone—even though society frowned on it and labels people who do it—I always thought even as a child that it was possible to embrace the world through a solitary lifestyle. I saw it in Greece, and it was peaceful."

For Christi freedom means the capacity to attach and detach, to strike a balance between being alone and being available. "Where do I locate my life?" she ponders in answer to one of my questions. At first she is stumped. She acknowledges that most women locate themselves in their roles as mother and wife. But what does she do? Doesn't she worry that she'll detach and fly off, so free that the social anchors that typically ground other people won't hold her? Not really, she says, nearly twenty years after her crisis at the bottom of the Grand Canyon. "I hope I *don't* locate my life," she decides. "Because to locate is to limit. So I hope always to remain open to dislocation."

In the stories they tell, in the feelings they express, the freedom to be oneself is the greatest and most treasured freedom of all, and that may be, as one researcher has pointed out, the single most salient characteristic of singular people. They have, M. Adams wrote in 1976, "a territorial integrity of the spirit."

I was surprised by the intensity of these stories. When I first started listening to these travel tales, I suspected that travel was a kind of consolation prize and the declarations of freedom were a well-developed defense strategy. But following these women through Greece and Brazil, through the woods of the Olympic Peninsula and the small towns of Spain, I have come to believe that the stories express something much more essential. I suppose you could call it a territorial integrity of the spirit, but there is probably a simpler way of saying it. There is in these stories the freedom for each woman to find out— *and celebrate*—who she is.

Simply that.

In the course of their lives, in adjusting to their marital status or handling their own personal histories, a few women have experienced clinical depression. Both Rachel Jacobs and Jillian Goodman have recovered from short bouts of depression, Rachel in her early thirties, Jillian in the midst of her fortieth-birthday crisis. Allie Ackerman is still struggling as she deals with her adolescent children and with her own retrieved memories of sexual abuse at the hands of her kindergarten teacher. Mary Stendahl has recovered recently. This incidence of depression is lower than the national average for women over the life course.

What does depression feel like? Jillian describes long days of sleep punctuated by short periods of activity. She describes anxiety, aimlessness, and oppressive sadness. Allie describes a sense of being overwhelmed. Mary Stendahl describes sleepless nights and a sense of emptiness. All four women have received treatment at one time or another.

Over the years the research on marital status and psychiatric disturbances such as depression has been contradictory. Typically the findings show that married women experience the fewest incidences of psychiatric disturbance, followed by ever-single women, then formerly married (divorced, separated, and widowed) women. Ever-single women report fewer problems than men in all categories.

But a study of nearly 18,600 adults published in 1992 found that in most categories, the differences between married and ever-single women were small. For instance, among white women, 3.5 percent of married women had been diagnosed with major depressive disorder (MDD), while 4.1 percent of ever-single women had. In contrast, 9 percent of the divorced/separated had been diagnosed with MDD. The minor differences between married and ever-single women shrank when researchers removed the influence of socioeconomic status. In fact, ever-single white women demonstrated a lower rate of anxiety than married women. Ever-single women did show a higher rate of alcohol abuse than their married sisters, white women more than black women. Overall, the researchers concluded that marriage per se was not health enhancing, as many have believed. Rather, the research group pointed out, the loss of a spouse is particularly predictive of poor mental health.

～

Why *don't* we feel worse? I wonder as I finish my last interview in a condo overlooking Lake Michigan. In these last two years, I have met many doubters, men who snicker and suggest that if I just got enough sex, maybe I wouldn't be pushed to thinking about such things; or women who squirm and fidget and tell me they could never talk about being single, as if talking about it condemns them to shriveling loneliness, to cold-hearted feminism, to loss, to grief, to a smaller, less feminine life. Clearly there are those who expect us to feel worse.

Then maybe we were self-selecting? Maybe women who volunteer to talk about their feelings are naturally women who are relatively happy. But that's not true, either: Roxanne Walters volunteered, Allie Ackerman volunteered,

Felicia Collinet and Nan Hansen agreed to talk. If self-selection is involved, it's that women who agreed to talk with me apparently don't subscribe to the superstition that naming one's status automatically condemns oneself to that status for life.

So why don't we feel worse? Of course, it's important to remember that a great many of us have felt pretty bad at other times in our lives. But why haven't these negative feelings lingered through our efforts to redefine family, to find friendship, to make a home? Why didn't they permeate work and prevent intimacy?

Often people tell me that it must be a matter of choice. Ever-single women have chosen not to marry, they say. Ever-single women have gotten what they want and that's why they're happier than divorced women who didn't choose to be single and widowed women who didn't choose to be single. Ever-single women are in their element; they're happy because they have achieved their goals.

There's something to be said for this theory. But the definition of choice is a slippery thing, and the question, have you chosen to be single? is rife with complication. Nonetheless, each of us did try to sort it out. To do it, we used a modified version of sociologist Peter Stein's model of single people.

Stein says that there are four different kinds of single people; each of his four categories expresses the nature and status of the choice to be single. In the model, the first category of single people is called "involuntary-temporary"; these singles have not chosen to be single and they see their single status as temporary. The second group is called "voluntary-temporary"; these singles have consciously or unconsciously delayed marriage for one reason or another and they see their single status as temporary. The third group is "involuntary-stable"; these people have not chosen to be single but they regard their situation as permanent. The last group is "voluntary-stable"; these singles have chosen to be single and they regard their choice as permanent.

"I can be in only one [group]?" asks filmmaker Roxanne Walters in disbelief. "Can I combine?" She is not kidding. In fact, she's expressing the majority viewpoint here. She'd like to combine groups 1 and 4, she says, but then she backtracks. "I don't know," she concludes helplessly.

"You know, in all honesty, I'd make five [categories]," says Lindsay Cordell. "[The fifth category] would be like involuntary-voluntary-undecided. Because it started out—I can definitely say that I am not married by choice. I've chosen not to be. I've had offers. But I didn't expect [it] to be this long. And now I'm undecided as to whether I want to be or not."

As it turns out, every word in the model finds a detractor. One woman grapples with *involuntary* for nearly five minutes. Another tackles choice. Then there's the issue of *permanent:* "How do we know it's permanent?" asks Mary Stendahl with a grin. "I mean, I am not married now, but that's not to say that I would never be married. How do I know? I may still, but it's not like I'm pining away to be married."

"'Voluntary-stable' would mean you've taken a vow of celibacy or something," observes Kate O'Connor, a practicing Catholic whose sister entered the convent as a young woman. "Like you're going to remain in the world but you're going to be celibate. And I never thought of that." She goes on, working through the words: "'Involuntary' makes it sound as if you didn't have any choice and still wished you weren't going to be single. I'm not looking to be married, but I don't think it's impossible. He'd have to be a prince for sure. . . ." she adds, noting, as Maureen Cabot has, that there is so much she'd have to give up in a marriage. "I don't see it [being single] as involuntary, like something I'm stuck in," Kate concludes without really concluding.

A few finally settle on group 2: voluntary-temporary. Caitlin McKuen is one of these. "And how I got voluntary is because I purposely dumped Gary [and] I purposely avoided relationships; and the place I'm at is voluntary because if I wanted to be married right now, I probably could be," she says. But as clear as she is, Caitlin soon muddies the waters by questioning the term *marriage.* "In the future?" she asks herself. "I don't know. Marriage is kind of— I don't know what it means." She soon settles on the same definition of marriage that nearly all the ever-single women I've talked with settle on—the notion of intimate marital friendship. "It's nice to have a friendship, a relationship with somebody." Does she expect to achieve that? Is she a temporary? "I don't know. Maybe."

A couple settle on group 1, involuntary-temporary. "Number one," Felicia says with absolute certainty.

"The first one," says Janice Patinkin, although she admits that her friends would disagree. "If you were to ask somebody those questions about me, they would say I chose it voluntarily, not to be married," she says. "Because they think that I've had so many chances that I have chosen not to be with those

[men]. That's true," she concedes, "but those chances weren't what I felt would have been a good marriage to me . . . so it was involuntary."

Two select group 4, voluntary-stable. "I think the last one would probably be the most honest," Melissa Van Lenten, who was in her late thirties when she left her career in marketing to get a master's in music, says quietly. Now in her seventies, she, too, qualifies her answer. "I think that at most stages if I had found somebody that was really challenging to me . . . I guess I always thought some of them were kind of boring." But it wasn't just boredom, she says. Like Caitlin, Melissa has a strong sense of what she needs and wants out of her life: "I saw myself getting into this situation and I thought, I'm never going to be able to do my thing, my music. I saw that as being stifled and I think that always made me back off." In the end she returns to the description that I've heard from two dozen other women across the generations: "I've often said I didn't meet the right guy at the right time, and I think that is probably it."

An important corollary of this familiar refrain is the idea that getting married isn't what's hard—making a good marriage is what's hard. Like Janice, just about every woman feels that she's had opportunities to make a bad marriage. Always succinct, Maureen Cabot puts it this way: "Almost any woman could marry if she didn't have certain goals of her own in mind as to what she wanted in a husband."

So what does that say about *her* choices? "I would say, if you mean by 'voluntary,' did I at one point in my early life say, 'I'm never going to get married'? No. I always did think, I was raised to think, that the proper life for a woman was married with a family," Maureen says. "But on the other hand, I never stood up and said, 'Oh, I'm getting desperate; I'm getting older.' It was not primary in my mind."

In short, she doesn't believe that life fits into these categories. "I look back and I don't know at which point I decided that I might as well plan the other way. I don't think that you can draw a hard, hard line." In fact, Maureen notes, two of her neighbors in her retirement community just married: he's seventy-eight and she's ninety-eight. (When I repeat this story to Lillian and Walter, the retired farmers, Walter shakes his head gravely. "I'd give up by *that* time!" he says at seventy-two. Sitting next to him, Lillian agrees.)

Not surprisingly, Karen King is probably the most articulate on the subject of choice; she analyzes the issue the way she probably analyzes her students' English papers: clearly, simply, picking it apart piece by piece. She soon casts this verbal nightmare we've developed in conceptual terms.

"There are things where choices are clear-cut," she explains. "Either you go to college or you don't. That's clear-cut. You cook dinner or you don't. That's pretty clear-cut. But when it comes to marriage, there are all sorts of variables that go into it." Already I can see that she's on the right track. In the last year I've heard hundreds of variables: whether you love him or not, whether you want the same things in life or not, whether his family will accept you or not, whether you agree on the position of women or the raising of children, whether sex is good, whether there's intimacy, whether he has just taken a job in Madagascar, whether you've just committed yourself to a Ph.D. program. As Karen points out, these variables are specific and situational, and they're caught in time. In her own case, choosing not to marry the prosecutor was not the same thing as deciding against marriage as a way of life. It was a specific choice and it can't be generalized.

On the other hand, Karen *has* made a general, clear-cut choice, and that is not to marry for the sake of marriage. In this she stands with the vast majority of ever-single women I've met. But coming from a woman, that choice is sometimes incomprehensible to other people and it's rarely validated.

"I had a girlfriend who once said, 'Why don't you get married? You'd make a good wife,'" Karen recalls. "And I said, 'Well, if I really wanted to get married to be married, I could have been married three or four, five, six, seven, or eight times. . . . You can turn over a pile and find someone who will marry you if you just want to get married," she says. "A lot of people do that." But not Karen.

Not Linda Schindler either. For all her focus on finding a marriage partner, for all the singles dances and matchmaking services, Linda has a bottom line. "If anything prevents me from getting married," she says, "it's not getting married just to get married."

And so went our exploration into choice. I confess my head was spinning, and I was frustrated. I felt a little like a camp counselor who can't get her campers to coalesce around the campfire, much less decide what they're going to sing. For every questionable word in the sociological model there was a camper off pursuing it in the woods. I was annoyed that we couldn't come up with a manifesto that said, Here is what we've chosen and that is why we feel the way we do. In fact, we could barely come up with a working definition of *choice*.

But looking back over the responses we made and the stories we shared, I've come to believe that we did stumble onto something—a key to why many of us don't feel as bad as the world thinks we do.

The operative element is not choice; *choice* is too big a word, too grand a posture. As Karen pointed out, there are too many variables for clear-cut choices to be made and claimed. It's more a matter of perceived control: women who feel that they exert some control in their marital status seem to be the happiest in the group. Those who feel that they have no control are the unhappiest.

Sadly, it's hard to feel control in this culture. Lack of control is at the heart of the images in the cultural mirror. In magazine articles such as *Newsweek*'s "Too Late for Prince Charming?", in movies such as *Sleepless in Seattle*, women are slapped around by an unfair and uncontrollable demographic profile that dooms them to be single. In movies such as *The Prime of Miss Jean Brodie*, in TV shows such as *thirtysomething*, in the pages of *Glamour*, the ever-single woman is at the mercy of a barely controllable fault inside her (controllable only if she loses ten pounds, buys the right makeup, or learns to flirt intelligently). Historically and currently, the culture suggests that women are primarily passive and without power in the marriage decision; it throws women—as writer Kate Hevner Mueller once noted way back in a 1955 issue of *Mademoiselle*—into a "ruthless market" created by "people who want to sell her something." If she's active at all, it's only as a consumer of a "packaged" identity.

Given this cultural message, it's no wonder that women sometimes drop their voices in shame and "confess" that they are involuntarily single. It's no wonder these women—women who believe that they have never had the opportunity to marry because of some external force or internal flaw—are apparently not happy. In contrast, women who say they are involuntarily single and then qualify their responses with anecdotes and caveats, with stories of men they've left or things they aren't willing to do for marriage, seem to be more satisfied. These quasi-involuntary types see themselves as part of the action, part of the story; their anecdotes speak of a self declared, a loss sustained, a person who was there, participating, deciding, exerting some taste, thought,

emotion. Apparently owning those stories and expressing those caveats con-
tributes to life satisfaction.

It's not surprising, then, that women who say that they are voluntarily
single—either in the general sense (I'll never marry) or the specific sense
(I've chosen on occasion not to marry)—show the most satisfaction. "I would
say 'voluntary-stable,' but then I wouldn't close the door," says Lisa Nolan,
forty-nine. "I kind of feel sorry for women who have that as a goal in life."

The level of control women express when they characterize themselves
as "temporary" or "stable" also seems linked to their level of satisfaction. The
happiest of the "temporarily single" seem to be those who would like to marry
in a general sense but nonetheless describe specific variables that defy an or-
derly time line. They do not seek to control the uncontrollable or hunt down
some unnamed, faulty variable within themselves. They say they are "temporary" because they believe that *if* the variables line up correctly, they'll exert
their control and marry. These hopeful, temporary types say things like,
"Who knows?" and "You can always hope!" Their marital status is temporary
within the context of a basically uncontrollable world: "Someday I'll meet
someone after four or five hours of putting up hay," says Marguerite, imagining the heat, the sweat, a conspicuous lack of romantic attire. "*That* would be
my luck."

Among women who say that their marital status is stable, the happiest
seem to be those who describe being single as the reasonable result of a series
of choices. As might be expected, those who dabble in the idea of perma-
nence—few actually commit to it in the end—are older women: "Involuntary
stable," says Diane Faverty, seventy-four, who thinks that her executive career may have gotten in the way of marriage. Marriage in retirement is possible, she concedes, but she would have to weigh her autonomy—especially her
financial independence—against the advantages of a marriage.

This sense of control seems to grow with age, as experiences mount, as
friends divorce, as men come and go, as women come to feel—as Diane, Kate,
Maureen, and Melissa do—that they have come to a place where marriage
doesn't offer what it once did. In this place, even without a proposal, the
knowledge that any proposal would require careful consideration is control
enough. "I mean, he'd have to be well nigh perfect for me to think it was
worth giving up what I have," says Kate, who takes her portion of control seriously. When a friend recently joked with her about a potential blind date,

Kate's temper flashed. "I am not going to be fixed up with anybody!" she tells me. "I still would say that it's not impossible that I would ever marry anybody, but it's not going to be somebody they fix me up with!"

In a sense, singular women are beam-walkers, carefully maintaining emotional position between extremes—between passive victimization on one hand (no control) and adamant rejection on the other (total control), between obsessive self-correction on one hand (no control) and absolute closure on the other (total control). Although many seem to swing between the extremes in those early scriptless years, few of the women I met have landed in one of those extremes and settled there, unhappily. Instead, most value marriage but say they won't marry for the sake of marriage; they hope but they don't hunt; they talk about potential but they do not wait for this particular potential to be realized. Singularity is a state of being open and yet being self-sufficient; it is a state of readiness, but not a state of desperation.

The movie *Rachel, Rachel,* which chronicles the struggle of a thirty-five-year-old ever-single woman to define herself and her future, ends with this emerging point of view. Rachel has decided to leave the town she grew up in and go west as an adult fully engaged in her own life adventure. We hear her thoughts as she sits on the bus, looking forward in a new, less desperate, less confined way: "Where I'm going anything may happen. Nothing may happen," she thinks. "Maybe I'll find a friend. Maybe I'll even marry a middle-aged widower and have children in my time. Most of the chances are against it, but not, I think, quite all. It may be that my children will always be temporary, never to be held—but so are everyone's."

In the last moments of the film, we see Rachel's image of her life with a child on a beach somewhere west. "I will be afraid always," she thinks meanwhile. "I may be lonely always." But that's not the dominant thought here; that's not the focal point of her life. For the first time in her life, Rachel is balanced on the beam, holding steady—and yet poised for change. "What will happen?" she asks herself. "What will happen?"

How does a woman get to this moment of balance? How does a woman achieve this singular sense of control and acceptance? I think as I walk down the lake shore with my dog. This is a good place for me to address this question: I have a dicey relationship with the city of Chicago and the lake shore, which is its primary asset. Fourteen years ago, I came here to get married; the relationship failed, and I stayed because I had a job and student loans to pay for. I was brought here and I was left here. I didn't choose this freezing winter rain, this solitary walk along a cold and whitened beach.

On the other hand, maybe I did. After all, my former fiancé has managed to marry and move to sunny California. After all, I've turned down three jobs out of state.

Okay, so maybe I did choose Chicago. But singlehood?

How does a woman come to feel that she exerts some control over her marital status? I wonder. But I don't wonder for long: in truth, I haven't met a woman yet who hasn't exerted some control. I haven't heard a life story that didn't have some decision, some twist or turn that the storyteller herself initiated.

Despite daunting demographics that put educated black women at a profound disadvantage in the so-called marriage market, Roxanne does not date—and believes she would never marry—outside her race. For twenty years, Gretchen Wentworth dated an unavailable man; for six years, Caitlin purposely kept herself at an emotional distance from men while she studied her art. Janice has turned down several proposals. In her college years Felicia Collinet found she couldn't stay with the man her family thought was the catch of a lifetime. More than forty years after her moment of loneliness in a New York hotel, seventy-six-year-old Louise Long remembers leaving a man who just couldn't understand the traveling part of her life and her character; he assumed she would happily stop if she married. In the vernacular, he just "didn't get it"—and she turned him down. Looking back, reserved, sensitive Nan says that she wasn't quite sure what she wanted until recently; only recently has she been ready socially and emotionally to marry.

It is this slippery portion of control that Heidi Holland, the art historian in the Broadway play *The Heidi Chronicles* (1989), fails to grasp. At the wedding of a former lover, ever-single Heidi learns that her bid for equality is the factor that doomed her relationship with Scoop. "We're talking about life choices," Scoop tells her, minutes after marrying someone else.

"I haven't made them yet," Heidi insists.

"Yes, you have," Scoop says, "or we'd be getting married today."

The interchange is quick and subtle. In her late thirties, Heidi still feels that she hasn't chosen (in the general sense) to marry or not; Scoop tells her that she has chosen (in the general sense) not to sacrifice who she is and what she wants for marriage. That is a life choice. But at this point, Heidi can barely admit her portion of control.

"I didn't marry Lisa because she's Jewish," Scoop argues.

"No," returns Heidi, flexing her nascent sense of control just a bit, "you married her because she's bland-ish."

In reality, these stories are everywhere, in every life. But some women have listened to their own stories and others, like Heidi at thirty-seven, haven't. And those who have listened carefully seem to feel that they have more control. Lindsay Cordell pointed that out in a letter. "I just wanted to let you know how I felt after our interview," she wrote. "It gave me a sense of empowerment and pride."

I think about Lindsay's letter as I walk along in a curmudgeonly mood, calculating the temperature in this freezing city and resenting it, resenting it and laughing at it. If there's a hidden process in my own journey this year, it's that I have come to listen to my own story as carefully as I have listened to the stories of these other thirty women. And in the listening, I have to come recognize my own moments of control (including Chicago; including not bending, shaping, or curtailing myself to meet the implicit terms of the marriage offer that brought me here). I've come to laugh at my changing foibles, reassess ancient caveats, grieve mistakes, and own the self who lives in those stories and carries them in her own personal backpack like a lone hiker crossing a wilderness plain on into her forties.

If there's a single silent change, it has been that. The unwitnessed life does have a witness: me. Of all the changes, this is the one that has made looking forward easier than ever: I've listened.

CHAPTER TEN

Looking Forward

🍂

*She'd always said that when she got older she'd move to be near her sister.
"One day I looked in the mirror and I said, 'Hey, you're getting older.'"
She smiles. "It was time to make the move." We're sitting in her new
place on the outskirts of Ann Arbor, Michigan, a large home fully
equipped with a substantial TV (no point in watching football on a small
TV, she explains) in a quiet suburban neighborhood that's fairly teeming
with single types, mostly widows and divorced women.*

*Of course, Melissa Van Lenten had some concerns about leaving
Milwaukee. "I said, when I move I'll lose my musical identity," she admits. But the worry was misplaced. Within months of moving, Melissa
had new piano students and a job playing organ at a local church. Today
the piano tuner is downstairs, and we can hear him working on her two
baby grands.*

*When I ask Melissa what the rough times in her life have been, she
mentions her father's death and her brother's. And she talks about scattered times, usually the summers, when she felt disconnected. "I would
sit in my studio and it would be . . . a kind of depressing time," she says.
"You have to reach out and get out of the house. For me, I can even do it
with just going out window shopping . . . so I think this is important."*

*But when I ask her what the best time has been, the answer comes
much faster. "I think I'm moving into some good years now," she says
at seventy. "At an exercise class somebody just had a birthday, and*

*she kept saying, 'Oh, it gets better all the time,' and I told her afterward,
'It really does.'"*

🦅

It's possible that if more of us were in the habit of wading through psychological and sociological studies, if we were given to studying census data or ran-
domly asking married and unmarried seniors at bus stops what their lives are
really like, we might not be so concerned about growing old in the absence of
a partner. The data are clear: in the generations of women who have reached
their sixties and seventies in the 1970s, 1980s, and 1990s, those who have remained single all their lives fare very well. To date, among older unmarried
women, ever-single women are often the best off financially, they suffer less
loneliness and dissatisfaction, and they demonstrate reasonably good health.
The data also show that a majority of women are unmarried in their later
years: among women sixty-five and above, 48.3 percent are widowed, 5.5 percent are divorced, and 4.9 percent are ever-single. Another 2.3 percent live
separate from their spouses. This leaves just 39 percent of women over the age
of sixty-five married and living with their husbands.

Of course, even if you are a fan of the mental health studies in the *Journal
of Gerontological Social Work*, you may still have difficulty embracing these
findings. Instinctively, younger women recoil. "I'm afraid of dying and being
alone," Roxanne Walters says bluntly.

That recoil is understandable among women who have grown up in a
"couple culture," as Marguerite Ramanis calls it; and it's nearly unavoidable in
a culture that values women most when their faces are unlined, when their
bodies are sleek and unsagging, when their presumed potential to marry is
greatest. Old age stretches before us, poorly understood and highly discounted.
If ever there was a time when the image in the cultural mirror—ugly and useless—looms larger than life, this is it.

The image in the mirror has deep roots and frequent expressions. Once
again Freud has had an impact. He saw the man of thirty as youthful, capable
of growth and development through analysis. But the woman, he said, "often
frightens us by her psychical rigidity and unchangeability. Her libido has
taken up final positions and seems incapable of exchanging them for others."

Psychologically calcified at thirty, she cannot be saved—even by marriage. That's partly why Alexandra Bergson, the heroine of Willa Cather's classic 1913 novel *O Pioneers!*, meets with ridicule when she considers marriage at a late age. "Everybody's laughing to see you get took in; at your age, too," sneers her married brother. "Why, Alexandra, you are nearly forty years old!" Alexandra has built a formidable farming empire, but it's too late for her to build a married life, says her brother, whose real worry is that, as a desperate middle-aged woman, Alexandra will pass her fortune on to an undeserving husband rather than her brother. Weak-willed sisters, bothersome mothers-in-law, out-of-date teachers, widows without lives of their own, aging wives with screechy voices: in books, movies, and TV shows, the older woman is pictured as a rigid and inconvenient intruder in a fleet male world. She's a barrier; she's an encumbrance.

It's no surprise, then, that the pretty thirty-five-year-old ever-single schoolteacher in *Rachel, Rachel* lacks a positive image for her aging. She has failed the purpose of her youth (marriage and children), and there is no purpose in later age. "This is the last ascending summer of my life," she says as she begins to close down her classroom for the summer. "Everything else from now on is just rolling on downhill into my grave."

So much for a sense of future.

As a result, I came to this question of future—of how women see themselves in the future and how older women have created and continue to create their futures—curious and cautious both. To age in America is to face a complex web of experiences and feelings, of emotional gains and losses, of finances, of questions of dependence and independence. To be an ever-single woman in the face of this web appeared daunting.

But what I found in those women who were born between 1917 and 1931 was not so much a matter of courage as continuity. Many of the emotional issues that younger women worry about had long since been resolved, and much of the work of old age—adapting to an aging body, shifting energies to different forms of work and play, maintaining and creating relationships, sustaining loss, managing finances—was familiar work for women who had independently changed jobs, bought and sold houses, and made and lost friends in the course of their lives. In fact, younger women would be wise to take note.

Among social scientists who study old age, one cause for concern is the emotional effect of retirement. When work plays a pivotal role in a person's identity and life course, how does that person adapt to the loss of work?

For years this concern centered on men, but lately the research net has widened to include women, particularly ever-single women who have typically worked all their lives. The findings are mixed: some studies show a heightened anxiety among ever-single women facing retirement; others show that ever-single women adapt to retirement very well. In one such study, researcher Laurie Russell Hatch was simply not able to account for the reasons ever-single women did so well.

One reason may be that they don't really retire. In Barbara Levy Simon's 1987 study, 51 percent of the women in her sample worked in paid jobs after retirement, a rate of employment seven times the national average. Similarly, among the older women I met retirement appeared to be a wildly inaccurate term. Rosalie Morgan and Melissa Van Lenten still work part-time; Rosalie, Melissa, Kate O'Connor, Diane Faverty, Maureen Cabot, and Lillian Salinger all donate considerable portions of their time to various organizations.

"You have to keep busy," Lillian explains as she serves her brother Walter and me the best homemade apple pie I've had since my grandmother died. According to IRS rules, she and Walter can no longer manage the land that they lease to a nearby farmer, and the farming discussions they do have with him must be initiated and led by him. Now what really takes up Lillian's time is her volunteer work at the local hospital, and she spends a lot of time with friends. "We are so busy with other people," she says, gesturing toward the upright piano where a dozen photographs of family and friends are displayed. "Sometimes you just gotta put a stop! We get invited to all the graduation parties, baby showers, weddings."

Forthright Maureen Cabot has been particularly strategic in her efforts to keep busy. After retiring from the utility company, she worked part-time in the office of her apartment building. Then she joined a retirement community, where she is the volunteer editor for the newsletter. In taking the editorship, she was following the advice of a friend's ninety-three-year-old mother. "She said the only thing she dreaded was waking up some morning and having nothing to do," recalls Maureen at sixty-eight. "Every once in a while I think, why am I knocking my brains out on this paper? It gets harder all the time. You have less and less help and fewer and fewer people around. The interviewing becomes harder because some of these people think I'm doing it more for myself than for them." In a sense, though, those people might be right—Maureen does have a hidden motive. "You keep your marbles longer if you use them," Maureen says unapologetically.

Typically women use the skills they developed in their professions. Melissa accompanies the church choir. Rosalie, once a full-time bookkeeper, does financial and administrative work for her church, although she has drawn the line at seeking donations door to door.

Kate, on the other hand, took off in a whole new direction. She retired early from the school system to take care of her ailing mother, who died a short time later. Rather than choosing to work with children again, she volunteered at a hospice. "They ordinarily did not take somebody who had suffered a recent loss," she observes, "but I was allowed to take it because Mother had been ill for so long." She sews, runs errands, provides company and emotional support. "I don't recall how I got interested in hospice," she says. "But it's just been wonderful. Probably the most fulfilling thing I've ever done as far as volunteer work—and I've done a lot of it." She also volunteers for the Catholic Church, spends time with her sister, and visits friends, who seemed to be everywhere we walked in her small Midwestern town.

Only Louise Long talks about missing work per se. She retired early from her job as an executive secretary to take care of her mother, who was in her nineties and fast losing her sight. Even then Louise believed that early retirement speeds decay: "My father left his job, he was either sixty-two or sixty-three . . . and I felt then and I still feel it more strongly than ever, it's a mistake to retire early. I think that physically, mentally, every which way you start to deteriorate." Although she didn't miss the early mornings or the winter commutes, she did miss the activity, the night classes, the contact with women at work. "I didn't do as much as I did when I was working. I guess a lot of times the more time you have, the less you accomplish." Now that her mother has died, she travels, often with her sister, keeps house, hikes, and takes a swimming class, and on some level she has adjusted. Occasionally, though, she still harks back to those first few years of retirement. "I missed it," she says. "I missed working very much."

But for most retirees, the shift away from full-time work is a welcome and sometimes subtle shift in lifestyle. Lillian and Walter still watch the fields that surround their farmhouse with interest, and they keep tabs on crop prices. This year it was a bumper crop in corn, Walter explains as we gaze at the harvested fields, and the federal crop program is just not worth the farmer's while. Lillian nods intently.

A corollary concern that social scientists raise is the financial effect of retirement. In the studies of older single people and single people in general, financial insecurity has a profound affect on psychological, emotional, and physical well-being; it's so powerful that in the 1970s, one study characterized it as "preeminently" tied to depression in unmarried adults. In Pat Keith's study of older adults, financial insecurity was a key factor in the overall vulnerability of the aged, and in David R. Williams's cross-racial study of adults, removing the factor of socioeconomic status narrowed the differences in mental health between married and ever-single women. Nationwide, finances are a vulnerable area for older women: because they made 57 cents (or less) on the dollar and because they typically interrupted careers to provide caretaking (for their children or their parents), their Social Security benefits are lower than those of men. More critically, they are far less likely to have held union jobs; only 13 percent receive private pensions. Rosalie gives some insight into what a female worker's pension can be: she was vested in the plan offered by the small company where she worked for many years and now receives $31.42 a month ("So I don't consider it a pension!" she says bluntly).

Nonetheless, most of the older women I met had planned ahead nicely. They're typical of this ever-single cohort, who, according to the Family Economics Research Group, characteristically have higher retirement incomes, lower housing costs, and a lesser dependency on Social Security benefits for survival than do their divorced and widowed sisters.

When she retired from her full-time job as a bookkeeper, Rosalie set up a corporation to handle the income she was still earning in her part-time work; this shielded her from the complicated ratio of paid work to Social Security benefits that has many retirees under seventy walking a thin financial line. And although the corporation had to pay tax at a corporate rate, it worked out. (I suspect it helps to have dealt professionally in finances for forty years to understand this arrangement.)

Lillian and Walter have come up with a seemingly less complicated solution. Part of their security lies in a series of land purchases they made some time ago. ("People thought we were crazy," remembers Lillian wryly.) They've figured out that selling the land wouldn't be wise ("because the capital gains will eat you up," explains Lillian), so they rent the land out to the farmer Lillian has worked with most of her adult life. "He started with me in the year of sixty-six. . . ." she says. "Either he has put up with me or I have put up with him." Lillian and Walter keep separate checking accounts, they have invested their money, and they hold life insurance policies on each other. They also help support an aunt and uncle, aged ninety-two and ninety-five respectively.

Of course, it's not all roses. Maureen Cabot jokes about her poor timing: "How should I put it? Murphy's Law! If I'd signed the retirement papers three years later, I'd have gotten a year's salary." Poor timing is a pattern with her, she says. The year she reached fifteen years' employment and achieved three weeks' vacation, the company's requirement dropped to ten years. "Before that, I graduated from college and during those union negotiations, they started to pay for work-related courses. But it's okay. I got it [the degree] anyway." Similarly, Melissa admits that she could have joined the college's retirement plan a lot earlier than she did. But both Maureen and Melissa feel secure; Maureen is able to reinvest some of her retirement income, and Melissa believes that she has made good choices. "We had a church retreat recently and we talked about what we would rather do. I said, 'Well, I'm pretty happy . . . where I am and with the things that I have,'" she explains, glancing around her fully carpeted house, which is perched on the top of a little rise. "I suppose if I had thought about it, I would rather not have all these stairs here. But I think this is a very good space for me."

Of far more concern to these women is the issue of caretaking—and for good reason. Caretaking is typically a family matter; on our targetlike map of relationships, it's the people who inhabit the rings closest to the bull's-eye— husbands, children, siblings—that typically provide care. They have close blood or legal ties that involve the moral and social obligation to provide care. Typically, Americans rely on their spouses and children (especially daughters) when the going gets rough. For the ever-single woman, spouses aren't a possibility, and children, especially among the women who are now retired, are a rarity. For ever-single women, the issue of caretaking is less clear than it presumably would have been if they'd married.

"I have friends who think, well, maybe I won't be alive three years or five years from now," says Kate, her brown eyes intent and clear. "I tend to think

I'll be alive until at least my mid-eighties. And the only thing that I—well, I don't fear it, but the only thing is that there will be no one to care for me." Kate doesn't have a solution: "When I say that to my sister, she says, 'Who's going to take care of *me?* You don't know necessarily because you have children that somebody's going to take care of you.'"

Nevertheless, the fear sometimes does play out; the worst that can happen sometimes does. In a small 1992 British study of ever-single women, researcher Christine Webb describes a woman who broke her collarbone and remained stranded without a phone until her eighty-year-old brother-in-law showed up twenty-four hours later. In his 1991 American study on kin and negotiated ties, Robert L. Rubinstein describes ever-single women who forged phenomenal non-kin ties—several actually raised other people's children—but do not expect to be taken care of as they probably would if they were blood mothers; ultimately they did not incur the moral obligation characteristic of a family tie. In the American study, at least, some of the problem lies in the culture itself, in the emphasis on independence that follows us throughout life and marks adult dependence (other than in marriage) as a shameful condition. Caretaking is a difficult issue for any American adult— and it is probably toughest for adults who find themselves unmarried in later life. This is partly why elderly ever-single women traditionally show high rates of institutionalization.

Even on this point, Kate makes a bold observation that reminds me of Caitlin McKuen's comment that she could put her "own self" in a nursing home. "I have said for years and I still mean it, that if I have to live out my last years in a nursing home and be isolated from people, I'm sure I won't like it well," she says. "But I hope I don't complain, because I've had such a wonderful life that I would sound like a crybaby if I couldn't take what other people have had to take for years and years."

Perhaps with caretaking in mind, many of these older women turned to siblings as they aged. Kate lives within a few miles of her sister; Melissa moved a few hundred miles to be near hers. By living with their siblings, both Rosalie and Lillian have achieved the same level of security that married women have (maybe more, since divorce is unlikely).

Although she is close to her extended family, Maureen Cabot took another path altogether. Two of her aged aunts had lived in Hillside Village, a retirement community that would provide nursing care as a resident's needs developed, but did not accept people with disabilities. When Maureen developed difficulties with her left leg and doctors began to search for a tumor in her spine, she quickly moved to Hillside. It was the best way to ensure her independence and not become a burden to her family, she felt. Ironically, there was no tumor: she now walks with a cane and rides an exercise bike regularly, although reluctantly. (Exercise, she asserts, doesn't make your life longer; it just makes your life *seem* longer.)

Hillside is a pleasant place with light and airy common areas, a tiny library, a convenience store, and a good restaurant. But it has its down sides: it's in a suburb far from the urban environment Maureen grew up in, and she doesn't drive, which means her family must come to pick her up for events. "It's the last place I will live," Maureen says with a frankness that surprises me. "With things the way they are today, perhaps I would not have done it," she observes, "but I did do it. It seemed the right thing to do then and . . . I'm happy here."

In contrast, Diane Faverty has held firm, living in the condo she bought nearly twenty years ago. A former executive with a quick wit and an urbane manner, she quotes National Public Radio reports and stories in *The New Yorker*, and she holds subscriptions to two or three theaters as well as the opera. Although she owns some farmland, she doesn't see herself living outside the city ("Small towns are death to a single person as far as I'm concerned") and she hasn't figured out quite what she'll do if she develops health problems. "Occasionally it comes to my mind," she says, noting that she is particularly concerned about leaving her estate in order. "My whole philosophy is I don't want someone to have to come in and take care of what I didn't do," she says. "I had to do that for my sister's things, who, as she got older, got very depressed. There was a lot to do in her home. I just don't think it's fair that the person . . . who's in charge of your estate has to come in. . . . So I hope I'm smart enough to have it done." As for caretaking in the case of illness— she gently skirts the issue.

Louise, who lives in the home her parents owned, has similar feelings. "People say to me, 'Why don't you move to Arizona? All your family is there. You're all alone here.'" But she is reluctant, and she's keenly aware that she could become a social obligation. "I say, 'I don't want anybody there to feel, you better call up Aunt Lou and see if she wants to do this with us,'" she says. "Not because they *want* to, but because they feel *guilty*." That's a strong and interesting position, especially in a woman who generously left the work she loved to take care of her ailing mother. And it's a position that a woman can hold only in the presence of good luck, reasonable finances, and continuing health.

꙳

In many ways, the younger women I've met have an advantage over these pioneers of feminine independence; in other ways, they don't.

Financially, most command far better salaries and most could end up far ahead of the women who came of age in the 1940s and early 1950s, when wages for educated women were particularly depressed. As a professor at Berkeley, Teresa Sanchez, for instance, has a good salary and a pension plan and she owns her own condo. In her fifties, she may or may not see reasonable Social Security benefits when she retires. Juillissa Rivera, Lisa Nolan, Susan Ryerson, Karen King, Mary Stendahl, Linda Schindler, and Ellen Adams are in similar positions.

But others are in less certain positions. Many of us have taken significant risks, and many have been caught in the downsizing of corporate America that marked the early 1990s. A former Digital employee, Marguerite Ramanis has started her own business; biochemist Rachel Jacobs is considering doing the same; filmmaker Roxanne Walters works free-lance, sometimes working on feature films that shoot for two and three months, other times working on commercials, a day here, a day there. Caitlin McKuen has chosen to live simply, and although her first major art exhibition was an extraordinary success, she nonetheless lives fairly close to the edge, and toys with dropping her health insurance. Nan Hansen has zigzagged across her field of marketing; she recently left a failing corporation only to take a lower salary with a nonprofit organization, and she is going to night school to switch professions entirely. "I'm kind of building back up," she says patiently.

Occasionally, they scramble. After all, there just isn't much room for maneuvering: without a second salary in the house, there isn't anyone to fall back on. Marguerite is sure that she would have launched her own business much sooner if she'd had the security of a second salary—a working marriage partner—on her side. But Nan, who hopes to start a business once she finishes night school, disagrees. "I think in some ways we tell ourselves, I would do this because I would have the financial and emotional support," she says. "But my gut tells me that it's probably much more difficult when you're in a marriage to say, 'Look, I want to risk all of what we have together. . . .' It may be a lot tougher to find a partner who's really willing to go along with that." Although taking a risk in the absence of marriage may feel more dangerous, at least the risk is being taken, she concludes.

Few expect Social Security to be there for them. The exception is Gretchen Wentworth, who retired from her career as a clothing importer at forty-five and lives largely on investments; she has actually written away to find out what's in her Social Security account. But most don't seem to think even that's worth the effort. "I don't think Social Security will be there," says Victoria Mason, who sees herself working two jobs for another few years. "I've been saying that for years."

Despite the belief that there will be no social safety net for them, most of these younger women have not planned. Strong-willed Karen King, the woman who once shocked her boyfriend by buying a house and adopting a child, is typical. "I have a thing about security," she says. "I don't believe there is such a thing as security. . . . When I retire, what am I going to do? I have some retirement money, and people say it's never enough, but it will be enough for me for what I want to do." Typically, these women work hard and try not to worry about what will happen twenty and forty years down the line.

But of course the inevitable does happen; it's happening to iconoclastic, independent Carrie Cunningham next month, when she retires early, mostly out of frustration. "I may be out on the street with a tin cup because I have not done anything about figuring out my finances or anything normal that you should do," she says frankly. I'm not sure how seriously to take this, but her situation is certainly more precarious than, say, Melissa's. For health insurance, she'll depend on COBRA, a federally mandated interim plan, but her pension is small. "I didn't sign up until late in the game so I had to stay five years to even be vested," Carrie explains. "And I thought, well, I'm definitely going to do that because I hated not to make them kick in *something*. But since I was only in it for a little over five years, it's going to be minimal."

The only exception to this pattern seems to be forty-two-year old Susan Ryerson, who will retire from her job at the fire department in a few years, taking with her a reasonable pension. Characteristically, she has studied her options carefully. Four or five of the books on her crowded living-room bookshelves are guides to retirement, and she has already determined where she will move. Her independence runs deep, and her determination to be independently secure may run even deeper. "I don't think many people do that [start planning] at the young age I started at," she observes. "That's strange. It could be because I saw how my mother's life was completely turned over when my father died." Later she adds, "You know, I've already outlived my father."

While although most of these younger women don't worry about finances, many do worry about emotional issues. Interestingly, even though we will probably resolve some of these fears in the course of our lives (just as our predecessors have), we do have additional reasons to worry. In contrast to the ever-single women who appear in the gerontological studies, women who came of age in the 1960s, 1970s, and 1980s are unlikely to share a household with another ever-single woman. We're also less likely to live with a sibling. Since we have the financial ability to live alone, we do, and that practice has implications for caretaking in our later years. It also puts us at increased risk of isolation, and although isolation does not necessarily translate into loneliness, it is certainly a factor.

Similarly, findings showing that ever-single women cope with their social status better than divorced women may also change. At the time that the women in those studies came of age, the stigma of being ever-single was not nearly as great as the stigma of being divorced; in the 1970s that cultural judgment flip-flopped. As a result, ever-single women in their thirties and forties suffer more stigma than their divorced sisters do—and they know it. "Divorce used to have a stigma," observes Teresa Sanchez. "Women used to hide that. . . . But now it's a *good* thing to say, 'I'm divorced.'" To Teresa, who values her perception and judgment, this cultural message is irritating. "[It's better to say] 'I was dumb, I made a mistake,'" she says with mock incredulity, "instead of saying, 'I was smart. I stepped back before it was too late!'" A scene in the film *When Harry Met Sally* confirms Teresa's evaluation. In a conversation about finding men, three thirtyish professional women discuss a man who has been recently divorced. "Don't wait too long," advises Sally's best friend, an ever-single woman who carries a dating Rolodex in her purse. "Remember what happened with David Warsaw? His wife left him. Everyone said, 'Give him some time; don't move in too fast. . . .' Six months later he was dead."

"What are you saying—I should get married to someone right away in case he's just about to die?" asks ever-single Sally.

"*At least you could say you'd been married,*" responds another (married) woman. In a movie peppered with comments like "Tell me that I'll never have to be out there [dating] again," the comment is an accurate reflection of the pressures resident in pop culture, written by the woman who later gave us *Sleepless in Seattle*. As Karen King puts it, "The fact that you were married at all validates you."

Lastly and perhaps most importantly, the younger women differ from the older women in that they seem to have a much weaker foothold in the community. Unlike the older women, most of the younger women have left the towns they grew up in and few are closely tied to a church or synagogue. The peace of mind that Lillian and Walter feel, the rootedness that Rosalie talks about, the quick and rewarding connection that Melissa made with her church in her new town; the way Louise counts on Carl, her postman, and Harriet, her neighbor of more than thirty years: this sense of community life does not often appear in the stories of younger women. Instead the younger women depend far more on work for their social identities. Diane Faverty, whose forty-year business career was certainly demanding, thinks this may be a mistake. "I had my own personal life, which is, I think, terribly important, to have it away from work, [so that] when you retire you don't depend on the people that you worked with for your associates," she says. "I think that's one of the reasons I've been so happy in retirement—because we [women] have a separate life from business; a man's whole life is tied up in business."

So if they don't marry, what will the younger women do? Ellen Adams, the woman who celebrates her birthday with a solitary walk, supposes that if she were unable to take care of herself in her later years, she would move back across the country to Connecticut, where her twin sister lives. Teacher Mary Stendahl thinks about moving from Maine to Michigan, where a married sister lives, and then equivocates: "I don't know, I'd probably move out there, and then they'd move somewhere else. [And then I'd] follow them, like a puppy dog or something." She shakes her head. "I'll let you know what happens," she concludes ruefully.

"I don't want to have to rely on my children to take care of me," Victoria emphasizes. "I would not like to be that type of burden." Nonetheless, like most of her cohort, she has no specific ideas on how she will live.

For those who don't have adaptive families and strong ties, the choices are particularly unclear. A baby boomer, Rachel Jacobs believes—and hopes—that the landscape will be different when she retires twenty-five years from now. "I don't know how it will be. There are so many of us," she says. "I think there will be living arrangements we can't even imagine right now." Others just have no idea. In answer to my question, Lisa Nolan, whose mother is in a nursing home, shrugs.

While many mention turning to friends for emotional support, few said they would turn to a friend—someone who inhabits an outer ring on the target—for caretaking or even for sharing housing. Perhaps the majority sense that such expectations might put them in the painful situation that Susan B. Anthony found herself in—hoping that her lifelong friend Elizabeth Cady Stanton would share her life in old age, and slowly realizing that Stanton, who had separated from her husband, would turn to her children, not her best friend. On the outer rings of the target, such expectations are weighty and difficult to negotiate. Thus, the most unconventional approach I heard came from Gretchen Wentworth, who lives in a condo building that has so many single women in it that one of her friends calls it "the sorority house." Deeply involved in a relationship but unsure if she will marry, at fifty-four Gretchen assumes that the mutual support these "sorority" women have developed among them may well suffice.

Not surprisingly, the strongest theme among these younger women looking forward is the theme of work: most expect to work in some capacity or to volunteer throughout their lives. "I can't imagine not working. I've worked for so many years and enjoyed it—I just can't imagine it," says Janice Patinkin, the high-energy hygienist, who at thirty-eight has put a "little bit" into a retirement account. "But if I were in retirement, I would first of all donate my time to a children's home," she says. Nan imagines a similar strategy. "I think this is part of the reason I would like to have my own business is to really have something . . . that can go on and be continued," she says. "I mean, I see so many people that are continuing to be productive in their seventies and even in their eighties. I would love that." Just as they have throughout their lives, they will find purpose outside the traditional role, and they will do what they can to have full and productive postretirement years.

All healthy people look forward in some way. At thirty, at forty, at sixty-six, that's the essence of being spiritually and emotionally alive. But for an ever-single woman, looking forward can be difficult. Soaked in fairy-tale expectations, trained by the adolescent crucible, buffeted perhaps by an unadaptive family or unaccepting friends, warned by the spinster image in the cultural mirror, she often finds imagining her later adult life impossible. For me, at least, that was the most painful aspect of my life: I could not look forward. I felt robbed of a sense of future because I was sure the future would be bleak.

One thing I've learned from the older women is that the ability to look forward comes with time and experience. It's something women learn as they survive the stigma (being unmarried at thirty-five, being childless, being a single mother). Surviving the stigma, these women learn to see themselves apart from it. More importantly, once they've discarded the stock images of fairy-tale marriages and Donna Reed lives, they take on the freedom to create their own images. "I would like to develop my own writing," teacher Pat McDonald, who recently turned down a state-wide early retirement program, says. "And I'd like to go to the northwest part of the country. I've been to New England and I'd like to go to Ireland." She would also like to share the wisdom that she has found in her own journey. "I think I'd like to work with adults who are maybe making discoveries in their lives and getting back to maybe things [that] they missed, like I did when I was younger. I didn't get into acting lessons until I was in my late forties," she reminds me. "I'd like to help other adults open up."

This hard-won peace appears never to be quite absolute, and it differs from the apparent adamancy reported in Barbara Levy Simon's study of ever-single women between the ages of sixty-one and one hundred. In that group, 76 percent claimed to have *chosen* the single life, mostly for the financial and emotional independence. More convincing is the profile Mary O'Brien paints in a 1991 study of older ever-single women living on Prince Edward Island. There, women said that their career interests had evolved and the marriage question had faded as time passed. Although nearly half of these women required help with shopping and transportation, nearly all considered themselves better off than their peers. They could concede that life had not been exactly what they had expected—yet life was nonetheless good. Having met the women I have and listened to thirty stories of pain and change and growth and resolution, I can only suggest that Simon's older group engaged in some significant (and probably unconscious) emotional editing.

Like the women in O'Brien's study, most of the singular women I met take an evolutionary approach to appraising their own losses and choices. Maureen Cabot, for instance, can look forward and back easily, and she speaks in a tense that tells you she is still creating her life and her self: "I pray that my sense of humor will not turn cynical or sarcastic," she tells me of the wit that has clearly helped her through rough times. Looking back, there have been regrets, times when she has looked at her siblings' children and thought that having children would be nice, but there were also times when they looked at her and wanted to trade places too. Mostly, Maureen has a philosophy that guards against unproductive second-guessing. "I'm lucky to have had all that I had and I'm certainly not going to spoil memories by thinking about what I did wrong—which," she says, laughing and tapping one of our interview transcripts demonstratively, "would take *quite* a number of pages!" The saddest phrase in the English language is "it might have been," she concludes. "That's true for *all of us.* They say, 'If we could do it again—' but unless we carried the experience and the knowledge back with us, we could make the same mistakes."

Melissa, who has lived alone since her father died, looks back with similar frankness. "[Not marrying] is probably one of life's disappointments—except that as I look around I find that there are a lot of people who are not in happy situations," she says. "There was a time when it bothered me very much. But I think at this point, while companionship would be great, I'm very independent. And I think it would be very difficult to have to live with somebody else. I eat when I want to and I eat what I want to. Just managing money!" She smiles. "There are some times [when] it would be nice to shove that burden onto somebody else," she admits. "But I think that—after all this time—I'm very independent."

❧

Yet as skilled as the women I met are, as game as they are to admit their losses and gains, they are reluctant to give advice. Perhaps they're reacting to the spate of books that shout shallow advice on how to live singly, most of it a poor match for their needs. Just a few that come to mind include humorist

Edan Schappert's counsel to avoid reading while eating, newspaper columnist's Ruthe Stein's advice on how to wear miniskirts to attract men, and Christian fundamentalist Luci Swindoll's advice on what music to listen to (she lists six piano concerti, six violin concerti, and six miscellaneous classical works—heaven help us if our tastes run to Mick Jagger, Ella Fitzgerald, or even Philip Glass). "It's arrogant," one singular woman tells me after reading Swindoll's prescriptive and chatty book. "How can she decide these things for me?"

Occasionally a singular woman will begrudgingly offer an ounce or two of wisdom. "Well, I don't know," begins Carrie Cunningham reluctantly. "It's almost like a parent talking to a child. Even in their thirties, they might think, 'What do you know? You're a fossil by now.'" With some encouragement, she continues: "Try to be kind. Not enough people seem to be kind anymore." And later she notes that keeping a sense of humor has been key for her. "I can usually see things that are funny even if it's something that's happened to me. I think that's true, if you don't have one you find you get too introspective and overly curious, and that's not me."

"Trust yourself that you have the strength," says reticent Pat McDonald, whose own journey from shyness has been arduous. "You don't need another person. . . . You can live alone . . . [but] you do need friends and family."

Take initiative, advises Melissa, who has often felt socially isolated by her seven-day-a-week job as a piano teacher and accompanist. "I'm perhaps somewhat aggressive about inviting people to my home," she says. "I think you need a social group."

"Don't pigeonhole yourself or other people," advises Christi Wagner, who has resisted labels and limitations all her life, in her teaching, in her travels, in her poetry.

But most hesitate to offer advice. What they offer instead is a rich and complex model, a model of continuity, of constant self-creation. To live it is to be adventurous, relatively forthright, and certainly forgiving. To describe it is messy. To derive three or four rules from it is just plain impossible.

I admit that this messiness has been a problem for me as a middle-aged woman writing about my journey toward singularity. Not only was I looking for simple models, but I had hoped to replace the distracting, nagging spinster image in the cultural mirror with a new one—maybe not as powerful as Miss Havisham, but certainly more real, more dimensional, and more positive than Alex Forrest. I had hoped to translate these lives, especially the lives of the older women, into bold pictures that could outlive and outshine the current pictures in the cultural mirror.

It isn't going to work. One reason is that Miss Havisham and Alex Forrest have a big advantage over anyone I've met in the last two years—Miss Havisham and Alex Forrest are not real. They're fantasies, they're fears, they're prejudices, they're social policies—but they're not people. That's partly why they live so long and so potently in our world. The women I met are too multifaceted to replace Miss Havisham, Miss Hathaway, or even Margaret Houlihan; they have pasts and futures, unlike Alex Forrest. They evolve offstage even as I'm writing about them.

As I write, the spinster image in the cultural mirror remains tied to the status of all women, and the changes that will give *all* women free access to work, to equal partnership, to a self-worth that is undominated by the marriage claim, are many years off.

Still, I share these stories of singular women and suggest that they offer all women a different kind of feminine narrative. I realize that it is in many ways accidental and messy, but here it is, living within a culture that portrays its women as dependent and passive, as happy only in marriage, as productive and fulfilled only in motherhood, as potent and interesting only in youth.

It's a narrative that is self-powered and yet connected. It's a narrative that may continue alone or in partnership. It's a narrative based on the feminine self—self-aware, self-directed, and valued—as we may see her in greater numbers, married and unmarried, far in the future.

I share it and someday soon I will achieve it: for now I know how that narrative could go for me.

Epilogue

So have you come to any conclusions? people ask as I pack up my interview transcripts and head for home.

First, the obvious one: it is possible, it is more than possible, for a woman to have a full and loving and productive life outside of marriage. I think of clear, intellectual Christi Wagner writing her poetry. Intense, dedicated Ellen Adams working in her waterfront home-office. Bright, commanding Karen King on one of her daughter's field trips. Reserved yet generous Melissa Van Lenten in between phone calls, exercise classes, and piano students, showing me how she freezes her casseroles in single servings. And Maureen Cabot, wise, acerbic, loved and valued by her family, always willing to share a moment—when she has one.

And there are other observations. The first is the worst: the twenties and the thirties are often the pits, mostly because of social forces and losses, sometimes because of family pressures. Other observations: women who come from adaptive families have a much easier time adjusting to a single life; women who like solitude or are at least resistant to loneliness are the most comfortable with life outside the normal social structures; finding good work is an important, though not necessary, ingredient in a singular life. But choice, choosing to be single, rarely has much to do with it. Feeling a sense of control does.

Nancy L. Peterson once concluded that straight and lesbian women who never married typically had someone in their pasts—most often a mother—who gave them permission to be single. I would amend that. Singular women typically have someone in their pasts—most often a parent—who has given them permission to be *themselves*. With that permission to pursue their own talents, desires, passions, and professions throughout life, the marriage question is no longer the preemptive, defining, long-awaited event, the fairy-tale question that makes or unmakes the woman. Now the marriage question appears in context, a context laden with timing, circumstance, chance, values, competing interests and responsibilities, and, not incidentally, a definition of intimacy that requires two whole individuals meeting somewhere in the middle.

Still, I suspect that there's another perception, something deeper and less articulate, beneath these observations. It seems that there is a bigger, more inclusive conclusion out there. So I pack my half-finished material and return to the beach I grew up on.

Twenty-five years ago, it was at a bonfire on this beach that I watched Tommy Piaget, the boy I adored, take Barbara Potts's hand and walk off into the darkness. It's here that my best friend, Nicki, and I watched the moon landing and toasted—with orange soda—to our honeymoons on the moon. We planned our waterfront weddings that day; the minister would be perched on the lifeguard stand.

It was here that eighteen-year-old Harry Duncan threw me down and lay on top of me, apparently to have his way with me—until I threatened to throw his glasses into the oncoming tide. And it's here that I have brought adult men to stay with my parents and walk the long stretch of beach north to the lighthouse. But I have always been careful about the unspoken, sparkling meaning of the place; I have guarded the place, the home of my hurricane nightmares and oceanside weddings at sunset.

The place has changed, of course. The beach has widened since I huddled around illegal bonfires watching boys and girls pair off. Today is gray and windy, a wet, off-season day exhaling the last gasps of a storm that blew through two days ago. It's the kind of day when locals dressed in rubber suits fish the breakers for blues, and people walk the shoreline wearing jeans and leather jackets. It's cold.

Then, suddenly, on the 17th Street beach I spot four men in tuxedos and four women in long, fancy dresses that trail in the sand. They're standing near the dunes, encircled by pots of purple, yellow, and orange mums; a Jeep stands by, ready to sweep them away if the weather gets any worse or the ocean gets any closer.

She is wearing white satin and a half-veil that attaches to her blond hair, which is swept up off her neck and twisted in a sophisticated knot. The groomsmen, the groom, and a bridesmaid—dressed in bright jewel blue, a fluffy dress she'll never wear again—are shuffling around while the photographer, a woman in pants, sets up the last shot. How the bride must have worried about the weather! I think, watching her consult with her maid of honor; she must have known that the northeaster would linger. Did she consider renting the Firemen's Hall? Did she worry about her dress, her hair, her mascara? Did she pack a few umbrellas in that Jeep, just in case? And when the vows came, did the wind whip away her words, and the guests lean in to hear better?

They're packing up the mums now, all those young, dark-haired men in formal suits, and the bride is climbing the dune to join her waiting bridesmaids. But she can't do it: her high heels disappear into the slipping sand, the wind fills her veil like a spinnaker, and she falters. Finally she takes off her white shoes, digs her stockinged toes deep into the damp sand, bunches up the satin skirts in her hands, and climbs. And as she climbs, the garter on her thigh peeks through a nearly full-length slit in her skirt.

It is a silly picture, this barefoot bride on the beach, and I wish I had a camera—to have the picture and to hold it, to keep it in mind as I walk to the lighthouse and later as I write. It is a moment, a confirmation, a challenge. It's a mirror, clean and fresh and accurate. Maybe it's a conclusion.

The conclusion is this: that a young girl dreamt of being a bride on a beach and she was; and another young girl dreamt of being a bride on a beach and she wasn't. But both have so many more dreams to create and fulfill, to dream and lose, to lose and recover, that this one dream cannot be the only determinant of quality in their lives.

For if it is, then we have each failed ourselves.

Source Notes

꽃

Introduction

Even recent feminists . . . : Pollitt, Katha. "Are Women Morally Superior to Men?" *The Nation*. December 28, 1992: 799–807.

Also see Hess, Beth B. "Friendship and Gender Roles over the Life Course." *Single Life: Unmarried Adults in Social Context*. Ed. Peter Stein. New York: St. Martin's Press, 1981: 106.

the common age of first marriage has drifted . . . : Crispell, Diane. "Myths of the 1950s." *American Demographics*. August 1992: 38.

Today in the U.S. . . . : "Marital Status and Living Arrangements: March 1992." *Current Population Reports* (Series P20–468). Bureau of the Census. December 1992: 1.

Our numbers swell . . . : Simon, Barbara Levy. *Never Married Women*. Philadelphia: Temple University Press, 1987: 19–20.

In Asia . . . : Watkins, Susan Cotts. "Spinsters." *Journal of Family History*. Winter 1984: 311.

Traditionally the psychologists . . . : Cockrum, Jean and Priscilla White. "Influences on Life Satisfaction of Never-Married Men and Women." *Family Relations*. October 1985: 551.

a phenomenon Samuel Johnson noted . . . : "Men know that women are an overmatch for them, and therefore they choose the weakest or the most ignorant." Quoted in Woolf, Virginia. *A Room of One's Own*. New York: Harcourt, Brace & World, Inc., 1957: 30.

some people argue . . . Gilder, George. "Still Seeking the Glass Slipper." *National Review.* December 14, 1992: 39–40.

Newsweek's article portrayed a slow, creeping panic . . . : The first line of the article begins, "Her sister had heard it from a friend who heard about it on 'Phil Donahue' that morning . . ." Solholz, Eloise. "Too Late for Prince Charming?" *Newsweek.* June 2, 1986: 55.

then Susan Faludi . . . : Faludi, Susan. "The Marriage Trap." *Ms.* August 1987: 62; 64. Faludi does discuss qualitative issues at the end of her article: 191.

Also: Faludi, Susan. *Backlash: The Undeclared War Against American Women.* New York: Crown Publishers, 1991: 3–27.

"Lashing Backlash." *New York Times Book Review* (letters). February 9, 1992: 31.

Does a forty-year-old never-married woman . . . : the answer is an unequivocal no and was no even using the statistical analysis *Newsweek* used. The quip, and it was apparently meant as a quip, appears in Solholz: 55.

In 1986 *Mademoiselle* . . . : Rozen, Leah. "The Great Man Shortage: Whatta Lie." *Mademoiselle.* September 1986: 246. So schizophrenic was *Mademoiselle*'s editorial policy that this article warns, "Remember that editors love national scare stories": 247.

the next year . . . : Wetzsteon, Ross. "Will the Man Shortage Spoil Men?" *Mademoiselle.* February 1987: 184.

even a bad marriage, is something all women . . . Solholz: 56.

often more satisfied than married women . . . Norval, Glenn. "What Does Family Mean?" *American Demographics.* June 1992: 34.

Chapter One

like to redeem the word *spinster* . . . : Opinionated Florence King has tried. See "Spinsterhood Is Powerful." *National Review.* July 19, 1993: 72.

in the U.S. the percentage . . . : Simon, Barbara Levy. *Never Married Women.* Philadelphia: Temple University Press, 1987: 19–20.

the marital use of the word *spinster* . . . : *The Oxford English Dictionary* (second edition) Volume 16. Prepared by Simpson, J. A. and E. S. C. Weiner. Oxford: Clarendon Press, 1989: 243.

A clearer explanation appears in Mills, Jane. *Woman Words: A Dictionary of Words About Women*. New York: Henry Holt and Company, 1993, 225–8.

Austen wrote *Pride and Prejudice* . . . : Honan, Park. *Jane Austen: Her Life and Work*. New York: Fawcett Columbine, 1987: 121–2.

and revised it sixteen years later . . . : *Ibid:* 308.

she'd had some field experience . . . : *Ibid:* 191.

"It is universally acknowledged . . .": Austen, Jane. *Pride and Prejudice*. Cleveland: The World Publishing Company, 1946: 11.

"the most Calamitous creature in nature . . .": quoted in Mills: 226.

The phrase is attributed to eighteenth-century traveler Nicholas Creswell in Doudna, Christine with Fern McBride. "Where are the men for the women at the top?" *Single Life: Unmarried Adults in Social Context*. Ed. Peter Stein. New York: St. Martin's Press, 1981: 30.

"maidens withering on the stalk . . .": Wordsworth, William. "Personal Talk." *The Poetical Works of William Wordsworth*. Boston: Houghton Mifflin Company, 1982: 346.

"uncultivated waste . . .": quoted in *The Oxford English Dictionary* (second edition) Volume 16: 244.

"My soul abhors . . .": Pope, Alexander. "January and May." *The Complete Poetical Works of Pope*. Boston: Houghton Mifflin Company, 1931: 36.

Pope reasserts the imagery of the spinster when he answers the question: "What is prudery?" Prudery is "a virgin hard of feature,/old and void of all good nature;/ Lean and fretful; would seem wise,/ Yet plays the fool before she dies." The poem is "Answer to the Following Question of Mrs. Howe." *Ibid:* 118.

"convenient stowage . . .": Milton, John. "Animadversions." *The Works of John Milton*, Volume 3, Part 1. New York: Columbia University Press, 1931: 151.

A more modern example of a structural need informing social opinion occurred in socialist East Central Europe, where being married or divorced assured women a socially acceptable role and economic position (in fact, some women married to obtain apartments). See Einhorn, Barbara. *Cinderella Goes to Market: Citizenship, Gender, and Women's Movements in East Central Europe*. London: Verso, 1993: 55–9.

It's also why Jane Eyre's evil . . . : Brontë, Charlotte. *Jane Eyre*. New York: The Book League of America. Georgiana is a "full-blown, plump damsel, fair as waxwork." Eliza is "very thin, with a sallow face and severe mien.": 183.

But first, within the first twenty-five words . . . : Brush, Stephanie. "Still Single at 38." *McCall's*. April 1993: 86.

Secret Finger-Pointing Syndrome . . . : *Ibid*: 88.

tribute to the sanctity of marriage . . . : *Ibid*: 89–91.

Brush wrote a follow-up piece . . . : Brush, Stephanie. "Living in the State of 'Unmarried-ness' Isn't That Bad." *Orlando Sentinel Tribune*. April 10, 1993: E3. Brush also makes it clear that she has a boyfriend.

On early television . . . : Spangler, Lynn C. "A Historical Overview of Female Friendships on Prime-Time Television." *Journal of Popular Culture* 22. Spring 1989: 15.

TV is not kind . . . : Meehan, Diana M. *Ladies of the Evening: Women Characters of Prime-Time Television*. Metuchen, NJ: The Scarecrow Press, Inc., 1983: 69.

When an attractive woman . . . : *Ibid*: 71.

This TV trend was so flagrantly . . . : interview with Freeman, Aaron. Studio A. WBEZ-Chicago. August 23, 1993.

When *Forbes* magazine . . . : Train, John. "Ma Bell an Old Maid?" *Forbes*. October 13, 1980: 250.

When *Business Week* . . . : "Stone Container: Caught Between Seeking a Merger and Going It Alone." *Business Week*. May 5, 1980: 90.

In the children's card game . . . : In 1993 Eisel-Johnston Games copyrighted Old Bachelor, "the 90s version of Old Maid." The bachelor is pictured as a middle-aged balding man in a crumpled suit who is just about to commit crossover combing to hide his bald spot. The women in the game include Colleen Carpenter, Consuelo Cardiologist, and Fannie Fire-fighter.

If ever there was a time to be a spinster . . . : Freeman, Ruth and Patricia Klaus. "Blessed or Not? The New Spinster in England and the United States in the Late Nineteenth and Early Twentieth Centuries." *Journal of Family History* 9. Winter 1984: 394.

"I want to be a spinster . . .": quoted in Freeman: 396.

an article in a 1917 issue . . . : An Elderly Spinster. "Tales of a Polygamous City I. Taffeta Trousers." *Atlantic Monthly*. December 1917: 721–30.

Ellen Key surveyed the scene . . . : Key, Ellen. *The Woman Movement*. Mammah Bouton Borthwick, translator. New York: G. P. Putnam's Sons, 1912: 71–3.

Although Key comes across as conservative now, H. L. Mencken thought her dangerously free-thinking; see Mencken, H. L. *In Defense of Women*. New York: Alfred A. Knopf, 1928: 183.

They were catching a ride on important historical currents . . . : Freeman: 397.

marriage was openly criticized . . . : *Ibid:* 396–7.

It was also during this period that a sort of sexual awakening occurred among married women, and it appears that they were dissatisfied in both the U.S. and Britain. See Holtzman, Ellen M. "The Pursuit of Married Love: Women's Attitudes Toward Sexuality and Marriage in Great Britain 1918–1939." *Journal of Social History 16.* Winter 1982: 39–52.

At the other end of the spectrum, a distrust of and/or disgust with sex was a major part of the female culture for both the married and unmarried. See Shade, William. "A Mental Passion: Female Sexuality in Victorian America." *International Journal of Women's Studies (Canada)* I, 1978: 19–20.

their more august contemporary Sigmund Freud . . . : Simon: 102–3.

Elisabeth Young-Bruehl makes the point that Freud did *not* see sexual expression between same-sex partners as perverse—at least homosexuals were expressing love to their love objects. See Freud, Sigmund. *Freud on Women*. Ed. Elisabeth Young-Bruehl. New York: W. W. Norton Company, 1990: 12–14. Nonetheless, most feminist scholars agree that in the popular mind, the specter of homosexuality that Freud raised made the lives of single women difficult.

the first pretty, competent ever-single woman . . . : Spangler: 16.

a good and steady friend . . . : *Ibid:* 17. Spangler makes the case that Mary Richards's friendship with Rhoda broke the TV mold.

Marriages began to dissolve . . . : "The Bargain Breaks." *The Economist* (American Edition). December 26, 1992: 37.

news reports falsely suggested . . . : Morin, Richard. "The Trend that Wasn't: Are Moms Leaving Work? Or Did the Dip Deceive?" *Washington Post* (final edition). July 14, 1991: C1.

Historically and cross-culturally, recession or contraction in the job market hits women first. See: Faludi, Susan. *Backlash: The Undeclared War Against American Women.* New York: Crown Publishers, 1991: 51–2; 393–8.

Also see Einhorn: 127–9.

Under similar pressures . . . : Spangler: 21.

Also see: Faludi. *Backlash:* 149–53.

Sally Rogers makes self-deprecating single jokes . . . : Meehan: 45–6; 56.

Mary Richards is flanked . . . : *Ibid:* 51.

a big body of evidence suggests that television . . . : *Ibid:* 114.

many women cope by changing the reflection . . . : Simon: 11–13.

not with a prescription . . . : remarkably, the marketing chief at *Self* magazine once noted that women are reluctant to swallow role models hook, line, and sinker. There is no female counterpart for Michael Jordan. See Warren, James. " 'Wife Test' Is No Test: *Self* Magazine Survey of 1,139 Women Shows a Widening Diversity." *Chicago Tribune* (Tempo). August 25, 1991: 2.

the cumulative social forces . . . : Cockrum, Jean and Priscilla White. "Influences on Life Satisfaction of Never-Married Men and Women." *Family Relations.* October 1985: 551.

Keith, Pat. *The Unmarried in Later Life.* New York: Praeger, 1989: 5–11. The model of stigma appears in *Ibid:* 16.

Chapter Two

when sociologist Ruth Sidel . . . : Sidel, Ruth. *On Her Own: Growing Up in the Shadow of the American Dream.* New York: Penguin Books, 1990: 48.

In *Private Pages* . . . : The diaries of young girls and women ages seventeen to twenty-eight appear at the beginning of the book. *Private Pages: Diaries of American Women 1830s–1970s.* Ed. Penelope Franklin. New York: Ballantine, 1986.

a series of profound crushes . . . : *Ibid:* 62.

fueled the essays of feminist . . . : Wollstonecraft, Mary. "Thoughts on the Education of Daughters." *Women in the Eighteenth Century.* Ed. Vivien Jones. London: Routledge, 1990: 110–12.

One of Wollstonecraft's concerns was that unmarried girls lacked the education to survive if their parents abandoned them. See Wollstonecraft, Mary. *A Vindication of the Rights of Woman.* New York: Penguin Books, 1992: 157–8.

justified in a series of essays . . . : Wolff, Cynthia Griffin. *Emily Dickinson.* Reading, MA: Addison-Wesley Publishing Company, Inc., 1988: 119–21.

training taught girls . . . : Newton, Sarah Emily. "Wise and Foolish Virgins: 'Usable Fiction' and the Early American Conduct Tradition." *Early American Literature* (Volume 25). 1990: 139–41.

Wilkes, Wendell. "A Letter of Genteel and Moral Advice to a Young Lady." *Women in the Eighteenth Century.* Ed. Vivien Jones: 30.

modesty is characterized by silence . . . : Gregory, John. "A Father's Legacy to His Daughters." *Ibid:* 46.

it was given to a young woman named . . . : Newton: 142.

Even proponents of women's education counseled girls to keep their mouths shut. The strategy was: educate her about the wider world but don't let her participate in it. See Lady Mary Wortley Montagu's 1753 letter to her daughter as edited by Olga Kenyon. *800 Years of Women's Letters.* New York: Penguin Books, 1994: 57.

Jane Austen read . . . : Honan, Park. *Jane Austen: Her Life and Work.* New York: Fawcett Columbine, 1987: 33.

so did the fictional Jane Eyre . . . : Jane is given conduct literature by the nasty Mr. Brocklehurst, who believes she is a born liar. Brontë, Charlotte. *Jane Eyre.* New York: The Book League of America: 24.

they turned it into bad fiction . . . : Newton: 150.

Even the ever-single, somewhat rebellious Louisa May Alcott was a participant in this trend; according to biographer Martha Saxton, *Eight Cousins* is essentially a piece of fictionalized conduct literature. See Saxton, Martha. *Louisa May: A Modern Biography of Louisa May Alcott.* Boston: Houghton Mifflin Company, 1977: 319.

In her preface to *An Old-fashioned Girl*, Alcott herself admits to writing conduct fiction. Alcott, Louisa May. *An Old-fashioned Girl.* New York: A. L. Burt Company. 1912: vi.

In the 1950s *Vogue* . . . : Brown, John Mason. "What Makes a Woman Memorable?" *Vogue.* November 15, 1956: 101.

The boy's success . . . : Erik Erikson's model of (male) development appears in Erikson, Erik H. *Childhood and Society.* New York: W. W. Norton & Company, 1963: 247–74.

Freud believed that a woman never . . . : Miller, Jean Baker. *Toward a New Psychology of Women, second edition.* Boston: Beacon Press, 1986: 73.

"It can never attain the strength and independence which gives it its cultural significance." Freud rightly observed at the time that feminists didn't like this portrait. Freud,

Sigmund. "Femininity." *Freud on Women*. Ed. Elisabeth Young-Bruehl. New York: W. W. Norton & Company, 1990: 357.

One social and public implication of her lack of superego is that women have little sense of justice. *Ibid*: 361–2.

it is probably her organic . . . : Freud: 345 ff.

In Miller's view . . . : Miller: 73–4.

"women's sense of self . . .": *Ibid*: 83.

that's very close to the point . . . : In fact, at the crux of the problem is the girl's discovery that it's impossible to be adult (autonomous) and feminine. Pipher, Mary. *Reviving Ophelia: Saving the Selves of Adolescent Girls*. New York: G. P. Putnam's Sons, 1994: 36–41.

As researcher Pat Keith has noted . . . : Keith, Pat. *The Unmarried in Later Life*. New York: Praeger, 1989: 8.

She was overweight . . . : Interestingly, Pipher believes that girls who are neither particularly plain nor particularly attractive have a developmental advantage. See Pipher: 56.

So little is known . . . : the work in female adolescent psychology has been pioneered by Carol Gilligan at Harvard and has been roundly criticized. Her first major work was Gilligan, Carol. *In a Different Voice: Psychological Theory and Women's Development*. Cambridge, MA: Harvard University Press, 1982.

Another study is recounted in Gilligan, Carol, Nona P. Lyons, and Trudy J. Hanmer (Eds.). *Making Connections: The Relational Worlds of Adolescent Girls at Emma Willard School*. Cambridge, MA: Harvard University Press, 1990.

One important pattern does appear . . . : typically researchers have looked for all sorts of indicators that might predict singleness. Some suggestions include being raised in a dysfunctional family and being the oldest in the family. But a study of older adults interviewed in 1972 and 1977 found that there were no apparent differences in background between those who had married and those who hadn't. The only indicator was education—ever-single women were more educated than their cohorts. Ward, Russell A. "The Never-Married in Later Life." *Single Life: Unmarried Adults in Social Context*. Ed. Peter Stein. New York: St. Martin's Press, 1981: 346.

Some of the other researchers who have noted the same pattern:

Cramer, Duncan. "Living Alone, Marital Status, Gender and Health." *Journal of Community & Applied Social Psychology* (Volume 3) 1–15. 1993: 5.

Rice, Susan. "Single, Older Childless Women: Differences Between Never-Married and Widowed Women in Life Satisfaction and Social Support." *Journal of Gerontological Social Work* (Volume 13). 1989: 37.

Simon, Barbara Levy. *Never Married Women.* Philadelphia: Temple University Press, 1987: 25.

education doesn't make spinsters, at least in the late . . . : However, you could make a case that education did make spinsters in the *early* twentieth century. In the general population 90 percent of women who came of age between 1890 and 1910 married at some point in their lives; meanwhile less than 50 percent of college educated women married. The trend continued for some years: only 50 percent of the women who graduated Radcliffe between 1911 and 1920 were married by the time the data were collected; and a mere 43.7 percent of women who graduated Oberlin between 1917 and 1921 married before the data were collected. In retrospect, the partial cause for these surprising stats may have been delayed marriage, but they caused quite a controversy back then. See Solomon, Barbara Miller. *In the Company of Educated Women: A History of Women and Higher Education in America.* New Haven: Yale University Press, 1985: 119–21.

negative correlation is fast diminishing . . . Moorman, Jeanne E. "The Relationship Between Education and Marriage." U.S. Bureau of Census. July 1987: 9. This is the census report Faludi claims was buried during the Reagan administration. It *was* hard to find.

It also makes supporting herself . . . : Pearlin, Leonard I. and Joyce S. Johnson. "Marital Status, Life-Strains, and Depression." Stein: 169.

Chapter Three

one half of all marriages . . . : "The Bargain Breaks." *The Economist* (American edition). December 26, 1992: 37.

asked 1,635 women what their goals . . . : Decker, Cathleen. "The L.A. Women: The Faces Behind the Statistics." *Los Angeles Times.* February 21, 1988: 11.

about 51 percent of the unmarried women . . . : Warren, Ellen. "More Women Calling Marriage a Tie that Binds Too Tightly, Survey Finds." *Chicago Tribune* (Section 2). July 29, 1993: 1.

many women make a distinction between wanting . . . : Kuriansky, Judy. "Results of the *New Woman* Singles Survey." *New Woman.* December 1987: 98–100.

It is, as researchers have noted . . . : Bass, Alison. "Working Women Fare Better." *Boston Globe.* September 17, 1990: 35.

Bass's article is based on Helson, Ravenna and James Picano. "Is the Traditional Role Bad for Women?" *Journal of Personality and Social Psychology*. August 1990. In the cohort they studied, part of the problem for both traditional, married women (who often suffered difficulties in their forties) and unmarried women (who suffered a psychological disadvantage earlier in life) is being out of synch with the cohort.

Barbara Levy Simon found that the thirties were particularly difficult for women who had wanted to marry. Simon, Barbara Levy. *Never Married Women*. Philadelphia: Temple University Press, 1987: 52.

In the *New Woman* survey, therapist Kuriansky found that older women are happier than younger women and notes that among her own clients the thirties are the rockiest period. Kuriansky: 102.

The highly traditional 1950s Broadway hit *The Tender Trap* makes the same point about the early thirties: "All we have to do to get married is stay home . . ." laments thirty-three-year-old Sylvia Crewes, a violinist who has moved to New York, where the glamour is. "We make a career; we find glamour and excitement . . . till one fine day we look around . . . and we haven't got a man." Later, when someone tells her that there are worse things than not being married, Sylvia—bright, accomplished, attractive—responds, "Name three!" See Schulman, Max and Robert Paul Smith. *The Tender Trap*. New York: Dramatists Play Service, Inc., 1956: 58; 69.

"her wild fears . . .": The poem "No Ring" appears in Cary, Alice and Phoebe Cary. *The Poetical Works of Alice and Phoebe Cary*. Boston: Houghton Mifflin Company, 1903: 85.

exhume every female fault . . . : check out the table of contents in Price, Stephen and Susan Price. *No More Lonely Nights*. New York: G. P. Putnam's Sons, 1988.

"Fantasize about being married". . . : *Ibid: 79*.

package themselves like a microwave dinner . . . : The consumer analogy is explicit in Gloria Bledsoe Goodman's 1991 book, *A Woman's Guide to Prime Time Dating* (Carol Publishing Group): "It's a buyer's market, and all the buyers are men." Quoted in Barbieri, Susan. "Advice for Re-Entering the Dating Game." *Chicago Tribune* (Womanews). June 9, 1991: 10.

"Never Meet Any Decent Men? . . .": coverline on *New Woman*, March 1988.

"How Intelligent Women Flirt" . . . : coverline on *New Woman*, May 1994.

"How to Get Him to Commit" . . . : coverline on *Mademoiselle*, February 1994.

Katrina's complaint recalls the story of . . . : Munsch, Robert N. *The Paper Bag Princess*. Toronto: Annick Press Ltd., 1980.

Source Notes

This exclusion was inevitable . . . : In *New Passages*, Sheehy highlights some differences between men and women, but the developmental scheme, which suggests predictable, indeed unavoidable, steps in the life course, does not elucidate the particular crisis women encounter *before* marriage. Sheehy, Gail. *New Passages: Mapping Your Life Across Time.* New York: Random House, 1995: 59. Her analysis of the ever-single feminist Gloria Steinem appears between 121–4.

Erikson's original framework . . . : Erikson's model appears in Erikson, Erik H. *Childhood and Society.* New York: W. W. Norton & Company, 1963: 247–74.

Because achieving marriage often requires . . . : Jack, Dana Crowley. *Silencing the Self: Women and Depression.* New York: HarperPerennial, 1991: 41–6.

One woman told Dana Crowley Jack . . . : *Ibid:* 47–8.

He understood that unequal relationships in society . . . : Erikson: 241–6.

Women in their twenties and thirties . . . : The college seniors in the 1977 Broadway play *Uncommon Women and Others* discuss their confusion quite frankly. "If I fall in love, it will be because I think someone is better than me," notes Holly. "And if I really thought someone was better than me, I'd give him everything and I'd hate him for my living through him." Kate, who is applying to law school, challenges her friend. "You don't really expect to live through someone else, do you?" she asks. "I think I'd like to very much," answers Holly, rather inexplicably. See Wasserstein, Wendy. *The Heidi Chronicles and Other Plays.* San Diego: Harcourt Brace Jovanovich, Publishers, 1990: 39.

poor ever-single Rebecca Ketchum . . . : Schlissel, Lillian. *Women's Diaries of the Westward Journey.* New York: Schocken Books, 1982: 100–101. Settling in Oregon, she achieved the marital status that would have made her trip easier. *Ibid:* 102.

In writer Richard Cohen's imagination . . . : Cohen makes it clear Alice is fictional. She doesn't exist, he writes, but if she did "she'd break your heart." Cohen, Richard. "What About Alice?" *Washington Post Magazine.* July 28, 1991: 3.

Response to Cohen was largely angry. One woman wrote: "Perhaps Richard Cohen's sympathy should be directed at the woman who finds, after the $1200 wedding dress and the $15,000 ceremony, that she has landed a man who has nothing to say to her at the end of the day." "Alice Doesn't Live Here Anymore." *Washington Post Magazine* (letters). September 22, 1991: 3.

Some women never face . . . : strangely, the recessive image of Catharine Beecher's mother is much like that of both Emily Dickinson's mother and Susan B. Anthony's mother. Beecher's mother's fate appears in Sklar, Kathryn Kish. *Catharine Beecher: A Study in American Domesticity.* New Haven: Yale University Press, 1973: 5. The struggles for her father's approval and against submission to the religion appear in *Ibid:* 28–33; 39. The marriage decision: *Ibid:* 34–6. The argument that women should be subordinated: *Ibid:* 156. The notion that women teachers should be paid less: *Ibid:* 182.

In fact, as a teacher, Susan B. Anthony did make less—about one quarter of what her father made and one half of what her brother made: Barry, Kathleen. *Susan B. Anthony: A Biography of a Singular Feminist.* New York: New York University Press, 1988: 47. Anthony's remark about Beecher appears in *Ibid:* 128.

The explorer Mary Kingsley . . . : biographer Katherine Frank attributes the failure on the part of Kingsley, Charlotte Brontë, Florence Nightingale, and even Queen Victoria to declare one's own self through one's own script to "a failure of nerve," and "a lurking fear . . . that they *were* unwomanly." Frank, Katherine. *A Voyager Out: The Life of Mary Kingsley.* New York: Ballantine Books, 1986: 209.

predicted that increased social fluidity . . . : See Stein, Peter J. "Understanding Single Adulthood." *Single Life: Unmarried Adults in Social Context.* Ed. Peter Stein. New York: St. Martin's Press, 1981: 18.

the younger ever-single women in her study . . . : Peterson, Nancy L. *Our Lives for Ourselves: Women Who Have Never Married.* New York: G. P. Putnam's Sons, 1981: 251.

Chapter Four

the percentage of single-parent families . . . : *Households, Families, and Children: A 30-Year Perspective.* Bureau of the Census, November 1992: 20.

America's cultural confusion over family . . . : Norval, Glenn. "What Does Family Mean?" *American Demographics.* June 1992: 30 ff.

Emily Dickinson spent seven years . . . : Wolff, Cynthia Griffin. *Emily Dickinson.* Reading, MA: Addison-Wesley Publishing Company, Inc., 1988: 44.

Catharine Beecher ran her sister . . . : Sklar, Kathryn Kish. *Catharine Beecher: A Study in American Domesticity.* New Haven: Yale University Press, 1973: 233–7.

Susan B. Anthony spent many months . . . : Barry, Kathleen. *Susan B. Anthony: A Biography of a Singular Feminist.* New York: New York University Press, 1988: 157.

At best, the spinster-aunt role . . . : Chambers-Schiller, Lee. "'Woman Is Born to Love': The Maiden Aunt as Maternal Figure in Ante-Bellum Literature." *Frontiers* (Volume 10, Number 1). 1988: 35–6.

According to Chambers-Schiller, the spinster-aunt as one-woman SWAT team began to disappear after the Civil War, when celibacy came under suspicion; it was believed that celibacy caused women's reproductive organs to atrophy, causing mental deterioration— not good qualifications for a childcare provider. *Ibid:* 41.

At worst, the family role was akin to servitude . . . : When Susan B. Anthony took care of her cousin Margaret during a difficult and ultimately fatal pregnancy and childbirth, it also meant actually running the household. She saw that she had two choices: remain a dutiful daughter and aunt and work like a "galley slave" and thus maintain a position in the community, or leave home, become a wage earner, and be exiled from the community of women—the quilting bees, the apple-parings. See Barry, Kathleen: 54–8.

Poor Mary Kingsley . . . : Frank, Katherine. *A Voyager Out: The Life of Mary Kingsley*. New York: Ballantine Books, 1986: 51–5.

the woman most angered . . . : Nightingale wrote her essay on women, family, and work, called *Cassandra*, just before she took a position. See Nightingale, Florence. *Cassandra*. Introduction by Myra Stark. New York: The Feminist Press, 1979: 37.

unable to break out . . . : Nightingale suffered many of the same ills other Victorian women suffered, including hallucinations, insomnia, and suicidal thoughts. Webb, Christine. *Ibid:* 1339–40.

Her illness, like her basic personality, seemed to be fueled by an overwhelming desire to control. A lacerating account of Nightingale's damaged personality and determined myth-making appears in Smith, F. B. *Florence Nightingale: Reputation and Power*. New York: St. Martin's Press, 1982. Her illness appears: 89–93.

Ellen Key talked about "ill-natured" aunts . . . : Key, Ellen. *The Woman Movement*. Mammah Bouton Borthwick, translator. New York: G. P. Putnam's Sons, 1912: 72–6.

Edith Wharton created exactly that kind of aunt . . . : Wharton, Edith. "The Old Maid." *Old New York*. New York: Appleton and Company, 1924.

Susan B. Anthony experienced such a shift . . . : Barry: 36. In fact, she dreaded both sisters' marriages, and both sisters withdrew emotionally before they married. *Ibid:* 42–3.

Being single in an adaptive family . . . : in Barbara Levy Simon's study, many women noted that the support they received from their families as they passed the common age of marriage was invaluable. Simon, Barbara Levy. *Never Married Women*. Philadelphia: Temple University Press, 1987: 66; 68.

Similarly, researcher Russell A. Ward found that older ever-single people were less likely to see their families than were the divorced or separated, the widowed, or the married, and he found that unmarried people were less satisfied with family life than married people were. More strikingly, he found that ever-single people were less happy than the married people, but that when he removed the factor of family life, the happiness scores of the ever-single and the married drew much closer—suggesting that family does have great significance. See Ward, Russell A. "The Never-Married in Later Life." *Single Life: Unmarried Adults in Social Context.* Ed. Peter Stein. New York: St. Martin's Press, 1981: 350–2.

in 1976, just 16 percent . . . : Weiss, Rich. "The Kidless Culture." *Health.* July–August, 1993: 40.

If trends continue . . . : Ambry, Margaret K. "Childless Chances." *American Demographics.* April 1992: 55.

In a 1991 *Self* magazine survey . . . : Warren, James. " 'Wife Test' " Is No Test: *Self* Magazine Survey of 1,139 Women Shows a Widening Diversity." *Chicago Tribune* (Tempo). August 25, 1991: 8.

Also in the early nineties, Leslie Lafayette founded a national group called ChildFree Network in an effort to support those who choose not to have children and to counteract the isolation that occurs with childlessness. Fulford, D. G. "Raising an Issue: Childlessness Is Definitely OK." *San Jose Mercury News.* October 19, 1993: 2C.

the fastest growing household . . . : Ambry: 55.

motherhood was a major issue . . . : Peterson, Nancy L. *Our Lives for Ourselves: Women Who Have Never Married.* New York: G. P. Putnam's Sons, 1981: 251.

and a number of studies indicate . . . : Besides Peterson's observations, Susan S. Lang mentions two studies; but she also points out that Pat Keith sees childlessness as benign. Lang, Susan S. *Women Without Children: The Reasons, The Rewards, The Regrets.* New York: Pharos Books, 1989: 70.

a well-publicized trend . . . : Teegarden, Carrie. "A Changing Nation: Traditional Clanlike Cleavers Now a Rare Breed, Census Shows." *Atlanta Journal and Constitution* (Section A). February 17, 1993: 4.

an estimated 29.7 percent . . . : *The Monthly Vital Statistics Report.* Centers for Disease Control. Volume 44, Number 3 (Supplement). September 21, 1995: 47.

during the Revolutionary era . . . : Shade, William. " 'A Mental Passion': Female Sexuality in Victorian America." *International Journal of Women's Studies (Canada)* 1. 1978: 15.

Despite recent politics, sex has been a part of courtship throughout U.S. history. See Trafford, Abigail. "Unwed Motherhood: Insights from the Colonial Era." *Washington Post* (Section 2). January 8, 1991: 6.

they had a greater tendency to give up their babies . . . : Speer, Tibbett L. "Why Single Women Keep Their Babies." *American Demographics*. June 1992: 9.

unmarried women have accounted for 53 percent . . . : The Alan Guttmacher Institute. *Facts in Brief: Abortion in the United States*. New York, 1994: 1. Rates are also high for married and unmarried women between the ages of forty and forty-four (44 percent) and married and unmarried teenagers (37 percent). The rate among all women is 28 percent: *Ibid:* 1.

"We were very poor . . .": Karen's comment is virtually an echo of Elizabeth Blackwell's comment to her own adopted daughter. In a letter written in 1887, the ever-single Blackwell wrote of her family: "I have always enjoyed one great blessing in life, *viz:* the fullest sympathy of my own family. The mother and nine brothers and sisters who were left to struggle through life on my father's death were a very united family. . . . We were all very poor in worldly goods." Blackwell became the first American woman to get a modern medical degree. Quoted in Payne, Karen (Ed.). *Between Ourselves: Letters between Mothers & Daughters 1750–1982*. Boston: Houghton Mifflin Company, 1983: 96–7.

This is a long and tragic dilemma . . . : in Charlotte Brontë's case, her minister-father was protected for quite some time from the fact that his daughters were writing famous novels; more to the point, Reverend Patrick Brontë had so confined his daughter in his own mind that he never understood her intellectual life and in the end nearly blocked her brief marriage. In fact, he refused at the last minute to give her away. See Fraser, Rebecca. *The Brontës: Charlotte Brontë and Her Family*. New York: Fawcett-Columbine, 1990: 286–7; 440; 443–4; 455–6; 466–7.

In Louisa May Alcott's case, the relationship was even more tragic, perhaps because the opinions about women that her philosopher father and his friends (including Ralph Waldo Emerson) held were so clearly contradicted by the fact that Louisa supported her parents for most of their adult lives. Prosuffrage but not feminist, Louisa never really found her self-worth and spent the last years of her physically difficult life tending her ailing father, dying only two days after he did, as if the framework of her life had dissolved beneath her. See Saxton, Martha. *Louisa May: A Modern Biography of Louisa May Alcott*. Boston: Houghton Mifflin Company, 1977: 162–4; 182–3; 295; 335–66.

In a series of "Cathy" cartoons . . . : in one episode, Cathy's emotional upheaval is not caused by her recent breakup but by her mother's grilling after the breakup. Guisewhite, Cathy. "Cathy." United Features Syndicate, 1995.

This theme is a familiar one to Guisewhite, who published a similar Mother's Day card in the early nineties. More dangerously, this version enshrined the notion that the unmarried daughter is a burden or maybe an embarrassment to her mother. On the cover, the ever-single Cathy appears next to a marital checklist, including: "married," "engaged," "going

steady," "dating seriously," "dating at all," "still capable of occasionally speaking to men."
Inside the message is: "Happy Mother's Day. And thank you for your patience." Guisewhite, Cathy. "Cathy." Chicago: Recycled Paper Products, Inc.

even in the *New York Times* . . . : in an article about New Yorkers who spend Valentine's
Day alone, one line goes: "As their mothers will gladly attest, a lot of these single New
Yorkers are the sort who shouldn't have any trouble finding a partner." Not surprisingly,
the article concludes that these single New Yorkers aren't searching for a partner but for
loneliness. Tierney, John. "Picky, Picky, Picky." *New York Times Magazine.* February 12,
1995: 22; 24.

Amusing as these quips may seem . . . : one writer who actually touches on the impact of
this cultural norm is Rosemarie Lennon. See "Are You Seeing Anyone?" *New Woman.*
February 1988: 148.

victim of extraordinary abuse . . . : Carrighar, Sally. *Home to the Wilderness.* Boston:
Houghton Mifflin Company, 1973: 5–6; 31–2; 71–9; 86–8; 114–15.

Later, as an adult . . . : *Ibid:* 116–18.

As Carrighar suggests, it may have been easier earlier in the century. Certainly the Elderly
Spinster consciously adopts similar substitute families when she moves to India. An Elderly Spinster. "Tales of a Polygamous City I. Taffeta Trousers." *Atlantic Monthly.* December 1917: 727.

Chapter Five

old-shoe comfort of the friendship . . . : "And then back in that perfect house," recalled
Potter, "Maggie Harkness fresh from her novel-writing to greet me to chat on all subjects,
human and divine, and to play snatches of good music on the parliamentary piano. I, lying
the while on the sofa, watching the river and the barges on it creeping by. Happy fellow-
ship in work, rest, and also in memories." This and other observations are quoted in Nord,
Debora Epstein. "'Neither Pairs nor Odd:' Female Community in Late Nineteenth Century London." *Signs 15.* Summer 1990: 739.

In a 1990 Gallup poll . . . : Destefano, Linda. "All the Lonely People." *San Francisco Chronicle* (Section B). March 7, 1990: 5.

60 percent said that *if they never marry* . . . : Kuriansky, Judy. "Results of the *New Woman*
Singles Survey." *New Woman.* December 1987: 101.

unmarried people do rely more on . . . : among the studies that show this is the Gallup poll.
Destefano: 5.

G. Moore's findings on married and unmarried adults' social contacts are quoted in Hatch, Laurie Russell and Kris Bulcroft. "Contact with Friends in Later Life: Disentangling the Effects of Gender and Marital Status." *Journal of Marriage and Family*. February 1992: 223.

They also seem to show that women's friendships . . . : P. C. Cozby's 1973 review of the literature concludes that one-half the studies show greater female disclosure; half the studies reveal no difference; but none makes a case for more disclosure by men. See Hess, Beth. "Friendship and Gender Roles over the Life Course." *Single Life: Unmarried Adults in Social Context*. Ed. Peter Stein. New York: St. Martin's Press, 1981: 105.

Later studies seem to lean more toward the conclusion that women's friendships are more intimate. See Hatch, Laurie Russell and Kris Bulcroft: 222–3.

Hit by Cupid's arrow . . . : Christy, Howard Chandler. *The American Girl*. New York: Da Capo, 1976: 142; 146.

in the married woman's life, there's a "before" person . . . : Hess: 110.

few women wanted to make the move . . . : Schlissel, Lillian. *Women's Diaries of the Westward Journey*. New York: Schocken Books: 10–14; 28; 108–11.

women were psychologically incapable . . . Hess: 104.

watched her friendships dwindle . . . Wolff, Cynthia Griffin. *Emily Dickinson*. Reading, MA: Addison-Wesley Publishing Company, Inc., 1988: 113–14.

Frustrated, Stanton wrote to Anthony . . . : Barry, Kathleen. *Susan B. Anthony: A Biography of a Singular Feminist*. New York: New York University Press, 1988: 127.

Stanton's comment is ironic in the context of Anthony's life, in which Susan was often disappointed by married colleagues who left the movement to take care of their families. Both Antoinette Brown and Lucy Stone indicated that she would be better off (and have less of a tendency to nag) if she were married. *Ibid*: 117. In fact, she was occasionally excluded on the basis of her marital status. *Ibid*: 263. Yet she was the backbone of the movement, partly *because* of her status—only an unmarried woman could rent halls, enter into contracts, or handle finances. *Ibid*: 259.

Stanton herself once abandoned Anthony on stage, but the friendship remained close. "Nothing that Susan could say or do could break my friendship with her; and I know nothing could uproot her affection for me." Quoted in *Ibid*: 274.

one ever-single wit called the constant mother-talk . . . : quoted in Freeman, Ruth and Patricia Klaus. "Blessed or Not? The New Spinster in England and the United States in the Late Nineteenth and Early Twentieth Centuries." *Journal of Family History* 9. Winter 1984: 403.

only one third of married women . . . : O'Connor, Pat. "Women's Confidants Outside Marriage: Shared or Competing Sources of Intimacy?" *Sociology*. May 1991: 245–6.

Take the inaugural issue of *Married Woman* . . . : Haberstam, Joshua. "A Table For Four." *Married Woman*. February/March 1994: 92; 94.

has stooped to grapple with the issue . . . : Nemy, Enid. "New Yorkers, etc." *New York Times* (Section 1, Part 2). September 9, 1990: 46.

it's about a friendship between two ever-single women . . . : Benedict, Elizabeth. *Slow Dancing*. New York: Bantam Books, 1990.

"*All* the time" . . . : Benedict: 194.

There are no guidelines . . . : for instance, Rachel Kranz grapples with the idea that, as a single friend, she will never come "first." See Kranz, Rachel. "Toward a New Definition of Singleness: Building a Life with Close Friends." *Utne Reader*. March/April 1989: 60–1.

the way we behave with family . . . : In a study of thirty-one childless, ever-single women Robert L. Rubinstein's team uses the "folk model" developed by David Schneider to describe kinship in America. According to Schneider, the blood tie is the primary basis for kinship; secondary is the code of conduct, which includes loyalty, trust, and help. In the absence of a blood tie, the code of conduct becomes negotiated, and the tie becomes "constructed." See Rubinstein, Robert L., Baine B. Alexander, Marcene Goodman, and Mark Luborsky. "Key Relationships of Never-Married, Childless Older Women: A Cultural Analysis." *Journal of Gerontology: Social Services* (Volume 46, Number 5). 1991: S271.

intimate friendships were key . . . : Simon, Barbara Levy. *Never Married Women*. Philadelphia: Temple University Press, 1987: 95.

summarily kicked out of one house . . . : *Ibid:* 103–4.

the overwhelming majority counted their relationships . . . : Rubinstein, Robert L. et al: S275; S270.

may be an edge that ever-single women . . . : Cockrum, Jean and Priscilla White. "Influences on Life Satisfaction of Never-Married Men and Women." *Family Relations* 34. October 1995: 554–5.

Interestingly, Hatch and Bulcroft's longitudinal study of 1,435 older adults found no differences between never-married men and women in their willingness to leave friends for a new job or in the number of friends they had. But women did have significantly more contact with at least one friend. Hatch, Laurie Russell and Kris Bulcroft: 227.

Source Notes

Chapter Six

the U.S. population grew by 10 percent . . . : Teegarden, Carrie. "A Changing Nation: Traditional Clan Like Cleavers Now a Rare Breed, Census Shows." *Atlanta Journal and Constitution* (Section A). February 17, 1993: 4.

Single women are the fastest growing group . . . : Levin, Jayne. "Singles Make up 50% of First-Time Buyers." *Washington Post* (final edition). January 23, 1993: E1.

nearly one third of ever-single women . . . : Woodward, Jeanne M. "Home Alone in 1989." *Current Housing Reports*. U.S. Bureau of Census. October 1992: 5.

She is exhausted by this: Marek, Lynne. "Working Women Feel Beset by Job Stress." *Chicago Tribune*. October 15, 1994: 1; 10.

Also see Hochschild, Arlie. *The Second Shift: Working Parents and the Revolution at Home.* New York: Viking, 1989.

when Catharine Beecher set up her own . . . : Sklar, Kathryn Kish. *Catharine Beecher: A Study in American Domesticity.* New Haven, Connecticut: Yale University Press, 1973: 62. In later years Beecher struggled over her lack of a home, much as her younger nemesis Susan B. Anthony would, and she tried several avenues to attain one. *Ibid:* 220-1. Eventually, she retired to her brother's home, no longer "a trunk without a label," as her sister Harriet Beecher Stowe once called her. *Ibid:* 272.

Mary Astell blazed . . . : Astell's ideal community was outlined in *A Serious Proposal to the Ladies.* Rogers, Katharine M. *Feminism in Eighteenth-Century England.* Urbana, IL: University of Illinois Press, 1982: 71-4.

until she made a reluctant . . . : she was pregnant as well as reluctant. Eckhardt, Celia Morris. *Fanny Wright: Rebel in America.* Cambridge, MA: Harvard University Press, 1984: 213; 232.

In Italy . . . : Palazzi, Maura. "Female Solitude and Patrilineage: Unmarried Women and Widows during the Eighteenth and Nineteenth Centuries." *Journal of Family History.* Winter 1990: 451.

By the turn of the twentieth century . . . : Freeman, Ruth and Patricia Klaus. "Blessed or Not? The New Spinster in England and the United States in the Late Nineteenth and Early Twentieth Centuries." *Journal of Family History.* Winter 1984: 407.

more than half returned home . . . : Antler, Joyce. "'After College, What?': New Graduates and the Family Claim." *American Quarterly* 32. Fall 1980: 421-34.

less than 6 percent . . . : *Ibid:* 421.

"charming farmhouse [with] all the cares . . .": quoted in *Ibid:* 431.

"Most things have come to me . . .": quoted in *Ibid:* 432.

the first thing a single girl does . . . : Brown, Helen Gurley. *Sex and the Single Girl.* New York: Avon Books, 1962: 105.

an interior-decorated mantrap . . . : *Ibid:* 108–9; 119.

"A chic apartment . . .": *Ibid:* 106.

"I often believe . . .": Harayda, Janice. *The Joy of Being Single: Stop Putting Your Life on Hold and Start Living!* Garden City, New York: Doubleday & Company, Inc., 1986: 106; 107–10; 112.

Beware of chintz . . . : Stein, Ruthe. *The Art of Single Living: A Guide to Going It Alone in the '90s.* New York: Shapolsky Publishers, Inc., 1990: 17–18.

"I don't live anywhere . . .": Koller, Alice. *An Unknown Woman.* New York: Bantam Books, 1991: 2.

there are two kinds of loneliness . . . : Weiss, Robert S. "The Study of Loneliness." *Single Life: Unmarried Adults in Social Context.* Ed. Peter Stein. New York: St. Martin's Press, 1981: 158–9.

the emptiness inside is exacerbated . . . : Weiss says that being with married couples may only intensify the single person's feelings of "marginality" and "of having no place." *Ibid:* 157.

much as women answering a 1993 survey . . . : Warren, Ellen. "More Women Calling Marriage a Tie that Binds Too Tightly, Survey Finds." *Chicago Tribune* (Section 2). July 29, 1993: 1.

"That . . . is an awful kind of loneliness . . .": Although few admit it readily, loneliness in the context of marriage does exist—at least frequently enough to catch the attention of Dan Kiley, bestselling author of *The Peter Pan Syndrome.* Kiley actually proposes five stages of loneliness within marriage: Bewilderment (under twenty-eight); Isolation (twenty-eight to thirty-four); Agitation (thirty-five to forty-two); Depression (forty-three to fifty); Exhaustion (over fifty). He also offers a five-step method for recovery. See Kiley, Dan. *Living Together, Feeling Alone: Healing Your Hidden Loneliness.* New York: Prentice Hall Press, 1989: 13–14; 32.

they believed that living alone . . . : Staples, Robert. "Black Singles in America." Stein: 47.

ever-single women have higher rates of suicide . . . : Kong, Delores. "Medical Notebook." *Boston Globe* (National-Foreign). March 4, 1993: 3.

Warrick, Pamela. "Experts See Themes in Assisted Suicides." *Los Angeles Times* (Section E). April 14, 1993: 1.

According to a 1979 review of the literature, older ever-singles also have higher rates of depression, phobic tendencies, and passivity. See Stein, Peter. "Understanding Single Adulthood." Stein: 15.

they are less physically healthy . . . : the difference, however, may be overrated. See Ward, Russell A. "The Never-Married in Later Life." Stein. *Ibid:* 347.

In fact, among the unmarried, the healthiest are ever-single. See Cramer, Duncan. "Living Alone, Marital Status, Gender and Health." *Journal of Community and Applied Social Psychology* (Volume 3). 1993: 1.

they have higher morbidity . . . : Somers, Anne R. "Mental Status, Health, and the Use of Health Services: An Old Relationship Revisited." Stein: 179.

Also see: Watkins, Susan Cotts. "Spinsters." *Journal of Family History*. Winter 1984: 312.

he and his team point out that the definitions vary . . . : Williams, David R., David T. Takeuchi, and Russel K. Adair. "Marital Status and Psychiatric Disorders Among Blacks and Whites." *Journal of Health and Social Behavior* (Volume 33). June 1992: 142–3.

The studies on living alone . . . : a review of the literature appears in Cramer: 1–3.

he found few differences . . . : Cramer: 8–13.

Hetty Fifield finds herself homeless . . . : the story is "A Church Mouse" and it appears in Freeman Wilkins, Mary E. *A New England Nun*. Ridgewood, NJ: The Gregg Press, 1967.

Chapter Seven

a new Japanese dating service . . . : Goozner, Merrill. "Japanese Women Say 'I Do' to Careers." *Chicago Tribune*. November 25, 1994: 1; 24.

women in Japan have delayed marriage . . . : They're bucking a tradition that calls them "stale Christmas cake" when they're not married by twenty-five. Meanwhile, the government is concerned that too many men are left single, without full-time housewives, which in turn threatens the structure of the corporate powerhouses. Beiwen, John. "Marketplace." Public Radio International, July 5, 1993.

Anna Quindlen points this out . . . : Quindlen, Anna. "The Out-of-Work-Wife." *New York Times* (Section A). October 26, 1994: 27.

Freud believed women incapable . . . : the exception: women invented weaving. Freud, Sigmund. "Femininity." *Freud on Women.* Ed. Elisabeth Young-Bruehl. New York: W. W. Norton & Company, 1990: 360.

Former Texas governor Ann Richards . . . : the speech was partially reprinted in the *New York Times*, June 25, 1994: 15. The ensuing flap was reviewed on "The Mara Tapp Show." WBEZ, Chicago, June 28, 1994.

when a recent women's "career" program . . . : the leader of the seminar was a Northwestern graduate and coauthor of a book on the subject. See Neumeir, Kathleen and Janet Z. Giler. *Redefining Mr. Right: A Career Woman's Guide to Finding a Mate.* Oakland, CA: New Harbinger Publications, Inc., 1992. Although the book emphasizes that women should maintain self-esteem, tips include retaining "some aspects of femininity"; doing the things men do, including sailing, golf, and martial arts; and sending effective nonverbal cues, including the head toss, eyebrow flash, and arm flexion. *Ibid:* 133–4; 155. The protest made its way to the Chicago ABC television affiliate, April 3, 1995.

Another confusing message appears in Margaret Kent and Robert Feinschreiber's book *Love at Work: Using Your Job to Find a Mate.* New York: Warner Books, 1988. The authors openly discount the job-threatening disadvantages to conducting love affairs in the workplace and they apparently never notice the more profound threat this notion presents to women who might otherwise achieve something good and confirming out of work itself.

they got sick . . . : some, of course, didn't. For some, the necessary choice between the demands of the work they held to be sacred and the demands of marriage was made consciously. Mary Cassatt (b. 1845) felt that she had to make a choice, as did the writer Miles Franklin (b. 1879), about whom there is a charming film, *My Brilliant Career* (1980), and Simone de Beauvoir (b. 1908).

plagued by a great epidemic . . . : Strouse, Jean. *Alice James: A Biography.* Boston: Houghton Mifflin Company, 1980: 102–6. One contemporary specialist believed that its cause in women was early exposure to intellectual and emotional stimulation. *Ibid:* 107.

a well-established cult of female delicacy . . . : Banner, Lois W. *American Beauty.* Chicago: The University of Chicago Press, 1983: 45–57.

Alice James suffered from it . . . : Strouse: 109.

Jane Addams did too . . . : Although Addams, who was a lesbian, certainly had organic physical problems including back pain, she also suffered nervous ills apparently caused by the "family claim." See Antler, Joyce. "'After College, What?': New Graduates and the Family Claim." *American Quarterly* (Volume 32). 1980: 413–4.

Mary Kingsley . . . : Frank, Katherine. *A Voyager Out: The Life of Mary Kingsley*. New York: Ballantine Books, 1986: 59.

"Thus far I have done nothing . . . ," "I have not done any . . .": Quoted in Antler: 424.

"There is nothing significant . . .": Quoted in *Ibid*: 425.

"I was married to a lawyer . . .": Quoted in *Ibid*: 429.

This was a lonely and difficult path . . . : A brief but dismal description appears in Cogan, Frances B. *All American Girl. The Ideal of Real Womanhood in Mid-Nineteenth Century America*. Athens, GA: The University of Georgia Press, 1989: 220.

A more complete, and more dismal, picture appears in Goldin, Claudia. "The Work and Wages of Single Women, 1870 to 1920." *Journal of Economic History* 40. March 1980: 83; 86; 88. Between 1890 and 1900, Goldin writes, 75 percent of the female labor force was ever-single; most would marry and leave. *Ibid*: 81; 83.

In 1930, 61 percent . . . : the research is the work of V. K. Oppenheimer. Quoted in Simon, Barbara Levy. *Never Married Women*. Philadelphia: Temple University Press, 1987: 129.

To be a flight attendant . . . : phone interview with United Airlines corporate spokesperson, January 10, 1995.

These rules codified . . . : Weaver, Polly. "What's Wrong with Ambition?" *Mademoiselle*. September 1956: 191.

Victor Fuchs points out that 20 percent . . . : Fuchs, Victor. *Women's Quest for Economic Equality*. Cambridge, MA: Harvard University Press, 1988: 66.

A smaller 1992 study . . . : Norris, Kim. "Study Shows Difficulties for Women Execs." *St. Petersburg Times*, August 19, 1992: 1E.

In Canadian politics . . . : Fotheringham, Allan. "It's Always Lonelier for any Woman at the Top." *Financial Post* (Spectrum), June 19, 1993: S3.

Marital status also affects . . . : Fuchs: 59–60.

There is research that indicates the opposite. In particular, I looked at Landau, Jacqueline and Michael B. Arthur. "The Relationship of Marital Status, Spouse's Career Status, and Gender to Salary Level." *Sex Roles* (Volume 27, Number 11–12). 1992: 674. However, the data all come from one Fortune 500 company; given the nature of corporate culture, policy, and politics, it's difficult to draw major conclusions from the sample.

And plugging on seems to pay off . . . : the study is reported in Gilder, George. "Still Seeking the Glass Slipper." *National Review*. December 14, 1992: 40.

Susan B. Anthony believed that the whole image . . . : Barry, Kathleen. *Susan B. Anthony: A Biography of a Singular Feminist*. New York: New York University Press, 1988: 59.

H. L. Mencken noted that work provided . . . : Mencken, H. L. *In Defense of Women*. New York: Alfred A. Knopf, 1928: 182–4.

"If the work of the average man . . .": *Ibid*: 18.

Less offensively . . . : Harding, M. Esther. *The Way of All Women: A Psychological Interpretation*. New York: Harper Colophon Books, 1970: 87.

Simone de Beauvoir described . . . : de Beauvoir, Simone. *The Second Sex*. H. M. Parshley, translator. New York: Vintage Books, 1974: 151–4.

"Why are all the old hens abolitionists?" . . . : Quoted in Nies, Judith. *Seven Women: Portraits from the American Radical Tradition*. New York: Penguin Books, 1977: 6.

she'd had two marriage proposals . . . : Nies: 16–17.

Bravely, *Mademoiselle* tried to debunk . . . : Weaver: 191.

Simone de Beauvoir said it was rare . . . : de Beauvoir: 780.

Chapter Eight

The party is the brainstorm . . . : The four spent $4,400 for four billboards posted for ninety days. Three hundred women responded to the pitch "Emily" made on WLUP radio. Little, Heather M. "Extras for the Dating Game." *Chicago Tribune* (Section 6). June 26, 1994: 11.

an intimate relationship has three characteristics . . . : Barbara Levy Simon quotes George Levinger and Harold Raush in Simon, Barbara Levy. *Never Married Women*. Philadelphia: Temple University Press, 1987: 92.

Psychotherapist Stephanie Dowrick emphasizes that a real self must be available for true intimacy. See Dowrick, Stephanie. *Intimacy and Solitude: Balancing Closeness and Independence*. New York: W. W. Norton & Company, 1991: 3–21.

it would eventually reach women . . . : in their study of economic dependence in marriage, Annemette Sørensen and Sara McLanahan make the point that social and economic inequality in marriage was considered necessary for stability. See "Married Women's Economic Dependency 1940–1980." *American Journal of Sociology*. November 1987: 660.

Author and male-ist Warren Farrell sees the male as a victim of economics that force him to work extremely hard to support a family he's too fatigued to be intimate with. "She gets paid for intimacy," he writes: "He gets paid for staying away from it." UPI report, January 13, 1988.

in the five years between 1982 and 1987 . . . : Kolata, Gina. "Use of Condoms Lags, Survey of Women Finds." *New York Times* (Section B). July 28, 1988: 7.

the number of cohabiting couples . . . : Tanfer, Koray. "Patterns of Premarital Cohabitation among Never-Married Women in the United States." *Journal of Marriage and the Family 49.* August 1987: 483. Tanfer found that in 1983 about one-eighth of ever-single women between the ages of twenty and twenty-nine were cohabiting, and about one quarter had cohabited sometime in their lives. *Ibid:* 485.

in 1981 they formed . . . : The founder of Single Mothers by Choice has also written a book: Mattes, Jane. *Single Mothers by Choice.* New York: Random House, 1994.

Rather suddenly, the western marriage . . . : several writers from all over the political spectrum have written about this phenomenon. For an economic analysis, see "The Bargain Breaks." *The Economist* (American edition). December 26, 1992: 37.

For a feminist analysis, see Pollitt, Katha. "Today's Women Don't Connect Marriage to Maternity." *The Oregonian.* July 23, 1993: C9.

The number of social introduction services . . . : Reynolds, Gretchen. "The New Singles." *Chicago* magazine. February 1993: 57.

One very exclusive . . . : Jannot, Mark. "Love Brokers." *Chicago* magazine. February 1993: 67.

Linda was told that she was demographically . . . : so-called "demographic undesirables" include men under twenty-eight and women over forty-five. *Ibid:* 62.

hit-and-miss results . . . : *Ibid:* 62. Reportedly, at one of the nation's largest video dating services, just 30 percent of the requests for a date (based on viewing an introductory video) result in a date. *Ibid:* 65.

launching "a campaign of search . . .": Weiss, Robert S. *Loneliness: The Experience of Emotional and Social Isolation.* Cambridge, MA: MIT Press, 1973: 234.

One interesting note in the many "campaign" approaches is made by Rhonda Weaver, who teaches a course called How to Find the Right Man at a community college in Tempe, Arizona. In her course Weaver points out that most women put more time into buying a pair of shoes than looking for the man they'll spend their lives with—so much for intimacy! Bolyard, Paulette. "Male Order Course; Teacher Advises Women in Finding the Right Mate." *Arizona Republic/Phoenix Gazette* (Tempe Community). May 26, 1993: 2.

has had many more sexual partners . . . : Michael, Robert T. , John H. Gagnon, Edward O. Lauman, and Gina Kolata. *Sex in America: A Definitive Survey.* Boston: Little, Brown and Company, 1994: 102.

Typical of this preoccupation . . . : of particular note is that Alice Hindman is just twenty-seven years old when her spinster adventure occurs. Anderson, Sherwood. "Adventure." *Winesburg, Ohio.* New York: The Modern Library, 1947.

For a real-life version, look to Congress . . . : a blow-by-blow account of this tactic appears in Phelps, Timothy M. and Helen Winternitz. *Capitol Games.* New York: Hyperion, 1992: 361; 370–2; 375.

While her academic ruminations are apparently difficult to follow and easy to mock, Hill did note that her marital status made her vulnerable. See Leo, John. "Deconstructing Anita Hill." *U.S. News and World Report.* November 2, 1992: 18.

"Ask any woman . . .": Cantwell, Mary. "For Better or Worse, a Wedding Is Memorable." *Chicago Tribune* (Tempo Woman). February 18, 1990: 5.

Primary *does* mean marriage . . . : Weiss: 94.

"I think it would be horrible to be in a [nonintimate] relationship . . .": Weiss calls these "empty shell" marriages and notes that these can actually *cause* loneliness. *Ibid:* 90.

who defines cohabitation as a form of courtship . . . : Tanfer draws this conclusion from the fact that the women who cohabited were not content with the cohabiting state in and of itself—most hoped to marry soon. Tanfer: 490.

people must become primary in their own lives . . . : Andre, Rae. *Positive Solitude: A Practical Program for Mastering Loneliness and Achieving Self-Fulfillment.* New York: Harper-Perennial. 1992: 4–7; 188–93.

Stephanie Dowrick talks about the same phenomenon in different terms and she believes it to be a prerequisite for intimacy. Dowrick: 55–61.

Writer Cheryl Meiser explains the concept in lay terms: "When you live alone, you have to become both the giver *and* the recipient in your life." See Meiser, Cheryl. "Alone at Last." *Utne Reader.* March/April 1989: 62.

Chapter Nine

"On the whole, the women interviewed . . .": the article focuses on African American women. See Higginbotham, Elizabeth. "Is Marriage a Priority? Class Differences in the Marital Options of Educated Black Women." *Single Life: Unmarried Adults in Social Context.* Ed. Peter Stein. New York: St. Martin's Press, 1981: 265.

loneliness is seen as a shameful . . . : Weiss, Robert. "The Study of Loneliness." Stein: 154.

some people don't want to be reminded . . . : Frieda Fromm-Reichmann has made the same point. Quoted in *Ibid:* 152–3.

Some psychologists such as Rae Andre say . . . : Andre, Rae. *Positive Solitude: A Practical Program for Mastering Loneliness and Achieving Self-Fulfillment.* New York: HarperPerennial, 1992: 7–8.

while it's associated with other experiences . . . : Lobdell, Judith and Daniel Perlman. "The Intergenerational Transmission of Loneliness: A Study of College Females and Their Parents." *Journal of Marriage and Family* 48. August 1986: 591.

In depression, for instance . . . : Weiss. Stein: 156.

unmarried men were as lonely as unmarried women . . . : *Ibid:* 162.

in 1973 one expert estimated . . . : The researcher was Vello Sermat, who spoke before the Western Psychological Association. He's quoted in Weiss, Robert S. *Loneliness: The Experience of Emotional and Social Isolation.* Cambridge, MA: MIT Press, 1973: 89.

Studies conducted in the 1950s and 1960s . . . : Ward, Russell A. "The Never-Married in Later Life." Stein: 342.

the way the daughters perceived . . . : Lobdell: 592–3.

a couple of possible reasons . . . : *Ibid:* 594.

Interestingly, TV viewing was also correlated with loneliness. *Ibid:* 594.

we set our own standards for loneliness . . . : Keith: 151–61. Once again, divorced women were the most dissatisfied.

Susan Rice has come up with . . . : Rice, Susan. "Single, Older Childless Women: Differences Between Never-Married and Widowed Women in Life Satisfaction and Social Support." *Journal of Gerontological Social Work* (Volume 13). 1989: 41.

what we intuitively expect ever-single women to say . . . : of course, there are ever-single women who say and experience what we expect them to experience. Probably the most searing portrait of loneliness I found was that of Clelia Mosher, Stanford University's pioneering professor of women's hygiene. An M.D., Mosher was the first researcher to study menstruation on any scale and she was one of the first to study women's sexual attitudes and practices. But she was extraordinarily lonely and so created a fictional friend to write to. "I am finding out why I am so lonely," she wrote in one such letter. "The only things I care about are things which use my brain. The women I meet are not much interested and I do not meet many men." Another time, she wrote: "There is a kind of friendship which may exist, between two women, where their individual interests are so merged, that each has for the other the same vital interest. . . . It has all the wonderful committed interest one finds in ideal marriage and only differs in the absence of the physical relationship. . . . It supplies to the working woman and compensates her for what she has missed in not marrying but cannot make up to her for her lost motherhood." Sadly, she lived in a time when finding this friendship was nearly impossible. See Griego, Elizabeth. "The Making of a 'Misfit': Clelia Duel Mosher." *Lone Voyagers: Academic Women in Coeducational Universities 1870–1937.* Ed. Geraldine Joncich Clifford. New York: The Feminist Press at the City University of New York, 1989: 149–82.

If researchers such as Nancy L. Peterson . . . : Peterson's conclusion appears in Peterson, Nancy L. *Our Lives for Ourselves: Women Who Have Never Married.* New York: G. P. Putnam's Sons, 1981: 257.

wonderful roots in the nineteenth century . . . : an academic study of Kingsley, North, and Bird appears in Birkett, Dea. *Spinsters Abroad: Victorian Lady Explorers.* Oxford: Basil Blackwell Ltd., 1989.

Alice Koller, who planted herself on Nantucket . . . : Although much of what she struggled with on Nantucket went unresolved, Koller *did* resolve to live a solitary life. She continued to move around quite a bit, picking isolated places and apparently relying on her dogs for a sense of family and continuity — and as a hedge against loneliness. She has written two books on her life as an ever-single woman. The longer-term view appears in Koller, Alice. *The Stations of Solitude.* New York: William Morrow and Company, Inc., 1990.

"a territorial integrity of the spirit . . .": quoted in Ward. Stein: 343.

For instance, among white women . . . : Williams, David R., David T. Takeuchi, and Russell K. Adair. "Marital Status and Psychiatric Disorders Among Blacks and Whites." *Journal of Health and Social Behavior* (Volume 33). June 1992: 146.

differences shrank when researchers removed . . . : *Ibid:* 149.

that marriage per se was not health-enhancing . . . : *Ibid:* 153. The notion of loss as a major factor in the health and happiness of the divorced and widowed is critical, and loss apparently accounts in large part for the differences in experience and orientation between the ever-single and the previously married.

Stein says there are four different kinds . . . : Stein's typology is designed to describe *all* unmarried people. For the purposes of talking with ever-single women only, my wording is slightly different. For instance, in place of the oppositional word "permanent" in his descriptions, he euphemistically says "stables" are those who "accept being single as a probable life situation." In eliciting women's feelings about themselves and their status, it seemed important to use clear and dialectic language. See Stein, Peter J. "Understanding Single Adulthood." Stein: 10–12.

Lack of control is at the heart . . . : Among the ever-single women often portrayed as lacking control over their marital status are Emily Dickinson, who flirted with marriage on a number of occasions and consciously weighed it against her own spiritual and intellectual autonomy; and Susan B. Anthony, who turned down at least two proposals.

Dickinson's struggle is particularly apparent in these lines: "Born—Bridalled—Shrouded—/In a Day/'My husband'—women say—/Stroking the Melody/Is *this* the way?"

Biographer Cynthia Wolff sees the entire poem, which begins, "Title divine—is mine!," as a discussion of two potential and competing life titles, "poet" and "wife." Clearly "wife" loses out. See Wolff, Cynthia Griffin. *Emily Dickinson*. Reading, MA: Addison-Wesley Publishing Company, Inc., 1988: 396.

Anthony turned down a proposal from a man who seems to have taken pity on her: Barry, Kathleen. *Susan B. Anthony: A Biography of a Singular Feminist*. New York: New York University Press, 1988: 100.

Although as a young woman Anthony was amenable to marriage, as she grew politically, she came to feel that nineteenth-century marriage laws denied women psychological autonomy and she rejected it apparently on those grounds. *Ibid:* 37–8; 46.

"ruthless market" . . . : Mueller, Kate Hevner. "The Marriage Trap." *Mademoiselle*. September 1955: 187–8.

Mueller's article was met with an interesting mix of applause and dismay. Nearly two hundred readers wrote in: one third agreed with Mueller, but one half disagreed completely. Edith G. Neisser of Illinois was typical. "Creating a home . . . appeals to her as a haven and a challenge," she wrote of the contemporary college-educated woman. "Why shouldn't being married be her first concern?" "Is Marriage the Trap?" *Mademoiselle*. December 1955: 99.

Despite daunting demographics . . . : In 1990 four of ten black men were married, but three of ten black women were married. Burnett, Claudette et al. *We the American Blacks.* Bureau of the Census. September 1993: 6.

But the statistics are more complicated. In the remaining pool, many men, especially the educated men, will make interracial marriages, which shrinks the pool for educated black women, who traditionally have less access to interracial marriage. These kinds of social forces have led sociologist William Julius to conclude that young black women are facing a shrinking pool of marriageable men. He's quoted in Meisler, Stanley and Sam Fulwood III. "Number of Inner-City Single Parents on Rise." *Los Angeles Times.* July 17, 1990: A-14.

The trend is long-standing and leads to a low fertility rate among educated black women, a statistic sociologist Robert Staples called "subversive" in the 1970s. See Staples, Robert. "Black Singles in America." Stein: 49.

It is this slippery portion . . . : Later in the play, Heidi begins to hear her own voice. She tells a friend who is producing a sitcom about unhappy ever-single artists that she won't help her write it "Because I don't think we made such big mistakes. And I don't want to see three gals on the town who do." See Wasserstein, Wendy. *The Heidi Chronicles and Other Plays.* San Diego: Harcourt Brace Jovanovich, Inc., 1990: 202; 227.

Chapter Ten

ever-single women are often the best off financially . . . : Schwenk, F. N. "Income and Expenditures of Older Widowed, Divorced, and Never-Married Women Who Live Alone." *Family Economics Review* (Volume 5, Number 1). 1992: 5.

In Pat Keith's study, the incomes of older ever-single women even exceeded those of ever-single men. Keith, Pat. *The Unmarried in Later Life.* New York: Praeger, 1989: 54.

they suffer less loneliness and dissatisfaction . . . : Hatch, Laurie Russell. "Gender Differences in Orientation Toward Retirement from Paid Labor." *Gender & Society* (Volume 6, Number 1). March 1992: 75.

they demonstrate reasonably good health . . . : one indicator is their expenditures on health care. See Schwenk: 6–7.

a majority of women are unmarried in later years . . . : "Marital Status and Living Arrangements: March 1992." *Current Population Reports.* Bureau of the Census: 1.

Freud has had an impact . . . : Freud, Sigmund. "Femininity." *Freud on Women.* Ed. Elisabeth Young-Bruehl. New York: W. W. Norton & Company, 1990: 362.

That's partly why Alexandra Bergson . . . : Cather, Willa. *O Pioneers!* Pleasantville, NY: The Readers Digest Association, Inc., 1990: 112.

51 percent of the women . . . : Simon, Barbara Levy. *Never Married Women*. Philadelphia: Temple University Press, 1987: 150.

"preeminently" tied to depression . . . : the unmarried have both greater exposure to life strains and a greater vulnerability—but once again, the ever-single fare best. See Perlin, Leonard I. and Joyce S. Johnson. "Marital Status, Life-Strains, and Depression." *Single Life: Unmarried Adults in Social Context*. Ed. Peter Stein. New York: St. Martin's Press, 1981: 175.

financial insecurity was a key factor . . . : Not surprisingly, financial insecurity apparently caused older people to delay health care, and the ever-single were the least likely to delay care: Keith: 45. Also interestingly, previously married women *felt* more vulnerable than ever-single women, and divorced women (not necessarily the most vulnerable women), were most unhappy. *Ibid:* 61–5.

removing the factor of socioeconomic status narrowed . . . : Williams, David R., David T. Takeuchi, and Russell K. Adair. "Marital Status and Psychiatric Disorders Among Blacks and Whites." *Journal of Health and Social Behavior* (Volume 33). June 1992: 149.

because they made 57 cents on the dollar . . . : Porter, Allison. *The Path to Poverty: An Analysis of Women's Retirement Income*. Washington, D.C.: The Older Women's League, 1995: 3.

only 13 percent . . . *Ibid:* 8. The result: in 1993, 26 percent of older women living alone were poor. *Ibid:* 3.

They're typical of this ever-single cohort . . . : Schwenk: 6–7.

Christine Webb describes a woman . . . : all of Webb's women were living in precarious circumstances. Webb, Christine. "Mothers and Daughters: A Powerful Spell." *Journal of Advanced Nursing* (Volume 17). 1992: 1336.

Rubinstein describes ever-single women who had forged . . . : Rubinstein, Robert L., Baine B. Alexander, Marcene Goodman, and Mark Luborsky. "Key Relationships of Never-Married, Childless Older Women: A Cultural Analysis." *Journal of Gerontology: Social Services* (Volume 46, Number 5). 1991: S273–4.

at least the risk is being taken . . . : although Karen argues a good emotional case for entrepreneurship, on average, single women are *not* as commonly self-employed as married women—mostly because they don't have the access to capital and health insurance that husbands often provide. See Devine, Theresa J. "Changes in Wage-and-Salary Returns to

Skill and the Recent Rise in Female Self-Employment." AEA *Papers and Proceedings* (Volume 82, Number 2). May 1994: 108–13.

might put them in the painful situation that Susan B. Anthony . . . : Barry, Kathleen. *Susan B. Anthony: A Biography of a Singular Feminist.* New York: New York University Press, 1988: 300–1.

the apparent adamancy . . . : Simon: 31–8.

More convincing is the profile . . . : O'Brien, Mary. "Never Married Older Women: The Life Experience." *Social Indicators Research* (Volume 24, Number 3). May 1991. The evolution of choice: 306; 308–9. The life satisfaction: 303.

Edan Schappert's counsel to avoid reading while eating . . . : Schappert, Edan. *The Sophisticate's Guide to Living Alone Successfully.* Whitehall, VA: Betterway Publications, 1988: 63.

Ruthe Stein's advice . . . : Stein, Ruthe. *The Art of Single Living: A Guide to Going It Alone in the '90s.* New York: Shapolsky Publishers, Inc., 1990: 60–1.

Luci Swindoll's advice on which music to listen to . . . : Strangely, Swindoll seems to believe that single people, more than others, need more arts in their lives—but never examines why or how this "extra" might function. Swindoll, Luci. *Wide My World, Narrow My Bed: Living and Loving the Single Life.* Portland, OR: Multnomah, 1982: 106–7.

Epilogue

someone in their pasts who gave them permission . . . : Peterson, Nancy L. *Our Lives for Ourselves.* New York: G. P. Putnam's Sons, 1981: 250.

For Further Reading

🖝

The Historical Perspective

An Elderly Spinster. "Tales of a Polygamous City I. Taffeta Trousers." *Atlantic Monthly* (Volume 120, Number 6). December 1917: 721 ff.

Antler, Joyce. "'After College, What?': New Graduates and the Family Claim." *American Quarterly* 32. Fall 1980: 409–34.

Banner, Lois W. *American Beauty*. Chicago: The University of Chicago Press, 1984.

Barry, Kathleen. *Susan B. Anthony: A Biography of a Singular Feminist*. New York: New York University Press, 1989.

de Beauvoir, Simone. *The Second Sex*. New York: Vintage Books, 1974.

Birkett, Dea. *Spinsters Abroad: Victorian Lady Explorers*. Oxford, England: Basil Blackwell Ltd., 1989.

Brandon, Ruth. *The New Women and the Old Men: Love, Sex and the Woman Question*. New York: W. W. Norton & Company, 1990.

Brown, Helen Gurley. *Sex and the Single Girl*. New York: Avon Books, 1962.

Carrighar, Sally. *Home to the Wilderness*. Boston: Houghton Mifflin Company, 1973.

Christy, Howard Chandler. *The American Girl*. New York: Da Capo Press, Inc., 1976.

Clifford, Geraldine Joncich (Ed). *Lone Voyagers: Academic Women in Coeducational Universities, 1870–1937*. New York: The Feminist Press at the City University of New York, 1989.

Coy, Stanlee Miller. *The Single Girl's Book for Making it in the Big City*. Englewood Cliffs, NJ: Prentice-Hall, Inc., 1969.

Eckhardt, Celia Morris. *Fanny Wright: Rebel in America*. Cambridge, MA: Harvard University Press, 1984.

Frank, Katherine. *A Voyager Out: The Life of Mary Kingsley*. New York: Ballantine Books, 1986.

Franklin, Penelope. *Private Pages: Diaries of American Women 1830s–1970s*. New York: Ballantine Books, 1986.

Fraser, Antonia. *The Weaker Vessel*. New York: Vintage Books, 1984.

Fraser, Rebecca. *The Brontës: Charlotte Brontë and Her Family*. New York: Fawcett Columbine, 1990.

Freeman, Ruth and Patricia Klaus. "Blessed or Not? The New Spinster in England and the United States in the Late Nineteenth and Early Twentieth Centuries." *Journal of Family History* 9. Winter 1984: 394–414.

Goldin, Claudia. "The Work and Wages of Single Women, 1870–1920." *Journal of Economic History* 40. March 1980: 81–8.

Hayes, Harold. *The Dark Romance of Dian Fossey*. New York: Simon and Schuster, 1990.

Henderson, Paul. "What Made Her Stop?" *Life*. May 1992: 77 ff.

Holtzman, Ellen M. "The Pursuit of Married Love: Women's Attitudes Toward Sexuality and Marriage in Great Britain 1918–1939. *Journal of Social History* 16. Winter 1982: 39–52.

Honan, Park. *Jane Austen, Her Life*. New York: Fawcett Columbine, 1987.

Johnson, Rheta Gramsley. "Mourning a Still Magnolia: Miss Castle Saw a Delta Many Missed." *The Atlanta Journal and Constitution* (Section A). January 12, 1993: 3.

Jones, Vivien (Ed). *Women in the Eighteenth Century*. London: Routledge, 1990.

Kenyon, Olga (Ed). *800 Years of Women's Letters*. New York: Penguin Books, 1992.

Key, Ellen. *The Woman Movement*. Trans. Mammah Bouton Borthwick. New York: G. P. Putnam's Sons, 1912.

Matthews, Nancy Mowll (Ed). *Cassatt and her Circle: Selected Letters*. New York: Abbeville Press, 1984.

Matthews, Nancy Mowll. *Mary Cassatt: A Life*. New York: Villard Books, 1994.

Mencken, H. L. *In Defense of Women*. New York: Alfred A. Knopf, 1928.

Nies, Judith. *Seven Women: Portraits from the American Radical Tradition*. New York: Penguin, 1977.

Nightingale, Florence. *Cassandra*. New York: The Feminist Press, 1979.

Noddings, Nel. *Women and Evil*. Berkeley, CA: University of California Press, 1989.

Nord, Debora Epstein. "'Neither Pairs Nor Odd': Female Community in Late Nineteenth Century London." *Signs* 15. Summer 1990: 733–54.

Oates, Stephen B. *A Woman of Valor: Clara Barton and the Civil War*. New York: The Free Press, 1994.

Palazzi, Maura. "Female Solitude and Patrilineage: Unmarried Women and Widows During the Eighteenth and Nineteenth Centuries." *Journal of Family History* (Volume 15, Number 4). 1990: 443–60.

Payne, Karen (Ed). *Between Ourselves: Letters Between Mothers & Daughters 1750–1982*. Boston: Houghton Mifflin Company, 1983.

Perlez, Jane. "The Woman in Command in Warsaw." *New York Times* (Section A). June 9, 1993.

Pomeroy, Sarah B. *Goddesses, Whores, Wives, and Slaves: Women in Classical Antiquity*. New York: Schocken Books, 1975.

Rogers, Katharine, M. *Feminism in Eighteenth Century England*. Urbana, IL: University of Illinois Press, 1982.

Saxton, Martha. *Louisa May: A Modern Biography of Louisa May Alcott*. Boston: Houghton Mifflin Company, 1977.

Schlissel, Lillian. *Women's Diaries of the Westward Journey*. New York: Schocken Books, 1982.

Shade, William. "'A Mental Passion': Female Sexuality in Victorian America." *International Journal of Women's Studies (Canada)* I. 1978: 13–29.

Sklar, Kathryn Kish. *Catharine Beecher: A Study in American Domesticity*. New Haven, CT: Yale University Press, 1973.

Smith, F. B. *Florence Nightingale: Reputation and Power*. New York: St. Martin's Press, 1982.

Smith, M. B. *The Single Woman of Today*. London: Watts & Co., 1951.

Solomon, Barbara Miller. *In the Company of Educated Women*. New Haven, CT: Yale University Press, 1985.

Sørensen, Annemette and McLanahan, Sara. "Married Women's Economic Dependency, 1940–1980. *American Journal of Sociology* (Volume 93, Number 3). November 1987: 659–87.

Stein, Peter J. (Ed.). *Single Life: Unmarried Adults in Social Context*. New York: St. Martin's Press, 1981.

Strauss, Jean. *Alice James: A Biography*. Boston: Houghton Mifflin Company, 1980.

Trafford, Abigail. "Unwed Motherhood: Insights from the Colonial Era." *Washington Post* (Section Z). January 8, 1991: 6.

Vicinus, Martha. *Independent Women: Work and Community for Single Women 1850–1920*. London: Virago Press Ltd., 1985.

Warbasse, Elizabeth Bowles. *The Changing Legal Rights of Married Women 1800–1861*. New York: Garland Publishing, 1987.

Watkins, Susan Cotts. "Spinsters." *Journal of Family History*. Winter 1984: 310–25.

Weiner, Nella Fermi. "Of Feminism and Birth Control Propaganda (1790–1840). *International Journal of Women's Studies* (Volume 3, Number 5). September–October, 1980: 411–30.

Werness, Hope B. "The Modest Maiden in 19th Century Art: Evolution of a Theme." *Woman's Art Journal*. Fall 1984/Winter 1985: 7–10.

Wolff, Cynthia Griffin. *Emily Dickinson*. Reading, MA: Addison–Wesley Publishing Company, Inc., 1988.

Wollstonecraft, Mary. *A Vindication of the Rights of Woman*. New York: Penguin Books, 1992.

For Further Reading

Sociological and Psychological Readings

Adams, Rebecca G. "Patterns of Network Change: A Longitudinal Study of Friendships of Elderly Women." *The Gerontologist* (Volume 27, Number 2). 1987: 222–27.

Bagnall, Janet. "Living Alone: Morning is the Loneliest Time for Widow." *The Gazette* (Montreal). January 21, 1992: 1.

Bettelheim, Bruno. *The Uses of Enchantment: The Meaning and Importance of Fairy Tales.* New York: Alfred A. Knopf, 1977.

Brownmiller, Susan. *Femininity.* New York: Fawcett Columbine, 1984.

Cockrum, Jean and Priscilla White. "Influences on Life Satisfaction of Never-Married Men and Women." *Family Relations* 34. October 1995: 551–56.

Cramer, Duncan. "Living Alone, Marital Status, Gender and Health." *Journal of Community & Applied Social Psychology* (Volume 3). 1993: 1–15.

Delfaco, Jane. "For Many, Being in Mid-Thirties and Single Can Be a Lonely Stage of Life." *Ottawa Citizen.* (Section B). May 25, 1993: 3.

Dowrick, Stephanie. *Intimacy & Solitude: Balancing Closeness and Independence.* New York: W. W. Norton & Company, Inc., 1994.

Erikson, Erik H. *Childhood and Society, Second Edition.* New York: W. W. Norton & Company, Inc., 1963.

Freud, Sigmund. *Freud on Women.* Elisabeth Young-Bruehl (Ed.). New York: W. W. Norton & Company, 1990.

Gilligan, Carol. *In a Different Voice: Psychological Theory and Women's Development.* Cambridge, MA: Harvard University Press, 1982.

Hatch, Laurie Russell. "Gender Differences in Orientation Toward Retirement from Paid Labor." *Gender & Society* (Volume 6, Number 1). March 1992: 66–85.

Hatch, Laurie Russell and Kris Bulcroft. "Contact with Friends in Later Life: Disentangling the Effects of Gender and Marital Status." *Journal of Marriage and Family.* February 1992: 222–32.

Helson, Ravenna and James Picano. "Is the Traditional Role Bad for Women?" *Journal of Personality and Social Psychology.* August 1990: 311–20.

Jack, Dana Crowley. *Silencing the Self: Women and Depression.* New York: HarperCollins Publishers, Inc., 1991.

Keith, Pat. *The Unmarried in Later Life.* New York: Praeger, 1989.

Landau, Jacqueline and Michael B. Arthur. "The Relationship of Marital Status, Spouse's Career Status, and Gender to Salary Level." *Sex Roles* (Volume 27, Number 11–12). 1992: 665–81.

Lang, Susan S. *Women Without Children: The Reasons, the Rewards, the Regrets.* New York: Pharos Books, 1989.

Lobdell, Judith and Daniel Perlman. "The Intergenerational Transmission of Loneliness: A Study of College Females and Their Parents." *Journal of Marriage and Family* 48. August 1986: 589–95.

Miller, Jean Baker. *Toward a New Psychology of Women, Second Edition.* Boston: Beacon Press, 1986.

O'Brien, Mary. "Never Married Older Women: The Life Experience." *Social Indicators Research* (Volume 24, Number 3). May 1991: 301–15.

O'Connor, Pat. "Women's Confidants Outside Marriage: Shared or Competing Sources of Intimacy?" *Sociology* (Volume 25, Number 2). May 1991: 241–54.

Peterson, Nancy L. *Our Lives for Ourselves: Women Who Have Never Married.* New York: G. P. Putnam's Sons, 1981.

Pipher, Mary. *Reviving Ophelia: Saving the Selves of Adolescent Girls.* New York: G. P. Putnam's Sons, 1994.

Rice, Susan. "Single, Older Childless Women: Differences between Never-Married and Widowed Women in Life Satisfaction and Social Support." *Journal of Gerontological Social Work* (Volume 13, 3–4). 1989: 35–47.

Rubinstein, Robert L. "Never Married Elderly as a Social Type: Re-Evaluating Some Images." *The Gerontologist* (Volume 27, Number 1). 1987: 108–13.

Rubinstein, Robert L., Baine B. Alexander, Marcene Goodman, and Mark Luborsky. "Key Relationships of Never Married, Childless Older Women: A Cultural Analysis." *Journal of Gerontology: Social Sciences* (Volume 46, Number 5). 1991: S270–77.

Sidel, Ruth. *On Her Own: Growing Up in the Shadow of the American Dream.* New York: Penguin Books, 1990.

For Further Reading

Simon, Barbara Levy. *Never Married Women*. Philadelphia: Temple University Press, 1987.

Tanfer, Koray. "Patterns of Premarital Cohabitation among Never-Married Women in the United States." *Journal of Marriage and the Family* 49. August 1987: 438–97.

Traupmann, Jane, Elaine Eckels, and Elaine Hatfield. "Intimacy in Older Women's Lives." *The Gerontologist* (Volume 22, Number 6). 1982: 493–8.

Webb, Christine. "Mothers and Daughters: A Powerful Spell." *Journal of Advanced Nursing* (Volume 17). 1992: 1334–42.

Weiss, Robert S. (Ed.) *Loneliness: The Experience of Emotional and Social Isolation.* Cambridge, MA: MIT Press, 1973.

Trends

"Alice Doesn't Live Here Anymore." *Washington Post Magazine* (letters). September 22, 1991: 3.

Ambry, Margaret K. "Childless Chances." *American Demographics*. April 1992: 55.

Barbieri, Susan. "Advice for Re-Entering the Dating Game." *Chicago Tribune* (Womanews). June 9, 1991 : 10.

"The Bargain Breaks." *The Economist*. December 26, 1992: 37 ff.

Barringer, Felicity. "Rate of Marriage Continues to Decline." *New York Times* (Section A). July 17, 1992: 20.

Brown, John Mason. "What Makes a Woman Memorable?" *Vogue*. November 15, 1956: 100 ff.

Cantwell, Mary. "For Better or Worse, a Wedding is Memorable." *Chicago Tribune* (Tempo Woman). February 18, 1990: 5.

Cohen, Richard. "What About Alice?" *Washington Post Magazine*. July 28, 1991: 3.

Crispell, Diane. "Myths of the 1950s." *American Demographics*. August 1992: 38 ff.

Decker, Cathleen. "The L.A. Women; the Faces Behind the Statistics." *Los Angeles Times Magazine*. February 21, 1988: 11 ff.

Destefano, Linda. "All the Lonely People." *San Francisco Chronicle* (Section B). March 7, 1990: 5.

Edmonson, Brad. "Marriage, Home Ownership, and Other Recent Census Releases." *American Demographics*. September 1992: 16.

Einhorn, Barbara. *Cinderella Goes to Market: Citizenship, Gender, and Women's Movements in East Central Europe*. London: Verso, 1993.

Exter, Thomas G. "Home Alone in 2000." *American Demographics*. September 1992: 67.

Faludi, Susan. "The Marriage Trap." *Ms*. August 1987: 62 ff.

Faludi, Susan. *Backlash: The Undeclared War Against American Women*. New York: Crown Publishers, Inc., 1991.

Fierman, Jaclyn. "Why Women Still Don't Hit the Top." *Fortune*. July 30, 1990: 40 ff.

Fotheringham, Allan. "It's Always Lonelier for any Woman at the Top." *Financial Post* (Spectrum). June 19, 1993: 5.

Fuchs, Victor. *Women's Quest for Economic Equality*. Cambridge, MA: Harvard University Press, 1988.

Gilder, George. "Still Seeking the Glass Slipper." *National Review*. December 14, 1992: 39 ff.

Glenn, Norvall D. "What Does Family Mean?" *American Demographics*. June 1992: 30 ff.

Goozner, Michael. "Japanese Women Say 'I Do' to Careers." *Chicago Tribune*. November 25, 1994: 24 ff.

Hirshey, Gerry. "Coupledom Uber Alles: Tyranny of the Couples." Reprinted in *Utne Reader*. March/April 1989: 48–55.

Jannot, Mark. "Love Brokers." *Chicago Magazine* (Volume 42, Number 2). February 1993: 60 ff.

King, Florence. "Spinsterhood is Powerful." *National Review*. July 19, 1993: 72.

Kranz, Rachel. "Toward a New Definition of Singleness: Building a Life with Close Friends." Reprinted in *Utne Reader*. March/April 1989. 56 ff.

Kuriansky, Judy. "Results of the *New Woman* Singles Survey." *New Woman*. December 1987: 98–103.

"Lashing Backlash." *New York Times Book Review* (letters). February 9, 1992: 31.

Lennon, Rosemarie. "Are You Seeing Anyone?" *New Woman*. February 1988: 148.

Leo, John. "Deconstructing Anita Hill." *U.S. News and World Report* (Volume 113, Number 17). November 2, 1992: 18.

Little, Heather M. "Extras for the Dating Game." *Chicago Tribune* (Womanews). June 26, 1994: 11 ff.

"Is Marriage the Trap?" *Mademoiselle* (letters). December 1955: 99 ff.

Masters, Brooke A. "Single Life in Suburbia." *Washington Post* (Section C). March 17, 1991: 1.

Meehan, Diana M. *Ladies of the Evening: Women Characters of Prime-Time Television.* Metchen, NJ: The Scarecrow Press, 1983.

Michael, Robert T. , John H. Gagnon, Edward O. Lauman, and Gina Kolata. *Sex in America: A Definitive Survey.* Boston: Little, Brown and Company, 1994.

Morin, Richard. "The Trend That Wasn't." *Washington Post* (Section C). July 14, 1991.

Mueller, Kate Hevner. "The Marriage Trap." *Mademoiselle*. September 1955: 133 ff.

Norris, Kim. "Study Shows Difficulties for Women Execs." *St. Petersburg Times*. August 19, 1992: 1E.

Pollitt, Katha. "Are Women Morally Superior to Men?" *The Nation*. December 28, 1992: 799–807.

Pollitt, Katha. "Today's Women Don't Connect Marriage to Maternity." *The Oregonian*. July 23, 1993: 37.

Ray, Nancy. "Barred from Pageant, Mother Claims Bias." *Los Angeles Times* (Section A). February 28, 1992: 3.

Reynolds, Gretchen. "The New Singles." *Chicago Magazine* (Volume 42, Number 2). February 1993: 50 ff.

Rich, Frank. "The Best Years of Our Lives?" *The New Republic*. September 7, 1992: 38 ff.

Richards, Ann W. "Girls, Pull Your Freight." *New York Times*. (Op ed). June 25, 1994: 15.

Roeper, Richard. "Fed Up, Single Women Turn to Sign Language." *Chicago Sun Times.* February 9, 1994: 11.

Rozen, Leah. "The Great American Man Shortage—Whatta Lie!" *Mademoiselle.* September 1986: 246 ff.

Schwenk, F. N. "Income and Expenditures of Older Widowed, Divorced, and Never-Married Women Who Live Alone." *Family Economics Review* (Volume 5, Number 1). 1992: 2–8.

Solholz, Eloise. "Too Late for Prince Charming?" *Newsweek.* June 2, 1986: 54 ff.

Spangler, Lynn C. "A Historical Overview of Female Friendships on Prime-Time Television." *Journal of Popular Culture* 22. Spring 1989: 13–24.

Speer, Tibett L. "Why Single Women Keep Their Babies." *American Demographics.* June 1992: 9 ff.

Stanfield, Rochelle L. "Valuing the Family." *The National Journal* (Volume 24, Number 27). July 4, 1992: 1562 ff.

Teegarden, Carrie. "A Changing Nation: Traditional Clans Like Cleavers Now a Rare Breed, Census Shows." *The Atlanta Journal and Constitution* (Section A). February 17, 1993: 4.

Warren, Ellen. "More Women Calling Marriage a Tie that Binds Too Tightly." *Chicago Tribune* (Section 2). July 29, 1993: 1 ff.

"What Makes You Happy . . . 1,100 Women's Answers to Work, Love, Money, Fitness and Health." *Self.* September 1989: 161–8.

Weaver, Polly. "What's Wrong With Ambition?" *Mademoiselle.* September 1956: 191 ff.

Weiss, Rick. "The Kidless Culture." *Health.* July/August 1993: 40 ff.

Wetzsteon, Ross. "Will the Man Shortage Spoil Men?" *Mademoiselle.* February 1987: 184 ff.

Literature

Anderson, Sherwood. "Adventure." *Winesburg, Ohio.* New York: The Modern Library, 1947.

Austen, Jane. *Emma.* New York: Penguin Books, 1980.

Austen, Jane. *Pride and Prejudice*. Cleveland: The World Publishing Company, 1946.

Brontë, Charlotte. *Jane Eyre*. New York: The Book League of America.

Calder, Jenni. *Women and Marriage in Victorian Fiction*. New York: Oxford University Press, 1976.

Cather, Willa. *O Pioneers!* Pleasantville, NY: The Reader's Digest Association, Inc., 1990.

Chambers-Schiller, Lee. "'Woman Is Born to Love:' The Maiden Aunt as Maternal Figure in Ante-Bellum Literature." *Frontiers* (Volume 10, Number 1). 1988: 34–43.

Cooney, Barbara. *Miss Rumphius*. New York: The Viking Press, 1982.

Dickens, Charles. *Great Expectations*. R. D. McMister (Ed.). New York: The Odyssey Press, 1965.

Doan, Laura L. (Ed). *Old Maids to Radical Spinsters: Unmarried Women in the Twentieth-Century Novel*. Urbana, IL: University of Illinois Press, 1991.

Freeman Wilkins, Mary E. *A New England Nun*. Ridgewood, NJ: The Gregg Press, 1967.

Heilbrun, Carolyn G. *Writing a Woman's Life*. New York: Ballantine Books, 1988.

Joyce, James. "Eveline." *Dubliners*. New York: Penguin Books, 1976.

Munsch, Robert N. *The Paper Bag Princess*. Toronto: Annick Press Ltd., 1980.

Newton, Sarah Emily. "Wise and Foolish Virgins: 'Usable Fiction' and the Early American Conduct Tradition." *Early American Literature* (Volume 25, Number 2). 1990: 139–67.

Richardson, Samuel. *Clarissa*. George Sherburn (Ed.). Boston: Houghton Mifflin Company, 1962.

Schulman, Max and Robert Paul Smith. *The Tender Trap*. New York: Dramatists Play Service Inc., 1956.

Spark, Muriel. *The Girls of Slender Means*. New York: Avon Books, 1990.

Wasserstein, Wendy. *The Heidi Chronicles and Other Plays*. New York: Harcourt Brace Jovanovich, Inc., 1990.

Wharton, Edith. "The Old Maid." *Old New York.* New York: Appleton and Company, 1924.

Williams, Tennessee. "The Glass Menagerie." *The Theatre of Tennessee Williams, Volume I.* New York: New Directions, 1971.

Woolf, Virginia. *A Room of One's Own.* New York: Harcourt, Brace & World, Inc., 1957.

Woolf, Virginia. *To the Lighthouse.* New York: Harcourt Brace Jovanovich, 1955.